BEFORE

BEFORE & LAUGHTER

Jimmy Carr is an award-winning comedian, television host and writer, goddamnit.

One of the biggest-selling comedy acts in the world, Jimmy consistently does stand-up to sell-out crowds, performing his shows at venues in over forty countries. That's a lot of countries. In fact, the only thing that's been on a more extensive world tour in the last five years is coronavirus.

Before making the move to streaming, Jimmy was one of the bestselling acts in the comedy DVD market, selling over 2 million copies. And to this day his DVDs continue to form the centrepiece of many Oxfam Shop window displays.

Jimmy is a household name in UK television, well-known for hosting Channel 4's *8 Out Of 10 Cats, Cats Does Countdown* and *Big Fat Quiz of the Year*. He is a regular on all the top panel shows. Jimmy's hair has appeared in both *The LEGO Movie* (2014) and *The LEGO Movie 2* (2019).

He was also the first UK comedian to sign a stand-up deal with streaming behemoth Netflix in 2015.

Before & Laughter is his first attempt at an autobiography. He might even write another one. Depending on next year's tax bill.

JIMMY CARR

BEFORE & LAUGHTER
a life-changing book

Quercus

First published in Great Britain in 2021 by

Quercus Editions Ltd
Carmelite House
50 Victoria Embankment
London EC4Y 0DZ

An Hachette UK company

A CIP catalogue record for this book is available
from the British Library

HB ISBN 978 1 52941 307 6
TPB ISBN 978 1 52941 308 3
Ebook ISBN 978 1 52941 310 6

10 9 8 7 6 5 4 3 2 1

Typeset by CC Book Production
Printed and bound in Great Britain by Clays Ltd, Elcograf S.p.A.

Papers used by Quercus are from well-managed forests and other responsible sources.

For Karoline and Rockefeller

CONTENTS

PART 9
TALKING POINTS

PART 10
WORK IS MORE FUN THAN FUN

PART 11
DON'T LEAVE LUCK TO CHANCE

PART 12
LOVE IS REVOLUTION FOR TWO

A CARR IS BORN

INTRODUCTION TO THE CARR MANUAL

When I read an autobiography, my takeaway is always, 'Wow, this guy talks about himself a lot.' So I thought we might mix things up a bit. You might be a little interested in me but I'm damn sure you're a lot more interested in yourself. This book, then, is about both of us.

I wanted to write something that changes Western culture fundamentally and increases the sum of human happiness now and for future generations. But that was a lot of work, so I did this instead: I wrote about what I know. I know about me and I know about comedy and I know how to help myself. Everything I needed to be happy I learned from dick jokes.

You can't be a Marvel superhero, you can't be a Jedi knight, but you can be funny. As funny as anyone. I'm making a case for laughing your way through life – for seeing the funny side wherever possible. If you could see the world through my eyes, well, let's just say I laugh my funny laugh a lot.

Of course, my map of the world is not accurate, my world

view isn't the truth. But then again, neither is yours, neither is anyone's. As Tim Ferriss said, 'Reality is largely negotiable.' And how you see the world is how the world is … at least for you.

My point is, life can be hard, harsh and depressing but if you've got a light, funny disposition, you're better able to deal with every setback life will inevitably throw at you. I'd like to take the filthy pond water of life and filter it through the charcoal of humour so we can all drink it.

What the fuck does Jimmy Carr know about life? We'll see.

HELP YOURSELF

The reason I'm writing this book (other than the generous advance) is that I have a son now (congratulations me), and if I die, what will I leave him? Hours and hours of dick jokes.

'My father? I don't remember much, but he sure had a lot of dick jokes.'

'Boy, sit down. This is a funeral.'

Well, there's more to me than just dick jokes … slightly more.

I became a father in my late forties. When my son is twenty-five, I'll be seventy-five. Now, that's around the time he'll need guidance. He'll be on the first big adventure of his life; he'll be trying to find his purpose. I take a lot of omega-3 fish oils and I try to eat right and exercise, but let's face it, I may have forgotten all my wisdom by then and where I left my keys.

I think the reason so much wisdom is vague may be less to

do with 'the unknowable nature of being' and more because the old people dispensing wisdom might have totally forgotten what it's like to live.

At least I'll still look the part. Thanks to the wonders of my plastic surgeon, I'm hoping my son won't realise I'm older than the other dads. He'll come and talk to me about his problems because, unlike the other dads, I'll never seem shocked or surprised, disappointed or sad, primarily because Botox has robbed me of the ability to move my forehead.

Just like everyone else you know, I'm going to die, although in my case large parts of me will not biodegrade. But at least my son will have this book. This book and my teeth. I imagine my teeth will outlive us all.

Spoiler alert: all self-help books say the same thing – prioritise later over now.

That's it; there's a whole section of the bookshop based around that simple idea. You could actually edit those four words down to just two: 'prioritise later'. So, case in point, I'm writing this now, which is frankly a pain in the arse, because I want to enjoy having written it later.

ME FIRST

Covid-19 really helped. Not just the 'government-mandated paternity leave' (I never would've taken a year off to be a full-time dad if the world hadn't shut down), but also, it's good to stop and take stock once in a while. Covid was a sort of half-time whistle on life. An enforced break that made us all do a little audit: what am I like? What do I like? What's useful? What's next?

I can never travel back in time and talk to myself aged twenty-five. But there *is* such a thing as time travel – it's just that time only moves in one direction and at one speed. I will get to meet my future self – I mean, I'll have to wait, but I'll meet me in twenty years' time (albeit in twenty years' time). And I can bring gifts to myself in the future. I can give myself money, if I save, good health, if I take care of myself: you get the idea. Whatever I do 'now', I know I'm going to get back 'then'.

I think if we're being honest, we all have the same time preference: we all value today over tomorrow. That's why it's easier to sit on the couch and do nothing than it is to work or exercise. We all prefer comfort and pleasure right now, but we also understand whatever we do today, we have to live with tomorrow. And so the stronger your preference for the future, the better.

That's stating the obvious, but how much time do you actually spend thinking about it? Do you want comfort right now, or do you want happiness in life? Well, ideally, both – but it's a constant trade-off, it's a balancing act.

YOU TOO

Last, and let's face it, least, this book is for all of you, dear readers (yes, I'm putting myself and my son ahead of you – more about priorities later).

You may think I'm very talented, funny and charming, not to

4

mention the good looks and humbling modesty. And to you I'd say, 'Thank you. This book is for you.' Of course, you may think I'm an unfunny, one-note, talentless prick. In which case, when you think about it, my achievements must seem all the more remarkable and interesting. Look how far I got on one tank of gas? If you're one of those people, this book is definitely for you.

I don't think any of you are special, I don't think any of you are destined for greatness and I don't think it's going to just 'happen' for anyone. Please don't take that the wrong way. I don't think I'm special either and I don't think I was ever destined for fame and fortune. I don't think anything 'happened' to me.

Obviously, if you do think you're a unique human being, destined for greatness and it's all just going to 'happen' for you – well, good luck with that. You can stop reading this now and might I suggest something from the fantasy section?

The premise of the book is: if I did it, you can do it. Maybe not what I did exactly, but my story is: I had a boring life and now I have an interesting life. That's the abridged version; the publisher insisted I expand on that.

Lots of people want to make that transition – well, here's the 'how to'. 'The road' I took, 'the road' I'm still travelling on as a comic – it contains all the wisdom I ever needed. All the wisdom, and any advice I have to give, I learned it all from comedy.

My story is the story of a stand-up comedian. But just to be super clear in case you're reading this and you're 'hard of thinking', 'stand-up' is a metaphor for life. You know, a metaphor, like 'All the world's a stage'. You don't have to tell me, Mr Shakespeare, I'm on that stage and I'm working as a professional killer.

I hope you enjoy the read. And if you're not totally satisfied, if you don't feel that you've had a better life because of this book, check in again when you're 102 and I'll give you your money back. Now, some of you will die before you hit 102 and that's on you. Just know that I would have made good.

SUPERPOWERS OF THE AVERAGE COMIC

'If I could have any superpower I'd go for Cold War era Russia.'

I'm going to argue there are five superpowers that all comedians have, things that we do better than regular folk. Does that mean we're better than regular people? Yes. Yes, it does.

Comedians are stand-out human beings. We have so many superpowers we should wear capes.

If you've ever watched a comedian and felt envious of any of their skills – great. All of it's learnable, which means you can do it too. I hope I'm not puncturing too many illusions when I say, none of it is magic; it's all in the preparation.

Comedians are much like magicians: it can be difficult to see what they're actually doing. That's why asking comics to improvise a whole show is like asking a magician to do 'real' magic. What you see is the result of the trick. But what you don't see is the hidden craft that goes into making the trick look seamless. You see the ta-dah moment, not the guy cleaning rabbit shit out of a top hat.

What we comedians do is to take a group of people and we

change their state, their chemistry, their mood. But how is the comedian actually doing this?

Let's break it down.

First we have communication. The most obvious superpower of the comic.

You watch a comedian on stage, and they seem to be having a completely natural conversation with 3,000 people. That is a learned skill. Most people are terrified of being on stage, so the ability to simply get up there in the first place, let alone get across a point, to emote and convey nuance looks pretty impressive.

The key thing about communication is that the comedian is 10 per cent on send and 90 per cent on receive (just like you on your work social WhatsApp group). Comedians are constantly listening and observing; whether to our audience or simply to the world around us, we're always alert. That's how we're able to report back. A comedian's hot take on the news is only interesting because they're not just hearing the news passively, they're *listening* to the news actively. Listening out for anything that doesn't make sense, the logic flaws, the nonsense, anything that makes them think, 'hang on a second . . .'. Because where there are gaps there's also potential for humour.

Secondly . . . timing.

It's not only about *what* you're saying, it's about *when* you're saying it. Do you need to give them a little more time to catch up with your pace? Are you all in the same groove? A good, solid tempo makes everything you need to do a whole lot easier.

Thirdly, we have pattern recognition.

What comedians do is look at the patterns in life, and draw analogies. Pattern recognition has always been the key to survival for all living things. If it wasn't for pattern recognition we'd have to start from scratch every time something slightly new came along.

Comics get so good at pattern recognition that they're able to mess with the patterns. And patterns are what jokes are: the sudden revelation of a previously concealed fact – that's all of comedy right there. You need the jolt of a surprise to get them to laugh out loud. Without the surprise, it's 'nice', you might get a smile – it's a political cartoon.

You occasionally read something like there's only five kinds of jokes. It's nonsense but yeah, jokes have structures. And there are going to be similarities. Yet, there is an infinite variety of jokes out there. It's like telling someone, 'You know there's only twelve notes, so, I guess we're done with music.' Yeah, dummy, but with those twelve notes you can make anything.

Fourthly, comedians have a superpower when it comes to honesty. And that's no lie. There is a brutal honesty with comics when they get together. Which is refreshing and also kind of shocking and transgressive. Trust me, stick a couple of comics in a room, give it five minutes and call the police, because I guarantee you someone has said something unacceptable.

Observational comics' whole attitude is the embodiment of honesty. They look at the world and they're bemused by how crazy life is. But 'have you ever noticed' – their starting point – is always how things *really* are.

Recalibration is a part of honesty. If you can see the truth of a situation, you have a better chance of working with it to get to where you want to go. Comedians are constantly changing and adapting to make things funnier. The audience laughter, or more pointedly the lack of laughter, tells you what you need to change.

Sometimes you'll fall in love with a line and the audience doesn't like it. What do you do? What you do is change it. You'll change it, and you'll change it, and you'll change it and eventually, it gets a laugh. And then do you know what you have? A different line.

Audiences keep comedians honest. An audience's laughter is brutally honest. I can't think of another art form like it. Is my painting any good? It's hard to tell. Does my music connect? Maybe ... Are my jokes funny? Well, did they laugh or not? It's binary.

The audience is comedy's self-policing system.

Lastly, failure is a superpower. Every great comic is 'Captain Failure'.

Every comic writes more jokes that don't work than jokes that do. There's never been a comedian who is an exception to that rule. If you think about it, neither has there been a musician who's had more hits than misses or an artist that's produced nothing but masterpieces. With comedians, it's a shorter feedback loop, meaning they get less attached to the results. So they get less stressed by failure.

All failure is just feedback. You look at something and think, 'Okay, that doesn't work, I'll change it.' If something doesn't work, you change your behaviour, you recalibrate and make it better. You don't just fail the same way a thousand times; you fail differently each time until you run out of ways to fail. And at that point, it's called 'success'.

Looking backward and connecting the dots, I can see that

being a comedian is what changed me. Being a comedian is a whole mindset, and when I adopted that mindset my whole life changed for the better.

Learning stand-up has a *Karate Kid* aspect to it. You're given a task to do: you must go on the stage and make people laugh. That means you have to work on your communication skills, on timing, on being honest and accepting the world as it is. You have to recognise patterns in order to write the jokes. And you have to make friends with failure. That's what I had to do to be a comedian. I had to become good at these five things. That's the 'wax on/wax off' of comedy.

You're on a mission to become a comedian and as a result of that mission, you pick up skills, and those skills transfer to all human activity. Do you want to be a better lawyer, father, soldier, doctor, pizza delivery guy? All of these comedy super-powers are going to help. After all, without timing all the pizza delivery guy's got is cold pizza.

You start to become better at these things, and before you know it, it starts to bleed into the rest of your life. Your relationships become better, because your communication skills are better. As your timing improves, not only do your laughs become louder in clubs, but you notice at a dinner party that you're never talking over anyone. You start to recognise when you're in the pocket of the rhythm. You recognise what works and what doesn't and you adapt accordingly. And you work out that failure is not something to avoid.

All I was doing was trying to be a better comedian and I ended up having a better life. Stand-up comedy raised me. It taught me all the skills I needed for life, except for tax accounting.

PART 1
WHAT DO YOU WANT?

CHAPTER ONE

VERY MUCH ON PURPOSE

THE INEVITABLE CAR CARR ANALOGY

Warren Buffett is one of the world's wealthiest men – and no, it's not because he invented the buffet. I checked.

Buffett once gave the following piece of advice in an interview. Imagine he buys you the car of your dreams, whatever car you want. The only catch is that one car will have to last you the rest of your life.

How are you going to treat that car? You're going to read the manual, keep it garaged, fix any problems right away, right? You will baby that car, because it's for life.

Warren Buffett – a guy who could buy any car he wants, he could buy Ford, not a Ford car, the company Ford* – turns this little fantasy into an analogy: your body is the car, you are the vehicle. It's a great analogy, because it's all about the journey, not the destination (I see we're already ahead of our quota for

---

* Please buy the Ford Motor Company, Warren Buffett. And bring back the Capri.

self-help clichés). Absolutely true, especially if you remember the destination in life is death (bummer, right?).

Now, let's drive that analogy into the ground. Come on. This is a self-help book by a guy named Carr, what did you expect? You are the car. You have the car you have. The vehicle is you, your physical body and your mental health. Fill it with the cheapest, shittiest fuel, what do you think is going to happen? Yes, you can always get some work done under the hood, maybe pimp it up, but your car is what you're going to be riding in for the rest of your life. If you find a guy who does good bodywork, that's a personal trainer.

But of course, we don't start out behind the wheel. We all start out the same – as a passenger. You sit in the back seat of Mummy and Daddy's car shouting, 'Are we there yet?'

Then you turn sixteen, you have more freedom but really, you're just going on mini jaunts and maybe taking a joyride or two. You're pushing buttons wondering, 'What does this one do?'

An education is your first big toll road. Going to university is expensive. Is it worth it? I don't know, you tell me.

Around this point, you might want to ask yourself, 'Who's driving? Is it still Mummy and Daddy?' It's a bit of a grey area.

When you eventually settle on where you want to go, there are different roads. Some people keep on track, they stay in their lane. If you want to be a doctor, you know what route to take. That road has been taken many times before, they've got good signage up. You know you'll need excellent results in maths, chemistry and biology. The next step is pretty clear, and the next, and the next. Even if you fail, you can dust yourself off and get back on track.

Or maybe you're more like me, you go off-road. There have been other people who have become comics before, but the path isn't exactly obvious. It's there, but it's a single-track road, not a motorway, and there are no road signs.

I was driving in the wrong direction when I set out. And there's no roundabout on that corporate highway. I had to make a handbrake turn and drive across the central reservation. It was a little bumpy for a while.

And then there are some people who never even take the car out to see what it can do. They might have an Aston Martin and all they do is look at it. They polish it, but it just sits in the driveway. What a waste. You want to see how fast and how far it'll go, you want to know what happens if you floor it, right? Those are people who haven't fulfilled their potential and it's a heartbreaker.

Conversely, you meet people who were never going to make it – they had the wrong vehicle for the trip – but they had determination, and they ended up someplace further down the road. Great. Sleeper cars look like standard cars but with a turbocharged engine and a nitrous switch. These are people who maybe don't look like anything special, but then WOW – Ed Sheeran, anyone?

Some people's lives are a continuous car crash. You strain your neck rubbernecking to catch a glimpse of the ball of flames by the side of the road.

Sometimes, the car actually can't be for life, no matter what Mr Buffett says. If you kick your shotgun passenger out of the car halfway, you are going to have to stop and sell your nice car and buy two shittier cars. And if you have kids, that's going to be a lot of stopping on hard shoulders. Any baggage is 'emotional' baggage.

I'm really waterboarding the metaphor here.

There are detours. Some people decide to take the scenic route and that's always nice. But then some people take the scenic route and get lost. Those who get lost, run out of fuel and get stuck with no cell phone reception are the dumb fucks who never stop to ask directions.

Still other people get distracted and fall asleep at the wheel (clock watching in data entry).

And then some people are driving in circles. Comedy has a thing called 'the circuit' and at first, you are desperate to get on it. But you don't want to stay on it. You want to be on it and then, at some point, take off.

Ask yourself, what road are you on right now? Bumpy or boring? Heading in the right direction or have you ditched the map? And who's in the car with you? It's going to be a long trip. Four kids, huh? Are you sure? If you want to go fast, go alone. If you want to go far, go together.

Now I'm on a road, there's someone sitting in the passenger seat and a little guy in the back. Occasionally, there's some stopping for nappy changes but, luckily, just for this kid still. It's worth noting, if I'd got on this road in my early twenties, I'd be looking for the exit ramp right about now. It's all about timing.

MY LAUGH STORY

To thine own self be true . . .
– Yeah, but that only works if you already know who you are.

This is *Jimmy Carr: The Origin Story*: I landed from space in a cornfield and was immediately bitten by a radioactive spider, who shot my parents in front of me. They should really make it into a comic strip. And then a movie. And then another movie. And then fourteen more movies and a lunch box.

That's me. But who are you? Go ahead, answer. How well do you know yourself? If you've ever seen a superhero movie, you'll know: you can't really find your purpose until you know who you are. Take a moment, you may as well, you can tell me, there are no secrets here. Who are you? (And I'll also need to know, what's your mother's maiden name? And what was the name of your first pet? And your four-digit PIN code?)

Here's what I think: you are who you are when nobody's watching. It's not just stand-up comedians who put on an act, we're all doing it, we all act a certain way when people are around, and we act differently according to who we're with. Kids are vastly different with parents and friends and teachers. Think how inappropriate it would be for a thirteen-year-old to smoke and swear and finger blast in front of a teacher or a parent – that's clearly friend stuff.

The moments when we're really alone are revealing. When all pretence is gone.

If you want to know who you are, ask your priest. I don't mean literally ask your priest, but ask the one you tell all your deepest, darkest secrets to. You know who I'm talking about . . . Google.

Google knows who you really are. Google operates as a modern-day confessor. Show me someone's search history and I'll have a pretty good handle on who they are. Show me their Pornhub history, and that's who they are with their pants down. (Think no one is watching? How do you think they're suggesting all those videos that you just happen to be into? Do you think it's the same homepage for everyone? Guess again.) Between Google and Pornhub I'd know you better than your family and friends, maybe even better than you know yourself.

You might not have given your identity any thought for a while. When you're a kid, it's easy, you just list a few simple facts and that's you – name, age, where you're from, that's it:

Jimmy, 5, Slough.

The grown-up version just adds what you do into the mix, as if that's in any way revealing: Jimmy, 21, student, Cambridge. (Promising)

Jimmy, 24, marketing executive, Slough. (Slough again, fuck's sake)

I think your identity is about more than just a few facts, it's more than your behaviour. It's about your core beliefs and values. And those are things that change over time. You're not a noun, you're a verb (something I'll keep saying throughout this book). Which is good news, because if you're a doing thing, then you can do better.

LIES, DAMN LIES AND RÉSUMÉS

I'd been working on my CV since forever. It was a ladder I had constructed to help me climb to a better life, only my ladder was leaning up against the wrong wall.

Your résumé is a one-page document. There's a line in it for your education. It represents twelve years of your life and it's reduced to: I got this many GCSEs and this many A levels.

And then if you go to university or take on an apprenticeship, find an internship, whatever ... that's another line. All those memories and experiences and friendships. You get one line.

And then your work experience, just this cavalcade of bullshit written in language like 'bringing significant projects to fruition'. I mean, no one speaks like this. 'Projects to fruition.' What the fuck does that even mean? You get shit done. You're just bigging up your role. If you read anyone's CV it sounds like they were running the company. If you had read *my* CV and then heard I was leaving Shell, you would think, 'I guess Shell doesn't exist any more because they lost their guy. He did everything. I mean, now that Jimmy's left, who the fuck is doing all the liaising?'

It's such bullshit. You know the hobbies and interests section on the bottom? As if you could sum up your personality in five lines.

'I enjoy cinema.' Really? Who fucking doesn't? 'Long walks in the park.' 'I enjoy outdoor pursuits.' What the fuck, dogging? You might as well write, 'I am a human.'

I suppose it would raise eyebrows if you wrote what you actually spent most of your spare time doing: 'I enjoy internet pornography, binge-watching TV series and eating junk food.'

It's a great moment to look at your CV for the last time. You feel like a guy who's been on a diet, lost a half ton, and is posing in a photo with his old fat guy trousers. Yup. Won't be needing these any more. That's the *old* me.

NO BLACKS, NO DOGS, NO IRISH

> *Irish blood, English heart, this I'm made of,*
> *There is no one on earth I'm afraid of,*
> *And I will die with both of my hands untied.*
>
> – Morrissey

Although I was born in England, I think of myself as Irish. My parents were both Irish and throughout my childhood we'd spend six weeks every summer in a tiny seaside town called Kilkee, inhabited exclusively by people from Limerick, a good hour's drive away. After a month and a half, I would be immersed in Irishness. I would pick up the local accent, you know, like you do when you're a kid. Then every September I'd go back to school in Slough where the other kids would be like, 'What?' And I'd snap back into having an English accent pretty damn quick. I was always very aware of being a little different.

Anti-Irish prejudice is largely gone these days, but it was a real thing. People didn't like the Irish. It's hard to believe now; I mean, we're adorable. But it gives me hope: if that can change, why not other prejudices and isms? It feels like it's not comparable to the racism and prejudice suffered by other groups because it's gone now. And I'm not comparing my experience

22

to that of other minorities, I'm a straight white man for fuck's sake. But let me tell you a joke that was popular back then:

'How many potatoes does it take to kill an Irishman?

None.'

There used to be signs that said, 'No Blacks, No Dogs, No Irish'. I was six years old. We were in our local newsagent to buy sweets. The headlines at the time were about an IRA terrorist attack and the guy who owned the shop said loudly, 'These Irish fuckers should be shot along with their children,' something to that effect. And my mum reacted. 'Fuck off,' she explained, and proceeded to cause what polite English people would call 'a scene'. I don't remember the exact details, but I do recall the newsagent being super respectful after that.

I might seem urbane, but I'm the son of two immigrants from Limerick who moved to Slough (they moved from a shit town to another shit town, I guess they knew what they liked). When I open my mouth, I sound like I have had a very expensive education, when really I just went to the local school.

Despite being Irish, I come across as thoroughly British. I'm very fond of my status as a 'Plastic Paddy'. I have an Irish passport. And I only speak and carry myself in a terribly British way because I'm better than regular Irish people.

I know who I am and I also know how I'm perceived. I think you need both.

> *What's the world for if you can't make it up the way you want it?* — Toni Morrison

A QUARTER LIFE CRISIS

*True education is to learn how to think ... not what to
think.*

— Jiddu Krishnamurti

When I was twenty-five years old I had a quarter life crisis. A
quarter life crisis is about finding your purpose. See *Trainspotting*,
Fight Club and *The Matrix* and for heaven's sake, take the red pill.
The cliché of the quarter life crisis is travelling: you go on an
adventure to 'find yourself' and what you discover is: wherever
you go, there you are.

When you travel, you become acutely aware you are a story
you tell yourself.

In my story I was twenty-five, bored, frustrated and wanting
a life less ordinary. So, I changed my life and became a stand-up
comedian. When I was twenty-five I thought I was terribly old
to discover that I wanted to be a comedian. Twenty-five seems
incredibly young now, but when you're twenty-five, that's the
oldest you've ever been – it's a personal best. And if things
aren't going according to plan, if you don't even have a plan,
twenty-five feels horribly old.

It's easy to look back on my life and think, 'That's the only
way it could've gone.' But I'm acutely aware it could've gone
another way.

Life: it's either a wonderful adventure or it's a super fucking
boring trudge. I know because I very nearly had the boring trudge.

I love a good crisis. The word 'crisis' has a bad reputation. It has an image problem – 'crisis' requires some crisis management. A crisis suggests something terrible. A full-on, shitting-in-your-hand-and-clapping breakdown. It's a bad word. As a society we crave stability, but really a crisis is just a point at which we change and move on.

Change is always right around the corner. It's probably best to start thinking of it as a good thing because however comfortable and content you are right now, this too shall pass. However despairing and anxious you are right now, this too shall pass. Look! I've gone all fucking hippy and I'm leaning into it. Hang on a minute while I light a joss stick.

Sandalwood . . . Nice.

If you don't make it happen, life is going to happen to you.

When I was twenty-five, I was being cautious, I was living timidly. If I had continued that way, I'd now be writing a book called *The Road Most Travelled*. Never mind 'The Hero's Journey', I was living 'The Incidental Character's Journey'. Because here's the thing: in the first twenty-five years of my life, I didn't make any decisions. I did as well as I could in any given circumstance. I did well in school, because that seemed like the right thing to do, I went to Cambridge because that seemed sensible, and I got the best job I could at the end of it all: marketing executive at an oil company. There's no end to the obvious 'right thing' to do next. The only downside is, it isn't your life. It's that question again: who's driving? It's embarrassing to admit: back then I had no ability to think. I'm now a writer and performer in a creative industry, that is to say I have a pretty good imagination. But my problem was – somewhat ironically – a total lack of imagination.

What nobody teaches you at university or on the management

fast-track scheme, and what I had to find out for myself, was the practical application of knowledge. That bit is called living. I sometimes meet people who are fresh out of university and they're already having a crisis, they're flailing, and I think, 'That's impressive, you're getting this done early.'

WHY DO YOU DO?

People ask, 'What do you do?' But I'm going to ask you a different question: 'Why do you do?' And you're going to ask, 'What?' and I'll say, 'No, why.' Because problems happen when 'what you do' and 'why you do what you do' don't line up.

Ever met someone really fun, the life and soul of the party, a mad man, a drinking machine? And then you find out he works in middle management for a large, grey oil company? Something ain't right. There's been a mix-up, there's been a mistake. Get that guy out of there, he doesn't belong.

That was me.

Ever do that thing in the street when you realise you're heading in the wrong direction and you need to turn around, but instead of just doing that, you do a little pantomime for some reason, you look at your watch and you sigh and hope that explains your 180 to no one watching? Imagine that embarrassment, but apply it to your whole life.

There's a word used a lot in therapy: 'congruent'. It just means you make sense. It's when what you do, who you are and why you do what you do all come together seamlessly – you become a united, congruent you.

Why are you doing what you're doing right now? Where are you headed?

I get that all human behaviour is purposeful. I believe in rational self-interest. I believe people want to have happy lives. But they don't half go about it in some fucking stupid ways.

We will do harmful things to ourselves with purpose. The best examples are the most extreme and fuckwitted. Some people are shooting heroin into the last viable vein in their crotch, but not for nothing. Yes, they're doing it to get high, obviously. But beyond that there's purpose. They're looking for something, could be comfort or security, or maybe they're self-medicating trauma.

Ever wondered why trust-fund kids all end up miserable and addicted? It's their lack of purpose. Well, that and the fact no one likes white kids with dreadlocks. They've got comfort and pleasure, but it'll never fill their inner void. Or get rid of the lingering stench of patchouli oil and their dad's disappointment.

What I'm saying is, you're not crazy. Whatever you're doing, you're doing it for a good reason. But there might be a better way. You might smoke because you want to relax, but there are better ways to relax that involve less cancer, death and bad breath. Or you might work in a job you hate, because you feel you need the approval of others. That was me.

I believe we've got two big adventures in life: the first is finding your purpose and the second is pursuing that purpose. The sad fact is most people get to do neither. I'm hoping you get to do both.

WHO'S DRIVING?

Are you living your life or are you living for someone else?

Beauty pageants for children are the most obvious example I can think of of a life lived vicariously. You see a four-year-old child in full make-up and a ball gown, wearing a tiara. She might have an agent, but she's got no agency. She doesn't want to be there. Look at her mother with a real-life Barbie doll to dress up. It's not the little girl's dream, it's her mother's dream. I'm not throwing shade here; I was that little pageant girl, just not in a tiara. I was in a mortarboard and gown and graduating from Cambridge. I do enjoy a humblebrag.

Here's the truth of it: no one wants you to follow your dream. Best-case scenario, they'll want you to follow their dream for you. Mostly, though, nobody cares about your dreams, they're busy getting on with their own shit.

CHAPTER TWO

DECEPTIVELY HONEST

CLEAR AS THE NOSE ON YOUR FACE

A man goes for a job interview.

The interviewer, impressed with his résumé, asks, 'What's your greatest weakness?'

He replies, 'My greatest weakness is honesty. I'm just too honest.'

The interviewer says, 'I'm not sure you could really call honesty a weakness.'

He replies, 'I don't give a fuck what you think.'

Stating the obvious is devastating, that's how much we lie. Everywhere in the world people are peddling honesty. Trust me on this.

Comics have a pathological need to tell people the truth because, God love us, we're trying to understand life. Sometimes when we're with regular people, we forget that the rest of the world lives on a relentless diet of positivity and half-truths. Comics are blunt.

It's not for nothing that comedians have been around for a long time in one guise or another. Almost every culture had trickster gods: Loki, Coyoteman, Monkey King, Anansi, Roy Chubby Brown. They were powerful because they kept the other gods in check. Speaking truth to power, puncturing hubris and bringing balance is what comics have always done. Think of court jesters: if those guys misjudged a joke, they died. Literally. These days we only risk getting cancelled.

YOU COULD ALWAYS KILL YOURSELF

Most of comedy is saying what's happening. Comedy is all about looking at the world and then poking fun at it. If everyone else seems to have bought in to a system, comedians will go, 'Nah, I don't think so . . .' Comics call things as they are: the emperor's new clothes, the elephant in the room, the bollock-naked emperor riding an elephant in the room . . . Our job is to reflect people back to themselves. We acknowledge inconvenient truths and lay out grim realities, Thankfully we sugar the pill with laughs or we'd be strung up. Saying the unsayable is only the starting point for comics. Honesty is a superpower, but with great power comes great responsibility.

A few years back, I was doing a Comedy Central Roast of Rob Lowe. The right-wing political commentator Ann Coulter was there. I was pretty restrained, I felt. All I said was, 'Ann is one of the most repugnant, hateful, hatchet-faced bitches alive. But it doesn't have to be this way, Ann. You could kill yourself.'

I got my wish. Coulter fully died on stage that night. It wasn't surprising (she's no comedian); what was surprising was how her entourage reacted. The people she had surrounding her backstage told her how well she did. Well, Ann Coulter didn't do well. She was about as funny as a fire in an orphanage. What's the point of having people around you who aren't honest? I guess honesty was never high on her own agenda.

OWNING YOUR SHIT

Don't get me wrong, flattery is nice to hear, but it's dangerous. You could die of encouragement. I'll tell you what, I've never been to a meeting in Hollywood where they didn't say, 'I'm a huge fan, love what you do, it's not a question of what, it's a question of when . . .' and, uh, I'm starting to think they're not being entirely genuine. But I could have lived off that. I could go on believing that it's going to 'happen' for me in Hollywood. I could wish away a lifetime.

If you start with the bedrock of honesty, you can use the improv technique of 'yes and' to build on that. In improv you never contradict; you always say yes and build on what your partner sets up. The foundation stone has to be acceptance of reality and then you get to own that reality and choose your own adventure.

Comedians can help you shake off the feeling of life being unfair. It is. There is no justice. Because the flip side to the unfair, unjust world is that it's exciting, it's surprising, it's strange, it's funny and we're lucky to be alive and living in it.

There's always a glimmer of hope for comedians. Even on

a very bad day they're thinking, hey, this might make a good story . . . Comedians take tough times and turn them into anecdotes. They open up and share their stories. Sometimes it's no more than just a shift in intonation. They're no longer moaning at something awful, they're joking about it.

When you shit your pants, people will laugh at you. And it's 'when' not 'if' – we've all sharted. But when you tell people you've shat your pants they'll laugh with you (unless the person you are telling is your Uber driver and it's *just* happened). I guess my advice is don't shit your pants, but when you do shit your pants, own that shit.

Everything is funny later. Laughter is a way of processing the tough times – it's suddenly in the past. Now who's got wet wipes? Clean up on aisle two.

And if you think about it, opening and sharing creates intimacy. If you do small talk with someone and they do small talk with you, that's an acquaintance. If you tell someone your deepest, darkest secrets and they tell you you need professional help, that's a friend. As a comic, if you tell an audience your truth, they'll accept you. Comics want laughs and the funniest jokes are the ones that say something true about the world and the people in it. People like your slutty mum.

MY FIRST TESLA

'Practising honesty' sounds like a philosophy preached by crunchy-granola-eating, sandal-wearing, electric-car-driving hippies. That said, I like the idea of owning your mistakes, correcting them and moving on to fulfil your purpose – and I now own an electric car. I'll tell you how it happened.

I'm in Westfield London. There is nothing I want to buy, I'm not hungry, I've just had a coffee and am mooching around waiting for my girl. And then I see it, the Tesla store – you can buy a car in the shopping mall now, great.

I ask the salesman in the shop, 'What's the deal with the cars?'

And the guy goes, 'Do you want to take one on a test drive?'

'Yes!'

Twenty minutes later, my girl is sitting in the passenger seat, the guy from Tesla is in the back and I am driving.

The car's got these incredible doors in the back, like a Mercedes Gullwing or the *Back to the Future* DeLorean. When the doors lift up vertically to open, there's a bit of me that will forever be fourteen – it's just cool.

We drive around and it's fun, like driving a massive go-kart. After doing a lap of Shepherd's Bush we head back. Westfield London is a huge shopping centre and the garage there is a confusing maze. We get a little lost, take a wrong turn and the Tesla guy suddenly pipes up from the back, 'Wait, stop. I'll move those cones, we can take a left here.'

'Great.'

He opens the back door, 'wuhoosh', and it goes up like something from *Star Trek*. I feel like Captain Kirk. He runs over and moves the cones.

Now, I'm a nice guy, a super-nice guy – ask anyone, I'm a mensch. I wasn't going to make this Tesla bloke walk all the way back to the car. It's twenty metres, I'm in a car, I'll go pick him up, what could be easier?

The car's still in gear. I press the accelerator and FUCK!

I took the door off the car. I hadn't noticed that the back door was still open, and it hit a gantry above. Now, I hadn't taken the door clean off, it was still hanging by one piece of cable, so the door was twitching around like a half-dead Terminator – it was dying but it wasn't dead yet.

The Tesla guy was just staring at me, his jaw on the floor. You know that stare people give you when you've just broken the door of a brand-new Tesla on a test drive? You know, *that* look.

So I wind down the window, lean out, and say, 'I'll take it.'

I now own a Tesla. Not that one, obviously, that one was fucked.

The lesson is: sometimes you fuck up and when you fuck up you have to make good. Also, if you happen to be test driving a Tesla, remember to shut the fucking doors.

CHA-CHA-CHANGES

There's a point when you go with what you've got. Or you don't go.

> – Joan Didion (and Joan was a goer – that's a fun thing to say about any important feminist, right?)

You're going to have to be honest with yourself if you're going to find your purpose. Take your 'inner critic', and here's the truth of it (I hope you're sitting down for this, because it's bad news): your inner critic is right most of the time (I'm sorry, but I thought it was best to tell you straight).

Take the worst thing your inner critic says, walk back the cruelty and you'll find the truth about you. Accepting what 'is' doesn't exclude you from an exceptional life. You have to accept who you are now, but then you get to decide who you are in your future.

I believe you have everything you need to get through life. I can't tell you how long you have, I'm not a psychic (fun fact: no one is), but I do know you're all you've got. So why not go with that? Everything you need you have within you already. I mean, maybe it isn't, maybe there are bits missing and you're defective, but the missing bits sure as hell aren't outside of you. You're just gonna have to go with what you've got.

Life is a little *Wizard of Oz** – the answer was inside you all along. The Emerald City of your dreams was an illusion. It was the journey, not the destination, that mattered (here we go again).

FLAWED JENIUS

As soon as we comedians step on a stage, we have a crowd of people getting the measure of us. As a result, we become very

---

* *The Wizard of Oz* is actually a pretty interesting book – it's really an allegory about the American political system. The lion is a politician, he needs courage, the scarecrow is a farmer, he needs a brain, the tin man represents industry, which needs a heart, and Oz is the President, who knows the whole system is built on a story that only works if everyone believes. Every day is a school day, Dorothy.

good at acknowledging our flaws. We're the first to mention them: we'll turn them into a joke. A comic with big ears will make it funny, then move on. It's a way of saying, 'Yes, I'm aware of this thing you can clearly see. I'll acknowledge the bleeding obvious so you can all have a laugh, get it out of your system and move on.'

I'm pale, I'm redheaded. I don't tan, I stroke. – Woody Allen

I could never have a threesome, this is not a threesome body. This is a turn-off-the-lights body, leave-your-shirt-on body, this is a tell-no-body. – Felipe Esparza

I don't look older, I just look worse . . . Honestly, when I'm walking down the street, no one's ever like, 'Hey, look at that man!' I think they're just like, 'Whoa, that tall child looks terrible.' – John Mulaney

I'll move the mic stand so you can see me. – Jo Brand

Comics are honest about and embrace their imperfections. Hollywood is all about perfect. Over there, it's all beautiful, well-lit people succeeding, whereas comedy is a little rough around the edges. You can see by which comics succeed that comedy is as close to a meritocracy as the performing arts get. No executive in their right mind would decide to make these misfits stars.

All the attributes that are considered bad in the straight world become advantages in stand-up comedy. 'I have ADHD' – great, you'll do three jokes a minute. 'I'm impulsive' – that's always funny, we can use that right now. 'I have multiple per-sonalities' – great, you'll do voices.

It's you that must accept yourself; the rest of the world already knows. You might be in denial about your big nose, but no one else is. In the history of the world no one has ever been in denial about someone else's big nose.

THE KIDS ARE ALRIGHT

People complain about how 'all kids get medals nowadays'. They ask, 'How will they learn to compete? How will they know if they're any good or not?' You want to say to those people, 'You're crazy. Seriously, look around.' Not all kids go into sport – you wanna know why? Because kids aren't fucking idiots. They know. They know who's sporty and who isn't, they also know who's weird or unattractive. You will never meet a group who are more blunt and matter-of-fact than kids (okay, maybe roast comics).

They see a fat kid with an inhaler and they know they're going to be faster than them. You think the fat kid with the inhaler doesn't know they're the fat kid with an inhaler? You're dreamin'.

Being honest is incredibly hard in the short term, but I'll be damned if it doesn't pay out in the long term every time. If that fat kid with the inhaler is smart they won't even try and compete on speed – they'll pivot and go start Microsoft.

If you have people in your life you don't care about, go ahead and tell them they're amazing. But if you care, tell them the truth. In Australia, they have a great turn of phrase, one of my favourites: you call a cunt 'mate' and you call your mates 'cunts'. It's a very Aussie way of saying that, with those we're closest to, there's a level of honesty.

Of course, real friends make a little effort and dress up the truth. Not all honesty is created equal. If you take humour away from honesty, what you are is a brutal prick. I'm saying this with love: don't be a brutal prick. (Aussies are excused 'cause they're a bunch of funny cunts.)

THE FALL OF WESTERN CAPITALISM

Stand-up taught me to be honest with myself. Being honest with myself helped me find my purpose. Comedians have to be honest because they're not only questioning the status quo but also their place in it.

Most of the time we don't really know why we do stuff. Say someone buys a Rolex because they like flashy things. If that's the case, then great. No problem if you're aware of your motive. But self-awareness can stop you from getting stuck in the stupid cycle of buying shit you don't need. That trap isn't easy to avoid – I've got a hair transplant and a mouthful of handmade teeth to prove it. The whole of Western capitalism is relying on you falling for it. There are vested interests who don't want me to tell you this, so if I go missing you know who did it: those pesky Western capitalists.

Being honest with yourself gives you clarity. And clarity gives your choices.

You can live for the exciting emotions, chase the nearest thing that looks like it might feel pretty good, but then what? The 'then what' will always come. If you don't think about what you want, how will you know when you get it?

Honesty helps you see what you're doing and where you're headed. And honesty might just save you from walking into a fuck-up you can avoid.

WHAT'S YOUR DRUG?

Say you go out with your friends for a drink . . . what do you want out of that evening? Sure, you're excited about getting your first drink, but do you really want another? Are you there to catch up, connect and have fun? Or are you just repeating your first want without further thought until you're drunk? Suddenly the world is spinning. You've over-refreshed. You're not nineteen and immune to hangovers (unless you are, in which case have fun).

In my experience the opposite to addiction isn't sobriety, it's purpose. Once you've got something to do and someone to be, your 'why', the need to distract yourself diminishes. You've dealt with the root cause of the addiction, you're not just treating the symptom. I used to be a fun drunk, a little too fun: I remember drinking pints of White Russians at a party and jumping over rooftops with scant regard for personal safety. I don't remember much else about that night. That's the thing about being a black-out drunk: a distinct lack of detail.

It was after university and we all had jobs. At work, I'd

wonder, 'Is this it?' and go crazy at the weekend. Looking back, I realise it was 'problem drinking'. The amount was never the problem; it was the reason behind it. Why was drinking the thing I looked forward to doing?

What are you addicted to: money, sex, alcohol, power, control? If you don't think you're an addict, look at your interests. What do you think about all the time? Whatever it is, that's your drug. If all you think about is football, day and night – you're checking the results, obsessively watching it and living it – then that's your drug. Of course, if all you think about all day is injecting heroin intravenously, then drugs are your drug – well done, that's neat.

For me, it was comedy. As soon as I got exposed to stand-up, I got hooked. It's all I could think about, it's all I wanted to do and see.

THE TRUTH WILL SET YOU FREE . . . UNLESS YOU DID IT

> *Art is a lie that tells the truth.*
>
> > – Pablo Picasso (he's an artist
> > so that could be a lie, I guess)

Let me be clear here. Honesty is not the same as 'the truth'. There is no 'the truth'. And 'the truth' is not necessarily honest. When you enter into an argument, do not assume that you're right, even if you feel strongly that you're right. Assume you don't have all the facts. Because that is 'the truth'. Every motherfucking time. We're all acting based on partial knowledge.

You can only perceive what you can perceive through context: education, mental capacity, environment, physical limitations, all that. Now, you can have your truth – but please, can we not mistake it for 'the truth'? Comics know about being unreliable narrators. And acknowledging the limits of your understanding looks a lot like self-awareness, if I've understood that correctly.

THE SUDDEN REVELATION OF A PREVIOUSLY CONCEALED FACT

When a thing is funny, search it carefully for a hidden truth.

— George Bernard Shaw

Laughter is the shortest distance between two people. Whenever two people share a laugh, they connect and trust is built.

We interact thousands of times every day. Here's the thing about humour: you don't need marbles, you don't need a stick, a console or crayons, it's available all the time and it's free. Mary Poppins tried to teach the father in the movie that you need fun in your life or it's not worth living (Mary Poppins was 100 per cent fucking the dad, right?).

There's zero downside to play. All you have to do is let it in: it's a decision you make.

I'll bet the most popular joke in the world is the eye roll. It's a sign, a sign that says 'Look at this guy' or 'Not again!' If you do that on your morning commute ten times, you will arrive at work in a better mood and in a small way you're practising humour and fun. Here's a tip, though: when engaging with strangers on a train platform, an eye roll is good, a wink is risky, and licking your lips is best avoided.

To hear someone exhale loudly through pursed lips when the stripper farts – that's a meaningful human connection. And it's not about being irreverent (although I love that), it's about a nice attitude, it's about an openness, an openness to other people. People respond to openness.

Let me tell you a story from showbiz. Hugh Grant is a friend and Monica Lewinsky is a friend of a friend and if you haven't seen her TED Talk on being publicly shamed, may I recommend you stop reading, go and watch that and come back. Done? She's great, right? So, at a party at my place I introduced Hugh to Monica in the kitchen, 'Hugh, Monica, Monica, Hugh.' And he said, 'Hello, I'm Hugh, the other fellatio story from 1996.'

CHAPTER THREE

RESPONSIBLE FOR EVERYTHING

LOSING MY RELIGION

Israel changed my life. I came back from Israel a different person. Normally when you lose baggage it's bad news. I lost my faith in Israel and honestly, I couldn't recommend it highly enough. I was, maybe, twenty-four. So it comes as no surprise to me that scientists say that your brain isn't fully developed until you're twenty-five.

I wanted to go on holiday somewhere. I didn't have a partner at the time and all my friends were working and couldn't take the time off. At least that's what they told me. Going on a beach holiday didn't sound fun on my own. I thought, 'Yeah, I'm interested in Israel, I'll go there. It's more exotic than Magaluf and I'm way less likely to come back with super gonorrhoea.'

My trip was a revelation. It was like Paul on the road to Damascus, just the exact opposite.

It's funny, we always think of ourselves as smart – I did. Sure, school wasn't always easy (more on that later), but I had good test scores and got through entrance exams. Yet I had never really questioned the existence of God. If you grow up in a household where faith is the norm, then that's the norm. My mother was Catholic and she became steadily more religious as she got older.

I took the existence of God pretty literally too, not as a charming allegory. There was a lot of iconography around the house: statues and pictures. I remember my mother being keen on a guy named Padre Pio, an Italian friar who had a benevolent face and stigmata on his hands and feet. This guy loved Jesus so much he literally grew holes in his hands in solidarity. (I say 'literally', but I doubt it. In a more modern sense, I guess Padre Pio 'identified' as Jesus and had his body fixed to reflect that.)

It meant that I was religious as a young man, a real believer. Surely every kid who goes to mass must have thought about joining the priesthood at some stage? You'd be crazy not to consider it. Who doesn't want to dress up and be the only one allowed to talk, in front of a crowd? It's basically showbiz from the Middle Ages.

Eventually, I decided being a priest wasn't for me. Fundamentally I just don't find kids that attractive.

I remember praying that my exams would go well – time that would've been better spent actually studying. Because, unlike Nick Cave,* at the time I believed in an interventionist god. A god that could change things for you if you prayed to him.

Jerusalem was like fucking Disneyland. It turns out it's 900 years old, not 2,000 years old. They rebuilt Jerusalem on

---

* Nick Cave: 'Into My Arms', one of my mum's favourites. Apologies to Nick Cave for me and Mum aggressively complimenting you on the King's Road. You were very sweet.

Jerusalem after they burnt down Jerusalem and just went, 'Well, that's old enough, tourists will still come.'

When you go to Jerusalem, you're very aware of the Jewish faith and very aware of the Muslim faith, because all of the holy sites are within spitting distance of each other, although I don't recommend spitting when there – they take this shit very seriously.

You eventually realise as you're pottering around that inevitably if you're right about God and Jesus, then everyone else is, well, wrong about their gods. The Christian way seems to be: 'Have you heard the good news? Well, it's not good news for you, Mohammed, Ishmail, Moshe and Aziz.'

And then you talk to a super-smart Muslim dude or Jewish girl and think, 'Wait, somehow it's fine that us Catholics are going to heaven and everyone else can all go to hell? Like, the whole of fucking India? Really? Ninety-eight per cent of India is going to hell? Could that be right?'

Take the most religious guy in Catholicism. Let's say the Pope. The Pope is famously Catholic. He doesn't believe in Judaism, he doesn't believe in Islam or Buddhism or Scientology. The most religious guy in the world thinks I'm right about atheism only with one exception.

The Scientology thing is interesting. I read up on Scientology and I thought, 'Oh that's nonsense, that's just made up.' But then all religions are just made up. It was the fact that Scientology was made up so recently that makes its lunacy more obvious.

Have you ever looked into the mental health status of Catholic saints? (All credit to the Catholic Church: it's been integrating people with mental health issues into its workforce for 2,000 years.)

I think the Jewish faith hits the nail on the head because they actually call themselves the 'Chosen People'. All religions think of themselves as the Chosen People. (Except Druids. Even Druids think Druids are a bunch of cunts.)

Actually being in Jerusalem made me question how likely it was that a man who, crucified 2,000 years ago by the Romans, was resurrected and then ascended into heaven just for little old me. I wrote a joke about it years ago, about a cult based around a benevolent zombie. After all, if we're all God's children, what's so special about Jesus?

Still, credit where it's due. When it comes to dying on a cross for the sins of others, Jesus absolutely nailed it.

And yes, you're right, I wouldn't do a joke like that about Mohammed. Because it could be 'triggering' – but with literal triggers.

Anyway, I came back from Israel, and I found out that when religious faith goes, everything changes.

THE GOD COMPLEX

It took me about a year to lose my religion completely. Losing your religion is like seeing a magic trick and being captivated, and then finding out how the magic trick is done. I felt like a fool for ever having believed.

And actually, when I eventually completely ditched my faith, I felt a bit lost for a while. I missed the comfort of rituals. Of course, you can still do them, but if you don't believe in what the rituals represent, they lose all meaning. Like fairies in *Peter*

Pan – if you don't believe in them, they die. 'Whispering into the abyss' is how I now describe praying. I get that it's kind of meditative saying the Rosary or Our Fathers or whatever. It's nice to just chill the fuck out for a while. But when you take away the spiritual aspect, ritual ends up being like when you have OCD and think, 'If I don't wash my hands, something bad will happen.' OCD is the ritual of religion stripped bare of a belief system. And it looks a lot like crazy. It looks a lot like crazy. It looks a lot like crazy. It looks a lot like crazy. It looks a lot like crazy.

See?

I really dislike the phrase 'lapsed Catholic'. The assumption is that because you were raised a Catholic, you may have wandered off for a bit, but you'll be right back like the prodigal son, like Robbie and Take That. He says he's gone but you know he'll definitely be Back For Good. Nope. I don't believe in your fairy story any more. Sorry; not sorry.

When you lose your religion you lose God, yes, but you also lose the devil. Result. Hell, damnation, Dante's inferno, being punished for all eternity, all of that shit that's been shoved down your neck as a Catholic goes as well. And it's quite freeing. You lose both salvation and damnation. Religious faith had been debilitating for me. Everything was geared towards the next life; it's the ultimate in procrastination. It had felt wrong to be ambitious for this life. But without religion, you suddenly go from living for other people to living your own life.

Losing my religion meant that I had to take responsibility. For me, the whole point of life is that you just get one go. That's what makes it precious.

Whatever doesn't kill you – eventually kills you. But then,

everybody dies, man up. Religion is one of the great examples of beliefs that hold us in place. Religion is great for the community, great for the tribe, great for the family but terrible for the individual. When you lose religion, that's when *carpe diem*, #YOLO, any number of clichéd inspirational posters become real. The opposite of religion for me isn't some kind of dry, intellectual atheism; it's an incredibly empowering rush of blood to the head. Thank Christ for atheism.

THE ONE PERSON FACING THE WRONG WAY

We become brave by doing brave acts.
– Aristotle (Greek Cliff-Diving Champion 384 BCE)

There's more than a little rebel in comedians. It's easy to see. These are people who thought about what they wanted to do with their lives and then did stand-up comedy, even though no one thought it was a good idea. In a room full of 3,000 people, the comic is the one person facing the wrong way.

Comics are rule-breakers, they question the status quo, that's what they do. That's what we're doing right now. We're questioning your status quo.

The interesting thing about breaking rules is not breaking the ones you know about, it's the rules you didn't know were there. The ones that you made for yourself and are unwittingly following. Like 'I must be this way, because of that', or 'Because of my past, this will be my future'. You have certain expectations and habits.

Until relatively recently I couldn't cook. I viewed the kitchen as a white appliance storage unit. Why? Because I just wasn't one of those, a cooking type of guy. Dumb.

I didn't start going to the gym until I was forty – I wasn't one of those workout guys. Dumber.

I now have three Michelin stars and rippling abs of steel – that's to say, I'm better than I was.

Have you ever said, 'I'm not the sort of person that does that?' Really? Why?

All progress is about trying new things. It's human – in fact, that's exactly how humans did it. Trial and error built our cities, modern medicine and the sandwich toaster. There are things you've been told about yourself that are not real. You just have to question a little.

FUCK SACRED COWS

In *Paradise Lost*, John Milton recast God as an authoritarian fascist and the devil as a rebel with the best songs. Fucking cool, right?

There's adrenaline and joy and excitement to rebellion. Before I started stand-up I felt old – I was the oldest twenty-five-year-old you've ever met. You'd never have picked me out of the crowd as I commuted in my grey suit. But rebellion starts with an internal revolution: the start of a 'revolution for one' is a simple thought – *this has got to change*. You don't even need to wear a leather jacket. When I started out, wearing a suit on stage at a comedy gig was a bit punk, a bit counter to the culture.

Once I'd found meaning, I was like a whole other person. I had energy and drive and ambition. I fizzed. I went from black and white to Technicolor. I wasn't in Kansas any more.

The realisation that it doesn't have to be 'this way' is powerful. Most rules are self-imposed; it's you holding on to an old idea. Your preconceptions about how things 'should' be are what stop you from becoming a different person. You can change anything – your career, your circumstance, your partner, yourself – you just have to give yourself permission. (I feel like this paragraph could go nicely on an inspirational poster with a picture of a dolphin climbing a mountain at sunset – still, I stand by it.)

There are two schools of thought in politics (yeah, I'm simplifying). Conservatives want to keep things as they are, to 'conserve' the status quo. Progressives want to find a new way. Regardless of your political views, I think you should be a progressive when it comes to you. Because holding on to the past is a fool's errand. Change is inevitable (unless you're a homeless guy, in which case – shrug and tap pockets).

EXISTENTIAL FUCKING UP

It's never the wrong time to do the right thing.

– Martin Luther King

Talking Heads' 'Once in a Lifetime' is one hell of a song. Part of the new wave scene that started at the legendary CBGB nightclub in New York, the band really hit big with *Stop Making Sense*, a concert film directed by Jonathan Demme. Sorry, I've gone a bit *American Psycho* on pop culture there, I'll stop immediately.

There's a lyric in the song about wondering how you got to where you got to: 'And you may find yourself in a beautiful house, with a beautiful wife, and you may ask yourself, "Well . . . how did I get here?"' Well, that's where I find myself today. I'm asking myself the question, 'How did I get here?'

If you're reading this and you're a little older and you didn't have a quarter life crisis – don't worry. Life is full of second chances.

We've had self-help clichés but we've not had any Chinese proverbs. Let's remedy that right now: 'The best time to plant a tree is twenty years ago. The second best time is now.'

The French call a midlife crisis an 'existential crisis'. They've only gone and done it again, those clever French bastards. They've rebranded an embarrassing milestone as a glamorous, intellectual-sounding event: 'Le Fuck-Up Existentiel'. I feel better already.

A midlife crisis is your inner self rebelling against the choices you've made. For details see: *American Beauty*, *The Wrestler*, *The 40-Year-Old Virgin*, *Thelma and Louise*, *About a Boy*.

It's an opportunity to take control of your life. Of course you can avoid it for a while. You can escape in the following fun ways: drugs, alcohol, food, sex, video games. But if you're a fat, alcoholic junkie playing *Call of Duty* whilst looking at Pornhub, you may have a problem.

As I write this, I'm aware of being exactly the right age for a good midlife crisis. I could be buying a sports car, quitting my job and marrying a twenty-year-old with daddy issues. What am I waiting for?

THE ETERNAL RETURN

Let's talk about Nietzsche, tastefully ignoring all the stuff the Nazis liked. Nietzsche had a concept called 'eternal recurrence'. It sounds super fancy but really, it boils down to this question: if you had to relive your life over and over again for all eternity, would it be a blessing or a curse? A question that wasn't fully answered until 1993 with the release of *Groundhog Day*.

At first Nietzsche, the drama queen that he was, found the idea oppressive and weighty. According to Nietzsche, if reliving your life is 'a curse', you're not living the life you want to live. In order to accept this 'joyful truth' you have to embrace life and live it to its full. And I've got to say I like his idea of embracing risk and suffering as a part of life. It's all part of it.

TAKE MY ADVICE AND PLEASE YOURSELF

You have to go the way your blood beats. If you don't live the only life you have you won't live some other life, you won't live any life at all.
— James Baldwin (Alec's much older, way blacker brother is right on this – you've got to live your life.)

What do you want? That's the big question in life. Not 'Is there a god?' Not 'What happened just before the Big Bang?' Not 'Is there life on Mars?' The deceptively simple 'What do you want?'

is the big one. In any given situation and for the whole of your life, if you can answer that question, you'll do all right.

The point of asking 'What do you want?' isn't to fulfil a short-term desire; there are easy solutions available for being hungry, thirsty or horny and a Friday night in Las Vegas is a sure way to satisfy all three. This is about deeper desires. It's about asking, 'What's your life's purpose?'

The trick to asking yourself questions is to ask and not stop at the first answer. These are big questions. Big questions need a lot of little answers and then more questions.

So, what do you want?

Our deepest fear is not that we are inadequate. Our deepest fear is that we are powerful beyond measure. It is our light, not our darkness, that most frightens us. We ask ourselves, 'Who am I to be brilliant, gorgeous, talented, fabulous?' Actually, who are you not to be? You are a child of God. Your playing small does not serve the world. – Marianne Williamson (Oprah Winfrey's guru and one-time presidential candidate)

I love that quote: 'Your playing small does not serve the world.' I can tell you who is served by your playing small: it serves you, at least in the short term and that's what I did for a long time. But at some point something's got to change. You have to decide the narrative of your story. If you're in charge of your own destiny, then you get to be the hero, you get to be the protagonist. You get to choose. When things are happening to you, you live in a dreamlike state. But, as Rage Against the Machine likes to repeat, you may also 'Wake up!'

All Western literature can be divided into two halves: are we a victim of fate or master of our own destiny? This book falls firmly into the latter camp. And yes, this isn't just a book, it's now literature. (I should stop telling you about the book you're already reading. It's like a character in *The Godfather* looking straight into the camera and saying, 'This movie is about the mafia.')

BAIT AND SWITCH

I know I'm right about this shit because . . . advertising. Adverts used to be about products. They would tell you what the product did and you would either need that thing or you wouldn't need that thing. Real simple.

But then there was a shift in emphasis, a sleight of hand. The advert for the car is selling you a desire – power, success, peace of mind. McLaren, Rolls-Royce, Volvo, they pick a desire and they say, 'If you had this, then you'd have that.' Well, I'm not buying it. Of course, I buy it. I've got lots of silly shit but at least I know it's silly. (I'm not for one minute saying my Fabergé egg collection is silly, because when you care to buy the best bejewelled eggs from Russia's tsars, you buy Fabergé.)

The problem as I see it isn't desires, it's the pursuit of desires in ineffective ways. Noticing what does and doesn't really fulfil your desires will save you money.

Happiness and success and peace of mind are not for sale in the shops. The signifiers of security, power and self-worth – the Patek, yacht and Gucci swag – they're empty. That is to say, they're empty unless you project meaning onto them.

If you want something, ask yourself, 'What experience am I looking for?' Ever bought something and felt a little low afterwards? You saved up and you finally got it and you just felt 'blah'? That's it, that's what I'm talking about. You got the thing but it didn't deliver what you really wanted – it didn't scratch the itch.

CAPTAIN CAVEMAN

We have instincts hardwired into our minds from millennia of evolution. We're programmed to hoard scarce resources and maintain our status in the group. Because in caveman days (apologies if this is too much historical detail), if you ran out of resources or got kicked out of the group, you died.

But that was then. Now, we do things in order to get things. We work in jobs to make money to put food on the table and a roof over our heads. The pursuit of resources has fully taken over. Why are we spending our lives working to buy things we don't need to show off to people we don't give a fuck about?

We live in a material world and I am a material girl. Wait, no, that's Madonna. It's easy to think that we all want material possessions. Those material 'things' really serve a purpose, but they're only desirable insofar as they can satisfy our underlying desire. Money is a tool: it's a method, not a desire. Sure, you can build things with tools but it's not the tool you ultimately want.

'Ready money is Aladdin's lamp,' said Lord Byron. (Lord Byron had the intelligence and foresight to inherit a massive fortune.) I get that, you've got to know what to wish for with the magic lamp or all you've got is a fucking lamp.

WHO WANTS TO LIVE FOR EVER?

Here's a question that can help you work out what your priorities are: 'You only have six months to live: what do you want to do?' (The good news is you don't only have six months to live, at least I hope.)

You don't have to be dying before you start to think about living. We walk around like we're immortal, like we have all the time in the world. The truth is, time is running out. I think comics are more aware of this because we die on stage all the time. Figuratively, of course, unless you're the late great Tommy Cooper or my old mate Ian Cognito, then actually on stage. (I feel bad for them but worse for the poor sod that had to follow them.)

I think doctors should always work with actuaries looking over their shoulder. In case you don't know, actuaries are insurance people and their purpose is twofold: they work out when people are likely to die and they make accountants seem relatively exciting. It's the doctor's job to say, 'You'll live' and the actuary's job to add, 'But not for ever'.

When my mother died in my mid-twenties, I had to face mortality. That when you die, that's it. Before that I'd had a religious belief like the Pope, or Jihadi John, that there was a life beyond this one. Well, that belief left me during the Jerusalem trip about a year before I needed it. I would say 'Goddamn' but that doesn't seem appropriate.

And facing up to mortality, as sad and traumatic as it is, can push you into action.

GOD ONLY KNOWS

If my mother could see me now, I think I know what she'd say: she'd say, 'Whooooooooooo', because she's dead and that's what ghosts say.

It's hard to describe your mum without it sounding weird. Anything you say about your mother feels a little *Psycho*, like you're sitting in a rocking chair wearing her clothes. There are photos of my mother when she was a young woman, very much of the era, sort of like Jackie O. Mum had raven black hair, porcelain skin, high cheekbones and a good jawline. She was a looker and took care of herself.

My mother Nora Mary Carr (née Lawlor) was a nurse. She trained at the Regional Hospital in Limerick, Ireland, and came over to London in the early seventies. She was one of those migrant workers, you know the ones: 'These immigrant nurses, they come over here saving our lives.'

My mother was, how can I put this, fucking hilarious. Any innate talent I have in me, I got from her. I don't know what she'd make of my stage act, but I think she'd want a credit and royalties. Fun, loud and inappropriately sweary, she was the life and soul. She had a literally breathtaking laugh. If you really got her good, she'd fall completely silent, eyes half closed as she slowly rocked back and forth, looking like she was having some sort of fit. To be clear, this isn't what killed her, but what a way to go.

My mother used to sing the Beach Boys tune, 'God Only Knows', to me: 'God only knows what I'd be without you.' She changed the lyric (without permission from the music publisher, I might add) to '... where I'd be without you'. She sang it to me a lot.

Of course, as a child I took that to mean I was a precious thing, I was loved. Looking back, I can't help but wonder about the other possible meaning. 'Where would I be without these kids holding me back?' It reminds me of all she sacrificed to care for us.

There's something about being loved unconditionally that's like self-confidence, or rather it's a sense of security, where if you have it, great self-confidence doesn't matter as much. In show business, there's a lot of rejection. Being loved unconditionally doesn't make that go away, it just makes it easier to deal with when you have that firm foundation.

When Mum died, I was lost. We were close. I suppose a therapist would tell you I was 'enmeshed', a surrogate partner for my mother. Maybe. Maybe we were too close, but I don't see it negatively. She gave me self-confidence and a sense of humour – what's not to love? You're either going to be too close to your child or too distant. I'd say fucking up on the side of too much love is the way to go.

Having three kids, two of them sixteen months apart – that can be hard on a body. The great sacrifice mothers give is their bodies. You've ruined your mother's body. Chances are your mum used to have great tits and now, not so much. You took her tits. You did that. Every Mother's Day card should say, 'Thank you. I know you used to have great tits and now you don't and that's on me.' Buy her a nice lunch and some fucking flowers because you know what? Your mother used to be hot. (There's the *Psycho* paragraph.)

Later on, my mother put on weight and was never happy with the way she looked. I have very few pictures of her because she would invariably tear the photos up and throw them away, saying, 'I look like a whore at a christening,' one of her favourite phrases.

What I remember about her was that she was clearly attractive to people and she was different. She stood out, and it wasn't just her accent. She was not a run of the mill 'mum'; she had a magnetism, she was special. She was loud, personable, engaging: she would talk to anyone and everyone. She was tactile and a hugger. My friends used to come over just to visit her. I'd come home and they'd be in the kitchen, drinking coffee and chatting. I liked it. I liked that the most important person in my life was strange and unusual. My mum didn't get to have an interesting life, but she lived the life she had magnificently.

It didn't occur to me that my mum was depressed. People are complicated. On one hand, my mother would laugh all the time. She would make things fun and had the magic ability of making everything seem okay. I didn't know she was also desperate and lonely and felt unloved. I thought it was normal for your mother to be in a bathrobe, just exhausted all the time.

I guess I never got over wanting to make my mum happy. (Paging Dr Freud, is this why I do what I do?)

We listened to a lot of music. I remember my mother would take us to a record store on the Farnham Road in Slough and we'd buy singles. We'd take them home and play them and dance around. She had this weird dance where she would sort of groove with her hands up in a fist and I know, because it's *exactly* how I dance. It would be songs like 'Girls Just Want to Have Fun' by Cindy Lauper, or Kim Carnes' 'Bette Davis Eyes' or 'The Obvious Child' by Paul Simon. Sometimes I'll hear something and think, 'Mum would love that.' My younger brother and I will send each other songs we just know our mum would fucking love.

'Home Isn't a Place, It's a Person . . .' Well, my mother was my home and when she died, the grief pretty much broke me. She was young – in her mid-fifties – when she died in St Thomas' Hospital, London. Opposite the Houses of Parliament on the River Thames: you could scarcely find a more picturesque spot to watch a loved one fade away and die.

Twenty years later and I still feel the waves of grief. I'll find myself driving the route I took to visit her in hospital, and it'll hit me. I'm right back there in 2001. She died in September, just before 9/11. It felt like the sky was falling and the world was ending.

Pancreatitis isn't a fun way to die. There are false dawns, you're in and out of intensive care. It must have been hard for my mother to get the news. As a nurse, she'd have known the prognosis all too well. I remember at the end, another nurse told me that I should call my brothers. She said that my mother had around five hours left. Imagine that. The nurse had seen so many people die that she could say, with accuracy, what was coming and when. Mercifully, because she knew the signs it allowed us all to be there at the end.

If you can be with a loved one when they die, you should. Her hands getting cold as the circulation shuts down, her breathing getting heavy, the death rattle. Bearing witness to a death is an incredibly intimate thing. You should be there, not because it's easy – it isn't – but because one day you'll want someone to hold your hand.

'One day your mum put you down and never picked you up again.'

PART 2

FEEL THE FEAR AND SHIT YOUR PANTS

CHAPTER FOUR

BREAKDOWN AND RECOVERY

POOR LITTLE ORPHAN JIMMY

Imagine your mother has died and your father is estranged. That's what happened to me and I've got to tell you, it's very freeing. Sure, it's sad, but on the other hand, I don't have to give a fuck what my parents want, they're gone.

You may have noticed one of my parents, who isn't my mother, hasn't been mentioned. If you are thinking of starting a family and you haven't spoken to your father in twenty years, you're very aware things don't always work out. Having a child really brings it home to you: things can go wrong, you can fuck this up.

My mother is dead and my father is dead to me.

Without fail, the universal reaction from people when you explain you are estranged from your father is, 'You should fix that.' I think they think, 'Hey, we've all had arguments before, it'll work out.' No, no it won't. It's like people need to believe there'll be some Hallmark happy ending where love conquers all. Like there's a whole scenario in their heads where there are tears and forgiveness and hugs and . . . roll credits.

It's a natural reaction and an intuitive one. I understand that people mean well and I don't even bother trying to explain. If they knew the motherfucker (literally, that's what dads do, they fuck mothers), they'd go, 'Oh, I get it, I 100 per cent get it.'

It's impossible to know what a person is like until you meet them. Except for maybe Donald Trump. Whenever I see Trump on TV (my younger brother gets it as well), I'm reminded of my father. It's uncanny.

We all start the same: we all want the approval of our parents. Sadly, many of us never get out from under that. Pleasing your parents is hard – really, it's a young man's game.

I like the phrase they use in Al-Anon: 'detach with love'. No bitterness, no hard feelings, no grudges: I just can't have you in my life. And this is my side of the story. I'm fully aware there are three stories – yours and mine and then the truth.

It's not that I didn't need a father. I did. But you don't have to be stuck with the hand you're dealt. You can find what you need in a 'father figure'. Even when it comes to parents, you can be flexible. Nothing is set in stone.

If someone has narcissistic traits, they have the disease and you have the symptoms. Of course, if you asked Donald Trump about being a narcissist he'd probably not even deny it. He'd just say he was 'the best narcissist there's ever been and a lot of people have said that'. The problem with confronting narcissists is that you can't tell them to take a long hard look in the mirror. Because they love that.

ACCEPT THE APOLOGY YOU'RE NEVER GOING TO GET

At what age do you stop blaming your parents? St Peter is not going to meet you at the Pearly Gates and say, 'You were terrible, but your mum was kind of a bitch, you get a pass.'

That's not to say I lack sympathy or empathy for people who have had difficult relationships with their parents, but we need some tough love here too. It seems entirely legitimate for a sixteen-year-old to say they blame their parents for their problems but it looks ridiculous for a forty-year-old to say the same thing. Where do you draw the line? The answer is . . . somewhere. Somewhere along the way you have to take responsibility for your life.

Jesus Christ, you can't keep blaming your parents. I mean God, who is your father, who art in heaven . . . Jesus, a grown-arsed man, aged thirty-three, hanging on the cross and calling for his daddy, 'Why have you forsaken me?' 'Dude, if you didn't want a problem with the authorities, maybe you should've stuck to carpentry.'*

Maybe I'm being unfair to Jesus. He was in a pretty unique situation. We've all had to deal with cruel dads, uncaring dads or drunk dads. But only JC had to cope with having a dad who was 100 per cent imaginary. I'm guessing that's a difficult relationship to get right – talk about absentee parenting.

Here's my advice for dealing with family trauma: accept the apology you're never going to get and move on. There, I just saved you £25,000 in therapy. You're welcome.

---

* Note to the publisher: that's actual blasphemy.

For me, the 'somewhere' where I drew the line was twenty-five. I started taking responsibility – somewhat ironically for me, that involved very irresponsible decisions.

IT'S ALL YOUR FAULT

The truth will set you free but only after it's finished with you.

— David Foster Wallace

Luckily, it's all your fault. Even if it isn't, it's better to see it that way. It's interesting to me that 'It's your fault' is an incredibly negative way of saying 'You're in control.' When someone wins an Oscar, they never go, 'This is all my fault.'

Because I'm on TV people will ask, 'What do you prefer, stand-up or TV?' and it's not even close. I enjoy doing TV, sure, but I didn't do stand-up to get on TV. TV is great, but stand-up is my passion and I enjoy every part of it, the whole kit and caboodle.

Why? you ask. With TV, it's a crap shoot. I'm not willing to put my life in the hands of a TV executive – are you crazy? What if someday someone comes along with better hair and teeth and the executive gives them my job? (I'll buy new and even better hair and teeth – you'll see.) In stand-up, I'm in charge and with TV someone else decides whether or not I can play. With stand-up, I get to take responsibility. With stand-up, the 'locus of control' is inside of me.

BLAME IT ON YOU

If you take the blame, you don't just get the blame, you also get to be the goddamn hero. I'd rather be the hero than an incidental character blaming someone else. It's empowering to know that you are the person who's holding the gun pointed at your own foot and you get to decide whether or not you pull the trigger.

Your story is going to be long. I've got to ask you: is this movie going to be any good? How boring is it going to be? Are people going to say, 'It was nice, but it didn't really go anywhere'?

Take all the blame, but also, take the win. If you do anything, it is all you. Teachers won't make you smart. Doctors can't make you healthy. Gurus won't make you calm. Mentors won't make you rich. Trainers won't make you fit. Your partner won't complete you. Ultimately, it all boils down to you. So save yourself.

Take the blame for your life, it's more empowering than any quote. And you can quote me on that.

CHAPTER FIVE

THE FEAR

REGULAR-SIZED DICK ENERGY

Take chances, make mistakes. That's how you grow. Pain nourishes courage. You have to fail in order to practise being brave.

— Mary Tyler Moore

When I said I wanted to be a comedian they laughed. Well, they're not laughing now.

— Bob Monkhouse

There are lots of lives without pressure. There are people who have it easy, where nothing can go wrong. Sounds a little boring, no? 'Pressure is a privilege': yes, you might fuck up and fucking up is stressful but if you get to take a chance, you've already won.

Take my virginity. Please. Losing my virginity became a big deal because I left it way too late. By then it had built up into something so big and burdensome, someone could have lost an eye.

I was twenty-six by the time I had sex. For fuck's sake. There are nanas in Leeds younger than that.

I'd like to take a moment and apologise to all the girls I didn't fuck and who were baffled as to why it didn't happen. It really wasn't you. But the gift you gave me, the 'Hey, just between us girls' conversations, was life-changing.

Why did I wait? I don't know. Catholicism? The difficulty of forming relationships when you are a surrogate husband for your mother just as you're entering adolescence? Putting pretty girls on pedestals? Slow developer? It doesn't matter, I caught up eventually.

It was supposed to be great and it was . . . okay. Once I'd realised there'd be no actual fireworks, my feeling was, 'Damn, I waited all that time for this?' Don't talk to me about INCELs, I invented that shit. I had conflated sex with love and romance.

You don't have to have sex if you don't want to; you don't have to do anything if you don't want to. It's fine, you'll be fine.

But here's the thing about being human: if we put off doing anything risky for long enough, fear will attach itself. Then what happens is that fear will attract even more fear until the fear becomes so big it starts to obscure the thing you mean to do. Fuck that shit. Feel the fear and fuck it anyway.

IN PRAISE OF RIDICULE

Ridicule is nothing to be scared of.
 — Adam Ant (And just as well, as poor Adam had
to weather the storm of being publicly sectioned.)

The great thing about being a comedian is that you want people to laugh at you. As a comic, that's your actual goal. In all the other arenas of life, we're terrified someone might laugh. Maybe that's why people think being a stand-up is so brave.

Seriously, ridicule can't be taken any more to heart than praise. If you know what it is to be creative, you'll probably have already said all the worst stuff they're saying about you to yourself.

There will always be somebody out there who will sneer at you. All they're doing is making it harder for themselves to try anything new. It doesn't matter. They don't matter to anyone but themselves. As my mother would say, 'Fuck 'em and feed them fish.'

Look, if someone taking the piss out of your dream is enough to stop you, they just saved you time. You should thank them. Nobody dead set on anything will stop because of a little derision.

DID I MENTION I WENT TO CAMBRIDGE?

I think imposter syndrome was invented at Cambridge. It's where I caught it. Cambridge University. The university I went to. The super-good one. For smart people. Like me.

By the way, if you have imposter syndrome, chances are you're an imposter. You're not crazy, you're right. If you have a fear of being exposed as a fraud because you've managed to hoodwink everyone – congratulations. You, my friend, have lucked out, you are in a privileged position you probably don't deserve. At least, not yet. But if you work hard you might not be caught out.

Cambridge is like living inside a church. It's so goddamn beautiful. It's cloistered – both literally and metaphorically. You eat your dinner in a massive hall with dark wood panelling and stained glass windows. You sit at long tables with benches, and when I was there on the top table people like Stephen Hawking would sit with a bunch of others who were also giants in their fields. They all looked about 102.

Oh, and everyone is wearing gowns. Like, it's normal to do fancy dress every fucking night. On the first day they force you to buy a gown. A gown. Not like a ball gown, it's more like a cape. It goes over your shoulder and ties at the neck. Mine was blue. I wore a blue cape to dinner for three years. As if I thought I was Batman.

You would usually sit with your friends, but because you were sat on a bench, chances are you'd also be sitting next to a stranger too. Cambridge is a pretty sociable place and you'd get to meet people studying a wide variety of disciplines: maths, physics, chemical engineering, medicine and evolutionary biology. It was a great way to meet people from around the world with different backgrounds and interests and learn how to talk to anyone about anything. You'd look at the guy sitting next to you and think, 'Okay, what's this guy's story, what's he been doing?'

And what is a degree ultimately? Why go to university? To learn? Because you know they post the reading list online. You could always just buy the books and read them – or not read them, if you want to feel like a proper student. No, you go to university for the social.

The great thing about imposter syndrome is it'll make you

work your ass off. You will push yourself to get better and better until you finally do belong. Later on, you'll look back and think, 'I used to feel like an imposter but I guess I was wrong.' You'll forget all about the work you did precisely because you felt like an imposter.

SCARED STRAIGHT

Be bold and mighty forces will come to your aid.
— William Benjamin Basil King

Obviously, the kind of bravery we're focusing on is the kind where you live the life you want to live. It's not a running-into-burning-buildings kind of boldness (unless you're in the fire service, in which case, that's a requirement). What we're talking about is the kind of bloody-mindedness it takes to live your life your way.

Look, fear is not stupid. Fear is not just something to brush under the carpet; we have fear for smart reasons. If you're doing something risky and you have no idea of what the risks are, you're either naive or a sociopath.

What does bravery feel like? It feels like, 'Uh-oh, I did not think this through, but oh well, I guess I'm doing it.' And sometimes, 'Fuck everyone, I'm doing this.' It's very anti-establishment.

The most important thing to remember about bravery is that being afraid is a part of it. Maybe the biggest part.

Here's Mark Twain: 'Courage is resistance to fear, mastery of fear, not absence of fear.'

And there are countless first-hand accounts of soldiers in battle doing incredibly brave things that basically boil down to 'I was totally and utterly shit scared, and I did it anyway.'

Fear will help you do incredible things.

FAKE IT 'TIL YOU MAKE IT

We are what we pretend to be, and so we must be careful what we pretend to be.
– Kurt Vonnegut (Wait, was he just pretending to be one of my favourite writers? Damn.)

Comics know what comic-book heroes know: you don't need to feel brave to act. That's what brave is, an act and an action.

Stage fright – the thought of embarrassment and humiliation – causes the body to secrete the hormone ACTH* and this hormone causes adrenaline to be released. This is you at your most alert, this is you in a heightened state, in peak condition.

Yes, you might be shitting yourself, but understand this is your body putting on armour, getting ready for the fight. Embrace it. Fear is nothing to be afraid of. Fear is a performance-enhancing drug.

Of course, most comics I know have decided to go into full denial and call stage fright 'excitement'. It isn't, really – but whatever works. Bravery does not feel like bravery inside. Bravery is an illusion.

---

* Fucking Google it.

'Fake it 'til you make it' is all about pretending to be confident for long enough for the mask to become the face, a common fairy-tale archetype – the pretender who earns the crown. I have to say, it's slightly galling that no one notices the difference. I'm generally relaxed on stage these days, but when I'm not, when I'm trying new material that I'm not sure about, it looks about the same.

POWERED BY COWARDICE

Fear is a great motivator.

At nineteen I went to America for six weeks with my university friend, Henry. Back then Delta had something called a Standby Airpass. For $600, you could take an unlimited number of flights around the States (sorry, Al Qaeda, but you missed out on some incredible savings). The only thing was, you couldn't book seats in advance, so there was a lot of time spent waiting around in airports. I had a carbon footprint like a Wookiee.

I was excited to go to the cities, like New York, Chicago, San Francisco, LA. But Henry, a natural scientist, was like, 'No, where we want to go is Yellowstone, the Grand Canyon, Big Sur' – all the national parks. This we discovered on the flight over. And what we decided to do was *everything*.

Majorly sleep deprived after jumping around all over the place, literally Sleepless in Seattle 'cause we couldn't find a room, we flew to Miami, found a hostel in Key Largo and slept like teenagers, sixteen hours straight.

We woke up refreshed, it was beautiful out and we decided

to go snorkelling. We went out in a boat and they told us it was safe but we had to be careful because the reef was covered in fire coral. (Touching fire coral causes an intense pain that can last from two days to two weeks. It's kind of like seeing an ex in the supermarket.)

We were out there swimming with turtles and big fish – it was heavenly and we couldn't believe our luck. There were these baby sharks, like two, maybe three feet long, definitively shark-shaped but little, and we followed them around the reef.

Suddenly, we saw what looked like another baby shark, but was in fact a big shark (eight feet long) that was far away. It was swimming away from us. So what did we do? We swam towards it. Did I mention we were idiots? After a day in the water we were feeling super confident. Then the shark flipped around and started swimming right at us. And suddenly all I could hear was the sound of someone playing the cello underwater.

I made a calculation: this was not good. As a natural scientist, Henry had probably figured it out a bit quicker than me.

We turned around sharpish and swam as fast as we could back to the boat. And I remember thinking, 'I don't have to swim faster than the shark, I just need to swim faster than Henry' (sorry, Henry). It was like the old joke about the two hunters and the bear.

We ended up standing on fire coral, which, trust me, burns like, well, fire – they didn't call it that for nothing. Literally two fish out of water, trying to wave the boat over to rescue us. And they were like, 'No, you come to us.' We had to get back into the water and gingerly swim to the boat.

We tried to tell them that there was a shark chasing us and they were like, 'Oh, those, they're reef sharks, they're fine.' And we said, 'Oh right, grey with a black-tipped fin, those ones are fine?' And they said, 'Oh, shit.'

I don't know what that says about me exactly, but I learned that I can outswim a natural scientist and a shark. It's amazing what you can do when you're motivated by fear.

METHOD IN THE MADNESS

Van Halen famously used to request a brandy glass of M&M's with all the brown ones picked out in their dressing room. The story has become a rock and roll legend, a tale of diva-like ridiculous requests and excess. Yet, there was method in Van Helen's madness. It was to check that the concert promoter had fully read their contract. If there were no brown M&M's, the band could trust the promoter, and they could relax.

If they hadn't bothered with that detail, if there were brown M&M's backstage, the band knew that all the lighting and sound specifications had to be reviewed. The brown M&M's were an early warning system. Van Halen didn't care that they came across as mad or excessive; they knew the purpose, they knew the 'why' of their request, so they kept at it.

When you have purpose, there'll be times when people don't understand why you're doing what you're doing. I used to go on stage with a clipboard and occasionally someone would say, 'You can't be bothered to learn your jokes?' No, dummy, I'm doing brand-new jokes and I'm not going to learn them until

I know they're funny. Who's got the time to memorise stuff that doesn't work?

BRAVE NEW WORLD

If you looked at my new life the week after I left Shell, you'd have thought, 'This guy doesn't have a job, he's not earning, he's lost it,' and you'd be right. My life was in turmoil because it was a liminal phase: I was transitioning into something else.

My story of giving up the day job and leaving to join the circus seems crazy looking back. Most of my friends didn't really get why I quit my job to do stand-up. I think they thought I'd gone mad. I suppose if you manage to surprise your friends a couple of times in your life, that's a good sign. Unless you're surprising them by turning up at your high school with a pocket full of grudges and a shotgun.

It wasn't like I didn't have doubts. There were moments where I too thought I might have gone mad. I would wake up routinely at 4 a.m. and have (what I now know to be) a panic attack. My eyes would ping open and I'd think, 'What the fuck am I doing? I'm going to be a stand-up comic, I've never done this before. Do I have a history of doing drama and plays at school? No. Have I always been creative? No. Do I know how to write jokes? No. Have I got an incredible stage persona? No. Have I got a skill? Do I sing? No. No. What the fuck am I doing?' It felt like walking on a high wire with no safety net.

Fear is the thing that will make you work hard and train. It didn't feel like I had five years to make it, not even two years.

To me, if this didn't work, I was fucked. I would have to go back to the old job.

When I started comedy, part of the reason it was possible to leave my job was because I was living at home and didn't have to pay rent. That's right. I was a millennial before it was hip. I'm your wise old millennial. I'm Obi Wan to your Skywalker.

I had like, maybe, maybe like £5,000 in the bank when I started; a year into comedy my net worth was around £300. I was lucky I didn't need money to write –when you live at home there is always food in the fridge.

I was at the start of my journey, all I needed was fuel. And in my case, that fuel was a highly potent mixture of petrol and fear.

CHAPTER SIX

COMPROMISE, I INSIST

COMPROMISE IS GREAT . . . MEET ME HALFWAY ON THIS

Do you live in other people's world or do other people live in yours? If you live in other people's world, you're going to have to get along. If other people live in your world – good luck, my friend, you're in a battle. You're in a battle every day. There's 7 billion other people and there's only one of you. Personally, I don't like those odds.

Compromise is a word with a terrible reputation. But compromise is your friend. If you know what you really want, compromising to reach that goal just demonstrates your willingness to get it. If you've got the 'why', you can handle any 'how'.

Don't fear compromise – being afraid to compromise will only limit your choices. Recalibration and compromise aren't to do with a loss of integrity – if anything, they demonstrate integrity. Show me someone with a plan who is determined to only do it one way, and I'll show you a failure.

Behaviour flexibility makes my dick hard. I mean it. Literally.

The good people at Pfizer were working on a blood pressure medication. It had a side-effect. A frankly magnificent, throbbing, veiny, proud side-effect. Now, Pfizer executives understood that their true purpose wasn't to reduce blood pressure but to make money, so they compromised. You might say they 'pivoted'. And, speaking as a man in his late forties, thank fuck they did. Viagra was born, and it's the one time in life when you should take the blue pill.

What I'm saying is, compromise isn't settling; it's about getting what you want by any means necessary.

You can plan all you want. But as John Lennon said, 'Life is what happens when we're making other plans' (point in fact, I'm sure John Lennon had plans for 1981).

Compromise is rock and roll, it's getting shit done. It doesn't have to be perfect, it's punk rock. As the Sex Pistols didn't sing, 'We're so pretty, oh so pretty . . . flexible.'

A terrible storm came into a town and local officials ordered everyone to evacuate immediately.

A faithful Christian man heard the warning and decided to stay, saying to himself, 'I will trust God and if I am in danger, then God will send a miracle to save me.'

The neighbours came by his house and said, 'We're leaving and there is room for you in our car, please come with us!'

But the man declined. 'I have faith that God will save me.'

As the man stood on his porch watching the water rise up the steps, a man in a canoe paddled by and called to him, 'Hurry, get into my canoe.'

But the man again said, 'No thanks, God will save me.'

The floodwaters rose higher and higher and the man had to climb up to his rooftop.

A helicopter spotted him and dropped a rope ladder. A rescue officer came down the ladder and pleaded with the man: 'Grab my hand and I will pull you up!' But the man STILL refused, folding his arms tightly to his body. 'No thank you! God will save me!'

Shortly after, the house broke up and the floodwaters swept the man away and he drowned.

When in heaven, the man stood before God and said, 'I put all of my faith in You. Why didn't You come and save me?'

And God said, 'Son, I sent you a warning. I sent you a car. I sent you a canoe. I sent you a helicopter. What more were you looking for?'

You might have a 'line in the sand', but it's fucking sand, dummy, rake it over.

Behaviour flexibility is one of the core human skills. We managed to survive as homo sapiens because we were able to adapt. Homo erectus was not so flexible (the word 'erectus' should really be the clue there; 'erect' doesn't suggest flexibility). They were fussy eaters and they were set in their ways, so they died out. I'm just asking you to be as smart as a caveman.

WELL ADJUSTED

Recalibration is important in all our lives.

No one sets off on their way age twenty-one and just fucking nails it for fifty years straight.

You want an example? Okay, say you're a mass shooter, a psychopathic killer with a blood lust. You're up in a tower with a high-velocity rifle and you take aim. The tiny dot below doesn't move, nothing happens, you missed. What do you do? You adjust your sights. You're crazy, but you're not stupid. You fiddle with the scope and you try again. And what do you know, this time it's a bullseye. Well done you. Atta boy.

Whilst we're in this area, my least favourite crime is the murder/suicide. If you happen to be contemplating it, go for it, don't let me stop you. I'd just like to give you a little friendly advice about the sequencing: why not switch it round and just kill yourself first, don't be a dick (apologies if you've read that classic 'just kill yourself first' advice in a lot of self-help books).

LAUGH LIKE A HYENA

I went on a safari to see the Big Five, and it was pretty great. If you don't have a god, getting that close to nature feels pretty special. The animal that stood out for me, the coolest animal, wasn't the lion (the lioness is cool, the lion is a lazy fuck – you heard me, Simba), not the elephant (I don't care how much you poach elephants, you'll never properly cook it like that), not the hippo (they say the hippo is the most dangerous thing in Africa, have they not heard of Boko Haram?). No, the coolest animal, bar none, the rock star of the Serengeti – drum roll please – is the hyena.

The hyena is my spirit animal and not just because of its remarkable and beautiful laugh, but because it's a 'by any means necessary', get the job done, results-driven badass.

If you were to ask a hyena, 'What is your preferred method of survival?' it will say, 'What have you got? We can hunt in teams or we can go it alone, we'll hunt in the day or at night.'

'What will you eat?'

'We will eat anything: fresh, carrion, half-dead, weak, ill . . . if it's food, we'll eat it. We will do whatever we need to do to survive.'

They can compromise. Whereas the rest of the animals on the Serengeti, they're picky, fucking idiots. Endangered animals can fuck off. If they're not willing to be flexible about food (I'm talking to you, Mr Panda), if they're not willing to fuck (you again, Panda Boy), fuck 'em.

I tell you what's not endangered: the hyena. The hyena is like Walter White: 'Endangered? No, I am the danger.'

FOOL THROTTLE

If you go for something, it's not always success or failure – sometimes you get something unexpected.

I was on *Top Gear*, the old *Top Gear*. Jeremy Clarkson is a great example of someone who isn't what you might assume he is. He's interesting and engaging, adventurous, knows how to enjoy himself, generous and great fun. That's sort of a backhanded compliment. I'm implying you think he's a dick. Well, he's not a dick, he's a mate.

Top Gear had a segment called 'A Star in a Reasonably Priced Car'. You'd drive around a track and they had a leader board and, well, that was it really. On the day I was the said 'Star', I had a crash helmet on and I had a full roll cage in the car. And before I got in it, I asked them, 'Is that shatterproof glass?' And they went, 'Yep.'

What I was thinking was, 'If I go fast enough through the apex of that bend . . . I might be able to roll the car. And if I manage to roll the car, I'll be a legend on this show. They'll have to name the corner after me.'

I went as fast as I could, at breakneck speed, and couldn't do it. I couldn't get the thing to roll.

But as a result of that craziness, I held the record for the fastest time on the *Top Gear* track of 1:46.9 in 2004. (The other good news about not rolling the car is I'm not typing this with a fucking straw.)

I DON'T GIVE A FUCK WHAT YOU THINK; I HOPE THAT'S OKAY

Comics start out with a vision of what is funny, we write it down, we find what we think is the exact wording and then we have to test the new material out in front of an audience. We're always certain it's going to kill. Mostly it doesn't. If they don't think it's funny, we have to adjust. If it turns out it wasn't a joke, just a couple of random sentences, back to the drawing board where we rework it a little, try new words to express this brilliantly funny joke. And then nothing. Again.

Even when the joke does work, we need to polish it up, to get bigger laughs. Comics know that the audience helps us get better. That simple lesson is very transferable.

If you know what you want, if you know where you're

headed, it's easy to recalibrate when you go off course. Is this getting me closer to where I'm going or not?

Comics know what they want: they want laughs. Comedians need the crowd. We desperately and pathetically need the validation of a round of applause and a laugh. We need you to accept us, but not at any cost. We want to be loved for who we are. We have warring needs, an interesting mix of 'needy' and 'zero fucks given'.

Ultimately, if the audience doesn't laugh, the joke goes. But even more ultimately, it's important that I find my jokes funny. The audience only has to hear my jokes once, whereas I have to hear them night after night, 300 nights in a row – tickets now available.

What comics care about is getting a laugh from the audience but also about pleasing themselves. That's a very healthy attitude. We have to be both internally and externally pleased. It's good to have checks and balances. In comedy, if you just please the audience you're a hack and your peers will dismiss you, but if you just please yourself you'll disappear up your own arse.

CHAPTER SEVEN

RISKY BUSINESS

WHERE THERE'S A WILL, THERE'S A WAY

A man can do what he will, but not will as he will.
— Arthur Schopenhauer

What Artie is saying rather obtusely is, you're free to do whatever you desire, but you are not free to choose your desires. Basically, the heart wants what the heart wants, right, Artie?

If life is meaningless, that's on you. You fucked up. Take some responsibility and get a life. The meaning of life isn't a 'one size fits all' thing – you go get yours. I find meaning in laughter, joy, connection, dick jokes – in that order – but those are just my touchstones. You get to decide what they'll be for you.

Have you ever been to a wedding and seen two people proclaim their undying love for each other, describing their new spouse as the most wonderful person in the world? You know both these people and they're good people, but 'the most wonderful'? A stretch, right? But good for them, they found each other. The meaning of life is a lot like love: it's not the same for everyone and it's down to you to decide what's right.

What do you want? That's the key question in life. It's why I've already said it so many times. And don't worry, if you don't catch it this time, I'll be saying it again.

There's this fellow, Abraham Maslow, you may already be familiar with him and his hierarchy of needs. He was a psychologist who basically made his name on a triangle, like an Egyptian pharaoh. And he's the neediest motherfucker you'll ever come across – he literally wrote the book on being needy.

His insight is that you need to take care of certain shit before you can take care of other shit. Wait, it gets good. You need to sort out your food, shelter and basic hygiene first. The Bear Grylls stuff gets priority.

The next level is safety and security. Security and safety sound like the same thing. But really, safety is all about 'Is there a bear?'; security is all about accumulating wealth – there are scarce resources and we want our share. And for some people, that is their main drive: security. They don't ever get to the next level, because they never feel secure enough.

Once you've taken care of survival and security then you can move on to connection, that is, familial relationships, friendships and intimacy. Or as Maslow didn't put it, mums, chums and bums.

After that, you'll want to start working on your self-esteem and think about where you belong in the world. Then finally you can focus your attention on fulfilling your purpose.

I've got to say, this guy Maslow is right. You've got to take care of business before you take care of business. A Buddhist monk in a monastery in Kathmandu might tell me that all I need is spiritual enlightenment, but I'll also need the Wi-Fi code.

People sneer at first-world problems, but what are you going to do? You can only deal with what's in front of you. You know what they call self-help books in the third world?* Firewood. They need to eat, they're not worried about any of this shit. First-world problems are important: am I good enough, am I fulfilling my potential? Third world problems are urgent: will I eat today, where is the safest place to sleep and how is my ongoing relationship with the secret police?

As the dramatic hero in your story, you are out to get something. Like Homer in *The Odyssey*, the Golden Fleece is the MacGuffin, the bullshit to drive the story along – if you didn't study ancient Greek, it's like the suitcase in *Pulp Fiction*. The adventure is the thing. It's the journey, not the destination. (Fun fact: it's actually a legal requirement that every self-help book must repeatedly contain that sentence.)

EVERY DAY IS A SCHOOL DAY

If you work for a big corporation, there's always a training budget for the employees. I was working in the marketing department at Shell in my early twenties, and because my department was not on oil rigs, but in nice safe offices on the

---

* I know we're not calling the third world the third world any more. But there's clearly a disparity between the 'have' and the 'have not' nations. See *Guns, Germs and Steel* by Jared Diamond if you want to find out why, but finish this book first.

Strand, there was no need for us to take health and safety courses. Instead, they sent us on Away Days where we would do trust exercises and Myers-Briggs personality assessments, you know, the usual.

Myers-Briggs is a system used by businesses and other institutions. It assesses personality types and puts everyone into one of sixteen different categories. Of course, there aren't sixteen types of personality; there are only twelve. If Mystic Meg taught us anything, she taught us that.

In a weird way, Shell had a quite nurturing environment (not for sea life, obviously). I'd just like to take a moment and say, 'Thanks, Shell. Al Gore might see you as a planet-killing cancer factory, but you did all right by me.'

I was exposed to what you might call the West Coast Human Potential Movement. Which if you've never heard of it, is exactly what it sounds like: a movement that grew out of a series of Californian retreats full of kaftans, sandals and weapons-grade body odour.

At the Polish Centre in Hammersmith, a guy named Ian McDermot ran an NLP course. I got lucky, he was a great guy and a wonderful teacher.

NLP, which stands for Neuro Linguistic Programming, sounds smarter than it is – remind you of anyone? No wonder I liked it right away. Doing these courses was a way of doing therapy on the cheap. For me, it was a revelation. Like all the dissatisfaction I felt was no longer some amorphous fog.

'You can't beat your environment.' Well, I certainly couldn't. Your environment is always going to win. I was not the funny guy in the office, of course I fucking wasn't; the circumstances were stifling. I was grey and boring because I spent a lot of time in a grey and boring office.

The big transition I made on those courses was to work out what I really wanted: to live to work. I wanted to do something that would be a part of my life, not just something I had to do in order to do the things I really wanted to do.

If I was on *The X Factor*, Louis Walsh would be telling me I was at the start of my 'journey'. And Simon Cowell would be telling me, 'You can't fucking sing.'

FUNNY TURN OF THE CENTURY

> *Until you make the unconscious conscious, you will call it fate and it will direct your life.*
>
> — Carl Jung

When you look back at your life, you have a tendency to create a narrative. You're trying to make sense of it, so you turn it into a little story. Basically, I'm an incredibly lucky man and I'm trying to join the dots of how I got here.

The best part of my day used to be reading the newspaper on the way to work. I don't think I've *ever* been so well informed. Then on the journey home, I'd read a novel. Pure escapism. Incidentally, I stopped reading fiction after I started doing stand-up. That isn't like a cheat or a life hack; I'm just saying I stopped reading fiction because I didn't want to escape any more.

But if you are looking for a life hack, here's one: put a wooden spoon over a boiling pot of water to stop it boiling over.

Alongside the NLP courses, I was looking for something to do outside of work. There's a place called City Lit (an adult learning centre) and it runs a comedy course. I thought it looked interesting, I'd get to meet people I didn't already know and it would be a fun thing to do on a Saturday.

The course was made up of three types of people – nutters, people who had an interest in stand-up, and nutters who had an interest in stand-up. I fell into the latter category. All of them knew more about it than me. They knew what 'the circuit' was, what the unwritten rules of comedy were, and they knew the names of a bunch of comics I'd never heard of. I didn't even know how to hold a mic.

But I liked it and I started getting more and more interested in stand-up comedy.

It was late 1999 the first time I got up on stage. I told a few jokes and could see this glimmer, like, 'Oh, maybe I could do this.' I went all in real quick. I'm aware some comics take a year or two and wait until they have a solid hour of material before they quit their day jobs. I quit my job a month later. And honestly, when I left I had maybe ten minutes of jokes that worked on stage. Christ, what was I thinking?

YOU'LL LIVE

A hugely successful comedian walks into the Comedy Cellar. He runs into another comic he hasn't seen in twenty years. His old friend asks, 'So what have you been up to?'

The comedian says, 'Well, I just did a Spielberg film and it grossed a billion dollars.'

'I didn't hear about that,' his old friend replies. 'That's great.'

The comedian says, 'And I'm getting the Mark Twain Prize . . .'

'I didn't hear about that, that's great.'

The comedian says, 'And I just came from Gotham comedy club. And man, I died. Horrible show, they hated me.'

'Yeah,' the old friend says, 'I heard about that . . .'

If you're embarrassed by something, that's a good thing. You're acknowledging what happened. You can always relieve the tension by laughing about it.

Risk, anxiety and humiliation come with the job of being a comic. You can't avoid it. There's no styling it out in comedy, there's no 'Oh, I think the lighting was bad' excuses. Failing as a comic is very public, so humiliation is always involved and it's very clear, very, very clear what is going on.

There are the nights when you're not for everyone and there are nights you're not for anyone. There is a little something called 'corporate gigs'. Essentially, it's a private show for a company. Which roughly translates as a bunch of people who haven't paid to see you and who do not give a shit; they're just interested in getting drunk on the company dime.

Once, after a particularly rough corporate show, a nice lady came up to a shell-shocked me and said, 'Oh, I could never do what you do.' And I was like, 'It turns out, I couldn't do it, either.'

Incidentally, the reason it's called bombing is because when a comic dies on stage all there is is the silence. And the silence is deafening – it's like the silence after a bomb falls and everyone's eardrums are blown out.

UNEMPLOYMENT BENEFITS

Just as I was aware I was done with being a company man, Shell rolled out a voluntary redundancy scheme. Talk about timing.

I don't want to say the work at Shell was easy, it just felt a bit pointless. We were ultimately working to increase 'shareholder value' and in return we got a pay cheque. I was – understandably, I think – struggling to give a fuck.

I talked it over with one of my bosses and he encouraged me to leave and do comedy. He was a musician. His wife had just died and he was bringing up his kid alone. It was one of those things where he was broken-hearted so intimacy was allowed. I'm conscious now that I'm older and my role has changed, I can never pay back Mike Harle for his encouragement and kindness, but what I can do is keep paying it forward (that's why I'm writing this book, you're welcome).

When Shell rolled out their voluntary redundancy scheme, what they were hoping for were fifty-year-olds in dead-end positions to fall on their sword and retire early. That was the company's dream.

Obviously, when a large corporation tries to tempt people into unemployment, what they're really trying to do is cut away some of the dead wood, you know, thin the herd. What they weren't trying to do is get rid of the young and strong. They were not expecting someone on the fast-track management scheme to go, 'Yeah, I'm out.'

But it was open to everyone. How much you got depended on how long you'd been there and the five grand I received was enough to sustain me for a year.

It was a risk but it didn't matter; I would've done it anyway. I did it and I did it with no guaranteed outcome. Doing what you enjoy every day is success. How else are you going to judge it?

A man is a success if he gets up in the morning and gets to bed at night and in between does what he wants to. – Bob Dylan (Of course, by that measure, Josef Fritzl is a huge success.)

TAKE THIS JOB AND SHOVE IT

You get what you settle for, not what you deserve.
— Every Corporate Speaker Ever

By the way, quitting your job sounds way more dramatic than it is in reality. The fantasy you see in the movies where the rebel tells their boss to 'Take your job and stick it, fuck you guys, you can't fire me, I quit.' It's such a wonderful movie trope.

The reality is that your boss isn't Mr Burns. I liked my boss and respected him. I liked the people I worked with. I liked the little community we had there. But I liked me more, and I knew I didn't have to do right by them. I had to do right by me. I was never that much of a rebel at school so this was really my first little taste.

But the actual walking out knowing I wasn't coming back was exactly like being in a movie. It felt like I was getting out of prison, it felt like that moment in *The Shawshank Redemption*. Like I'd personally dug a tunnel and escaped, naked, to freedom through 500 yards of sewer and then stood there as all the grime, grit and shit of Shawshank washed off of me and suddenly, I'm on a fucking beach surrounded by clear blue water waiting for Morgan Freeman to show up.

Leaving that job, walking out, felt extraordinary. It was like the Beatles tune 'You Never Give Me Your Money'. Do you know the lyrics?

> *Out of college, money spent*
> *See no future, pay no rent . . .*
> *But oh, that magic feeling, nowhere to go . . .*

LAUGH: THE MAN I USED TO BE

What's scarier is this: I could have stayed.

The first weekend before I officially started at Shell, I got a phone call from a woman saying, 'I believe you're starting with us next week. Do you have black trousers and black trainers?' And I said, 'I think I can get some black trainers. Why?' And she said, 'It's the Italian Grand Prix and we sponsor it and we think you should fly out to Modena and be with us in the pits to look at some of the branding.' And I went, 'Yeah, I should, I should totally do that.'

I met the Ferrari driving legend Michael Schumacher on my

first day and remember saying to him, 'Oh hey, how are you doing? I work for Shell,' and shaking his hand. Flying back in business class, I thought, 'Well, this has gone well.'

I'll tell you what, I wouldn't have thought about doing comedy that week.

How much 'interesting' does it take to keep you distracted in life? What would it take?

I've got some friends who work at companies like McKinsey and Boston Consulting. I think if I had gotten one of those jobs, it probably would've been good enough. Flying around to places, spending time in New York and San Francisco, yeah, that would have distracted me from following my purpose.

Now, there are not a lot of interesting, fun careers out there, but there are a lot of boring careers that pay pretty good money. How much money do they have to pay you to compromise on your dreams? In my experience, not as much as you think.

£30k a year, some perks and a little status was enough for me to compromise on everything. Not that I was compromising on a dream. At the time I didn't even have a dream.

If I'd bought a house in 2000, it would have been a good little investment, there would have been a nice return, but I couldn't have quit my job. The mortgage alone would have run my life. It's no accident that the 'mort' bit of mortgage comes from the French word for death. The things you own end up owning you.

I've got to ask you then: are you doing what you want with your life or are you merely being distracted enough?

It's a chilling thought, isn't it? I still measure success in life by what the alternative might have been. Like in *Sliding Doors* or *Spider-Man: Into the Spider-Verse* (if you're Gen Zed).

HEEEERREEEEE'S JIMMY!!!!

I mean, where would you rather be? Would you rather have a nice quiet desk job with security and a pension or . . .

The Tonight Show is the longest running late-night talk show in America. They have movie stars, celebrities, musicians and, occasionally, they even stoop to letting a comedian on to do a little stand-up.

Back in the day, a good set on *The Tonight Show* meant overnight success. Nowadays, not so much, but it's still a huge deal in my world.

The first time I did it was back in 2003 – I would have been thirty at the time. Jay Leno was hosting. I get called a hard worker here, but this guy . . . This is a quote of his: 'If you have time to complain, you don't have enough work to do.'

And Jay Leno is super friendly, like pretty much every other comic I have ever met. It's like there's a scent or something and we can sniff each other out. He makes it feel like: 'You're a comic, I'm a comic, great, we both know this is ridiculous.'

When you do *The Tonight Show* you are ludicrously well prepared. I mean, you've kind of been building up to these five minutes your whole career. But when you get there, before you do the show, the booker takes you out in Los Angeles for three nights in a row. They'll take you to the Improv, the Comedy Store and a couple of other small clubs to run your set, the exact set you're going to do on the show.

For some comics, it can be difficult to do four and half minutes. If you are an observational comedian, you might have barely said 'hello' in four and a half minutes, but I'm a one-liner guy which makes it comparatively easy for me. I pick twenty-one, twenty-two gags I think are gonna work that aren't too rude for television and line those jokes up. You don't even have to remember the jokes in that order because there's a cue card guy on *The Tonight Show* prompting you.

On the day of shooting, you go in at maybe two in the afternoon, you get dressed up, you meet the cue card guy, you give him the jokes, five jokes on each card. 'Perfect,' you think, 'this is gonna be easy.'

When I got my make-up done, the guy doing it gave me a little bit of colour in my face, a little tan, and it looked pretty good. I held up the back of my hands next to my face and I said, 'My hands, they don't match my face?' And the make-up guy said, 'Oh, if people notice that, you have done very badly. If anyone notices that, then you are not funny.' Harsh but fair, make-up guy – I'll stay in my lane and leave the make-up to you.

And then you're left alone. They tape at, like, five in the afternoon, which is way too much time to have on your pale hands. You're kind of just hanging around backstage getting nervous.

Before the show, I'm kicking around all made-up, suited and booted in the dressing room. When you're in a dressing room, unless you have an entourage, which I don't, you're just sitting there on your own in a room.

The thing about *The Tonight Show* is it's taped in front of a studio audience and they tape it 'as live'. The stakes are raised for you because if you fuck up a joke, they won't edit it out. You've got five minutes and that's it.

I'd been fine up until now, but in a little dressing room

backstage I was getting in my head, getting nervous. I couldn't settle. I couldn't eat, didn't want to drink, yet I inexplicably peed 500 times, then I did a little dry-heaving before deciding, 'Fuck this, I'm going to walk around.' I stepped out into the hallway, to hang out and chat to people, like, 'Oh hi, I'm Jimmy, I'm the comic on tonight . . .' just to distract myself from the nerves.

The other guest on the show that day was Cameron Diaz, the legit movie star Cameron Diaz. She was there to promote *Charlie's Angels: Full Throttle*. She walked down the corridor with her people towards me. I stood there staring at her. She said, 'Hey, can you do me a favour, if I . . .' She was wearing an incredible backless dress with just two small strips of material covering her chest. She said, 'If I lean forward . . . can you see my nipples?'

And I went, 'What?'

And then she leant forward. Her dress sagged a little. And there they were, I could see her, uh, perfectly pert, uh, boobs. I said, 'Yeah, no, I can see them. I can see both, erm, both yer boobs.'

And she turned to her agent and said, 'I gonna need some tit tape.'

They then proceeded to tape Cameron Diaz's boobs to her dress. Again, she bent over to test the tape. And she was good to go. I gave her a thumbs-up and made my face, the 'I don't know what to do with my face' face which, incidentally, is the same as my 'I just saw tits' face.

My nerves? Gone.

PART 3

HAPPY DISPOSITION

CHAPTER EIGHT

A PENIS . . . WAIT, NO . . . HAPPINESS

GREAT EXPECTATIONS WASN'T AS GOOD AS I THOUGHT IT WAS GOING TO BE

You want the key to happiness? I'll give it to you. Happiness is expectations exceeded.

Happiness is the gap between what we thought might happen and what actually happened.

School days are the happiest for some of us, partly because our expectations were pretty low. Double geography has a very low bar in terms of expectation. You think it won't be fun and then a little fun happens and suddenly you're thinking, 'This is pretty good,' and you're happy.

If you thought the new Saint Laurent shirt would make you feel like a rock star, you're going to be disappointed. If you were shooting for 'warmer' you might just be happy with your purchase. But if you had higher ambitions for it, you'll be frustrated. (Of course I'm not so shallow that I judge people by the clothes they wear. I judge people by how famous they are, and how much money they've got.)

Similarly, if you're expecting to be a movie star and marry Angelina Jolie, then anything but Brad Pitt's life is going to be disappointing. (Come on, we're all a little disappointed we're not Brad Pitt. And I bet even Brad Pitt gets a little disappointed sometimes when he realises he's not Leonardo DiCaprio.)

If you're not expecting much from life, you might just have gamed the system. Ever wondered how some people with nothing are happy? Well, they weren't expecting much in the first place. If you want it all, if you set the bar ridiculously high, then life is going to be a little bumpy. If you want to be a billionaire and you become a millionaire, that is a let-down. Poor you and your shitty little yacht.

Your ego is the bit of you in charge of unreasonable expect-ations. But for happiness, ego sucks balls. Egos do incredible things. They're useful early on, because they believe in you and have faith in what you can achieve. If you're looking for motiv-ation, the will to win, a push from hard times to greatness, God love your ego. But it's a killer for enjoyment. If you want to enjoy where you're at right now, you can't let your ego get in the way.

Have you ever met someone dying? My God, do they have perspective – I'd die for that kind of perspective. But what the dying don't have is ego (or much of a Christmas list). They're just grateful to have that day (unless of course they're bitter and angry – that's always an option).

It's why dads are so easy to buy for (assuming you know who your real father is), because their expectations are so low. 'A mug, I love mugs, thanks. And look, you've put a pair of novelty socks inside the mug? Truly my mind is blown.'

And while you're at it, maybe you should lower your expectations for what's happening in the future. The rest of this book is not that good.

HAPPY-GO-LUCKY

Here's a question for you. Is this the unluckiest man in the world, or the luckiest?

Tsutomu Yamaguchi was on a business trip to Hiroshima when the atomic bomb hit the city. By some miracle, he survived; 146,000 people didn't, but this guy did. He literally walked away from Hiroshima. And walked all the way home, despite the fact that he was wounded. Incredible.

He goes to work three days later. Tsutomu is an OG. He turns up and he gets berated by his superiors, who call bullshit on his story of a single bomb destroying a whole city. Right on cue a second bomb hits – I should have mentioned he walked from Hiroshima to his home city of Nagasaki. Here's the thing: he survives again. Eventually, of course, he dies. He dies of stomach cancer ... at ninety-three, ninety-fucking-three. There are cockroaches looking at this guy and thinking, 'Wow, that's a survivor.'

If you think he's unlucky, I think you're a fool. He's the luckiest guy in the world.

And I would say that having a positive disposition has the most profound effect on the *quality* of your life. It's actually your attitude that matters the most.

For me it was simple. What I did was talk myself into thinking I could, and then I did. Once I changed my mind, everything changed. I changed my mind, changed my job and changed my world.

You can change the world, or you can change how you look at the world. It's not easy to change your disposition – in fact it's hard, really hard. But it is a hell of a lot easier than changing the world.

Now, if I'm wrong about attitude then I just happen to have a magical, God-given talent that I also just happened to discover at twenty-five. If that's true, then good luck everyone, this is all fate, this is all meant to be. That can't be the case. I'm no better or worse than anybody else. I believe I'm what happens when you believe what I believe, believe me.

HELL-BENT ON CHANGING YOUR BENT

Disposition is as important as position.

— Susan Sontag

Five per cent of life is what happens to you, 95 per cent of life is how you react to what happens. It doesn't seem that way. It sounds like bullshit, but it's true.

What is disposition? Well, it's what you believe to be true. Perception is reality for me, and it is for you too. The world isn't happy or sad, serious or fun – it depends on how you see it.

We do not see things as they are, we see them as we are . . .
– Anaïs Nin

Surprisingly insightful for a child pornographer. Actually, the first pornography I ever read was Anaïs Nin's *Little Birds* and when you come across that book aged twelve, you literally come across that book. Anyway, I digress.

You might think someone with a happy disposition is only happy because they have a happy life. Or you might think someone with a happy life is only happy because they have a happy disposition. It's another loop – get on any place you choose.

Nature is just 'what is' – you're made the way you're made, it's the hand you're dealt, it's you as a noun. Go to a zoo and take a look around – that's what you are working with. That's your nature bit. The good news is, if you compare yourself to the animal kingdom, congratulations, you're smarter than all the dolphins, and I'm comfortable saying that – no dolphins are reading this book.

There's a huge debate on nature vs nurture. Frankly, it doesn't matter: nature is very important, but if we're dealing with just nature, then we might as well give up.

There's not much you can do about the nature bit, it's all preordained. Nature is very, very important but what the fuck are you going to do about it? Accepting that is an important step, but there's also stuff you don't have to accept.

Nurture, now that's more interesting. After you accept your nature you get to focus on the nurture side. Nurture is the only bit we can change. Nurture is the place where you get to fiddle with yourself. And I've always been a huge fan of fiddling with myself.

I'm not interested in the cards you're dealt. Life is like a game of professional poker: it's all about how you play the cards you have in your hands. If there's one thing I'm saying in this book, it is that changing your beliefs will change your disposition and if you change your disposition, it will dictate how your life goes (I suppose I could have just said that and saved us all a lot of time).

I remember my mother saying, 'If you keep making that face, it'll stay like that.' And she was right. I just didn't understand that it takes a long time.

'If you wear the mask for long enough, it becomes your face.' I'm certain the professional façade I was presenting to the world when I was at Shell was fooling some people. It sure as hell fooled me. We all wear a mask, we all present a version of ourselves to the world, but you do get to at least choose the mask you want to wear. If you choose to wear the mask of a happy disposition, that could become your face (Covid has rather changed the mask metaphor, but you get it).

Your face will give you away, the body keeps a record – if you're a miserable sod we'll see it. Your attitude is the key factor in your life. Which puts an awful lot of power in your hands. Or more precisely on your face. If you've got a 'resting bitch face', people will assume you're a bitch. Is it fair? No, but life's a bitch.

There are so many influences on you: the year you were born, your nationality, the political climate of the time, your peer group . . . they all affect how you turn out. But people seem to think nurture is something that happens to you when you're a kid and then stops.

They fuck you up, your mum and dad.
They may not mean to, but they do.
They fill you with the faults they had
And add some extra, just for you. – Philip Larkin

That's a super-famous poem – I bet Larkin's folks were proud. Larkin is spot on.

But that's not the end of it; nurturing is a lifelong pursuit. Your parents probably did the best they could, but I think you can do better. Who is to say you can't nurture yourself? Who's to say you can't be who you want to be in the future, who's to say you're done? Only you get to say that. So here's a tip: don't.

The last of the human freedoms is to choose one's attitude in any
given set of circumstances. – Viktor Frankl

And I am not about to quibble with Mr Frankl, he'd know, he was in a concentration camp (and no, he didn't work there – stop it).

JUST SAY 'YES'

Humour doesn't make light of serious situations, it enables us to move forward in spite of how serious things are. It is a lubricant for life. Lubrication is important. You have to lubricate for everyone's pleasure; you can't just keep stabbing at a dry gap.

Laughter bonds us together and shapes our relationships. Laughing in the good times helps us weather the tough times, filling up a reservoir of goodwill. Ask yourself, 'Who do I laugh with the most?' and spend more time with those people. You don't just decide one day to see the world full of happiness and levity, just like you don't just decide one day to have a six-pack, and instantly get one. You gotta put in the hours, you gotta exercise, and going to the humour gym is way more fun and easier than a regular gym (and if weightlifting was easy it'd be called 'your mum').

A sense of humour is a tool and using humour doesn't start with being a comic. You start as a consumer by laughing more, sharing a joke, being proactive. Humour requires you to get involved. Humour isn't passive; having fun and laughing is a choice you make.

Why do I keep telling you to laugh? Because happy people laugh more. It's a feedback loop – you laugh and you're happier, then you laugh more because you're happy. It can start anywhere, you can jump in at any point.

A happy disposition is everything. Your disposition is the key ingredient to how you experience your life. It is simply my suggestion that you pick 'happy'.

GET OVER YOURSELF

Don't judge me by my past. I don't live there any more.
— Zig Ziglar

Your past is important because it got you *to* here. But how you see your past affects where you go *from* here.

When it comes to memories there are all kinds of ways to fuck with your own head. You're already doing it, because every time you remember something, it changes unconsciously based on where you're at right now. And if that's the case, why not change it on purpose?

You can retrain negative memories. I learned this back when I was taking those courses in Hammersmith. It's the basis of Cognitive Behavioural Therapy and NLP. Using your mind to act as a camera lens means you can change your focus. This is great news. It means you can manipulate painful memories so that they're less painful by dissociating, or you can see them from another perspective, you can turn down the brightness, make them black and white, turn down the volume . . .

You can gain control of your memories and make them useful. Wouldn't it be nice to have a past that helped you in your present, a past you can learn from, scenarios you can replay with different endings? So why not take a trip down your own personal Memory Lane and say to yourself, 'Isn't it time this whole street was gentrified?'

Think back to the memories of bullies and assholes and bad parents and terrible weather and sketchy work conditions and the times in your life where it looked dark. No matter how bad the past was, it wasn't the end of you. You made it through – congratulations.

TEMPERAMENT TRAP

What I know for sure is that external factors don't change your disposition. You can get rich and famous and still be miserable, and you can be content sweeping the streets.

Do you believe that we're all born with a certain disposition? That some people are born happy-go-lucky, whilst the rest are doom and gloom and there just ain't a damn thing anyone can do about it? If that's the case, why bother with life? Why bother if your happiness is predetermined? If it's not the case, if you can change your disposition, then there is hope.

Your mood is everything. Not your mood right now but your 'factory settings' mood. Your base mood. How you feel most of the time. If you're in a bad mood all the time, that's not a mood. Guess what you are – an asshole. Apologies to any assholes reading this, I know you're a key demographic for me.

If you're an asshole, not only is your quality of life worse, but you also inflict your assholery on everyone else including the people you care about. What an asshole.

So, assholes, why not change your disposition? Rather than just allowing yourself to be in a bad mood, wouldn't it be smarter to ask yourself what's the matter? Maybe it sounds full-on mental. Maybe it *is* full-on mental, but I genuinely find it works. You might not want to try. You might be embarrassed to ask yourself questions. Well, why? Why are you embarrassed? (Obviously don't ask yourself out loud on a busy commuter train, that would be embarrassing.)

You may find you have constructed a whole philosophy that

supports your dickishness. Maybe you believe that you're being 'real' and 'authentic' and that makes you better than other people.

Maybe you believe it looks fake when people are happy or kind or nice. Maybe assuming the worst of people makes you feel safe. And if it works for you, then fine. But if you notice it doesn't really work for you, you may want to ask yourself why you hold those beliefs. And also, why don't you have friends and how come your kids don't visit?

Sometimes we're just afraid. We'll think if we're happy about something, that's a risk, that thing could be taken away from us. But coming at it from a different angle: if you are unhappy for no reason, it means you could be happy for no reason. And if you're happy for no reason, nothing can change that. Your default mood could be happiness.

We don't have to wait for something to happen to be happy. You can just be happy. If you want to, you can live an unreasonably happy life.

PERFECT DAYS

The first few years of comedy were a revelation.

Sleeping is incredible. Have you tried it? You've got to try it. After quitting my job to concentrate on comedy, I discovered that lying in was amazing. I'd have a couple of gigs in the evening, but the whole day was my own. Time expanded when I didn't have to be in an office or do the commute. Not being exhausted all the time, I'd recommend it. You don't get tired of that.

The thing that was the most emblematic of this newfound freedom was going to the movies during the day. I've always been obsessed with cinema, always loved going to the movies, but if you can see one during the day, it's the best. Anyone who goes to see a film during the day has come to see the film. They haven't come to talk to their mate on their phone, or to see if their date is up for a little light finger-blasting. They're just there to watch a movie. I know, right? And then, walking out into sunlight, your eyes adjusting, and then off you go to a show – just great.

I'd get up late, about 11 a.m., get a coffee, see a movie, maybe chat on the phone with a friend and do a couple of shows later, try new jokes. And the whole time, I'd be thinking about jokes. And then I'd end up eating Chinese food in Soho with Daniel Kitson and Russell Howard and the crew that used to hang out in Shoreditch. And you'd think, does it get any better than this? 'Did you have a good day?' Awesome day.

And everyone spoke like a human being. Suddenly, the language changed. Comics will talk about anything. And they're funny. You go from using business-speak to talking about who you really are – you go from being a one-page CV to everything you've ever experienced in your life being valid.

I learned how to wear a mask in order to be a marketing executive. But now I was learning how to be myself. Being a funny fucker felt authentic, it was authentically me.

I didn't just find my sense of humour, I found myself.

I'M THANKFUL FOR MY GRATITUDE

A study was done in 1978. Two groups were compared. There were people who had won the lottery and people who had just had a life-changing accident which left them paraplegic. Within a couple of years, the lottery winners and newly paraplegic people had returned to their 'base level' happiness. Sure, you're elated when you win the lottery – but you're still you, your disposition returns. Of course, you're devastated when you become paralysed but you're still you – your disposition returns. (In fact, the paraplegic group was actually very slightly happier. Obviously, the study is not telling us we don't need our legs. Legs just make us less happy.)

People are awful at predicting what will make them happy in the long run. It's called 'affective/hedonic forecasting', if you like looking things up. We get used to our circumstances pretty damn quick, so fantastic strokes of luck only make us short-term happy.

Robert A. Emmons wrote a book, *Thanks!*, on how gratitude can change your disposition. By merely spending time thinking about what you're grateful for once a week, you can change your world.

Changing your disposition sounds impossible, but it really isn't and, well, you're the one that bought a self-help book. It's easy to think of ourselves as a thing in the world, a solid-state item. But really, what is your personality made out of? Some beliefs, a couple of prejudices, accumulative actions and a few habits. All of those can be changed. How many do you think you have to change before you have a different outlook, before you become a different person? I'm not suggesting you can change everything overnight, but you're a process and you're not done yet (it's the verb/noun thing again). None of us are.

I was once asked, 'What have you got to be so happy about?' What I should have said was, 'Well, I've got a great attitude.'

PART 4

THE BEST MEDICINE

CHAPTER NINE

LAUGHTER LIFE

YOU GOTTA LAUGH

The best heckle I've ever heard of happened at the Glasgow Empire on a Saturday night. Ken Dodd is on stage and he's killing it. It's a notoriously tough gig. There's a brief lull between the laughter and before Dodd delivers the next joke, a voice from the crowd shouts, 'It's all very funny if you like laughing.'

When we're kids, we laugh all day long. At school we laugh and at university we laugh, but as soon as we start to work, we only laugh evenings and weekends, which is not enough to be happy. We're all born funny and growing up ruins us.

Ever wondered why you like to laugh? Of course not, it would be weird if you had. No matter. I'll tell you why you like laughing: laughing does a lot. It pretty much does everything that having sex does but without anyone getting an STI, although laughter can be infectious. And much like having sex, you can do it alone if you want, but it's more fun in a group and best with a professional.

Being credible and serious is an act. We're putting on a show for others and for ourselves. But that doesn't mean that's all we are. That's a good thing to know. It means we can put on other, more fun, shows.

Let's start laughing again, please. You can just decide to do it. You can choose to laugh at any time, you just have to see the opportunities. As we just saw, once you change the way you look at the world, the world will actively change the way it looks back at you. It's fucking magical. Physicists call it 'complementarity' because they're smarter than us, I guess. It's a fancy word that means the way you look at things actually changes those things. And it means you can change the world – at least for you.

Laughter is about a million years older than language. It's been with us from the jump, it's evolved with us. Imagine one of our ancient ancestors casually passing by a bush. He hears something rustling inside and freezes. Maybe it's a tiger? But then a small bird hops out. He laughs, and laughing relaxes him and it signals to the rest of his tribe to go ahead and relax too. We still signal to one another through laughter. Laughter means it's okay. Laughter helps us to connect with one another. It's part of our culture. You were born to laugh.

ALL COMEDIANS ARE DRUG DEALERS

> *Life does not cease to be funny when people die any more*
> *than it ceases to be serious when people laugh.*
> — George Bernard Shaw

I'm a drug dealer. I deal in endorphins, the same stuff that makes cocaine so very moreish. And I'm not just dealing to a few close friends; I'm really involved. To make matters worse, I've broken the first rule of dealing, I'm also a user. I've got high on my own supply. I'm hopelessly addicted to the drug I push.

The genius move, my customers already have the drug on them, they just need me to tease it out. Of course, I won't go to jail, they'll never catch me. There's no smuggling involved, no gangland hits and no one ever ODs. (I guess an asthmatic could feasibly pass out and die at one of my shows – hang on, have I just created the perfect murder? Yep, I have.)

IN PRAISE OF DRUGS

Laughter is good for you. It increases blood flow and muscle relaxation and it reduces the arterial wall stiffness associated with cardiovascular disease.

Humour uses different parts of your brain at the same time. That's why people think you're more intelligent when you make jokes: you are.

If you have a normal emotional response, it is confined to specific areas of your brain. But laughter is different; laughter produces a circuit that runs through a whole bunch of regions. Here we go: it starts in the left side of the cortex, where words and the structure of the joke is analysed. Then it goes to the frontal lobe and it picks up social and emotional responses and then it scoots over to the right hemisphere for the intellectual analysis required (when you 'get' the joke). Then you push it back to the occipital lobe to process the visual signals (you visualise the joke), right before you stimulate the motor section to get the physical response to the joke (you laugh). Also, I'm assuming that at some point it hits your funny bone. You do all of that in two-fifths of a second. Damn. I told you, super smart.

'Fight or flight' are your 'basic bitch' responses. Laughter suppresses cortisol and epinephrine, our fight or flight hormones, so you can actually deal with shit.

Laughter is intimate, it's physical. We vibrate, it involves the whole of you. You cannot laugh without moving your body. By laughing, you activate your vagus nerve and the vagus nerve will tell your nervous system it can relax, which in turn will tell your gut to go ahead and digest your food and later, you can sleep better (so, despite what you've heard, what happens in the vagus nerve does not stay in the vagus nerve).

When we laugh, our brains release dopamine, which makes us happy and lets us bond, along with oxytocin, which makes us more trusting. You believe me when I say that, right?

If there was a pill you could take that would do what laughter does, you'd take it, wouldn't you? Of course you would, there is no downside.

The problem with drugs is the impurities and processing. It's a filthy business, and you want a nice clean high. Where do you get that? Well, from your own central nervous system. Laughter is a ridiculously wholesome way to get lit.

GOOD MOURNING

The source of all humour is not laughter, but sorrow.
— Mark Twain

Mark Twain, the famous humourist, lost his sense of humour when his daughter died. But eventually, he regained it, phew.

I'm grateful for humour and laughter; they helped me through tough times and bereavement. That's not to say when my mother died I laughed – that would be psychotic. But in the act of remembering her and talking about her, I laughed as much as I cried.

The only place I found where grief couldn't find me was on stage. Performing required so much of my body and I was so mentally busy, there was simply no room for grief.

BETTER THAN SEX

Laughter in comedy is like orgasms in sex. In the words of the comedian Alan Driscoll, 'They're an essential part of it but it's nice if you're feeling some other stuff as well.' Pun after pun, one-liner after one-liner, joke after joke feels dirty, so I apologise. My shows are a filthy business.

Culturally, comedy is the canary in the coal mine. Comedy is the anal thermometer that takes the temperature of 'now'. Comedy lives in the space between public and private discourse. And right now the space between the two has never been wider.

The boundaries of appropriateness are constantly shifting sands. Comedians are trying to hit a moving target.

Whilst we're talking cancel culture, could it be the new book burning? And if it is the new book burning, are you sure you want to be part of the pitchfork-wielding mob?

'Cause here's the bad news: you're going to fuck up. Yeah, we all fuck up.

And cancel culture breaks the golden rule – do unto others as you would have them do unto you. (Who says 'unto'? But otherwise, smart.)

There are lots of things you can't say or that you might be scared to say because of societal pressure. Thankfully, comedians are willing to take the fall for you. You're welcome.

TRIGGER HAPPY

Humour is by far the most significant activity of the human brain.

— Edward de Bono

I used to think that the human brain was the most important organ in my body, but then I thought: look who's telling me that.

— George Carlin

Comedy is like sex or food in that how spicy you like it is very personal; laughter is an involuntary response. You don't choose your sense of humour, but you can develop it.

Everyone gets 'triggered' and we all get a little trigger happy when we're going through a hard time. Being triggered is saying you overreacted to a stimulus. Something pushed your buttons and you're all upset.

'Triggering' is the new and improved way to say 'pushing your buttons' – I prefer 'pushing your buttons'. Notice, it's 'your' buttons, not theirs. They're doing what they do, so don't worry about them. You take the responsibility, take the power back.

You have other buttons. When comedians make you laugh they're pushing one of those buttons.

Comedians reveal who they are with their sense of humour and I'm no different. I've been pretty consistently dark. That is who I am, that is my soul. And if you share my sense of humour, that is intimacy. Because for me, showing your sense of humour is an incredibly intimate act. My way of exposing myself is with my jokes. I learned that you don't even have to tell the truth as a comic for the audience to figure you out.

Some people find edgy humour cathartic, and some people don't. There are different audiences, different friends and different rooms.

You can laugh about anything but not with anyone. – Pierre Desproges (French-speaking stand-up comic. Apologies for my rough translation – I'm sure it's an even cooler quote in the original French with a Gauloise hanging out the corner of your mouth).

YOU HAD TO BE THERE

Everything is funny if you can laugh at it.
— Lewis Carroll

Sometimes, the good people at the *Daily Mail* or the *Guardian* will accuse me of punching down. Once in a while, they'll pretend they're offended. They'll say things like, 'Oh my God, he told a joke I did not witness, at a comedy show I did not attend.' But expecting political correctness at a comedy show is like hoping to find health and safety at a rodeo.

It's hard to convey tone or irony when it's written down. You haven't heard the joke when you've just seen some words written in black and white. Just like seeing lyrics is not the same as hearing a song. Our aim, as comics, is laughs. What would be the point of offending an audience we haven't met? Are you crazy? That's our livelihood. We wouldn't be able to survive.

Context is a factor: a guy online said he was offended by one of my jokes (he'd not been to a show, he read a review). He told his eight-year-old niece the joke I had performed on stage, and she got upset. She was a dwarf and it was a joke about dwarfs. I was horrified. Yeah, of course she got upset. What kind of fuckwit tells a little girl (very little in this case) a joke like that? 'Look, I heard this joke, it's sort of about you.' That someone would do that to a child is straight-up crazy. She's eight years old, and you're an adult. It is one thing to tell jokes to a paying audience, it is another matter to shout them through people's letterboxes, and an entirely different thing to tell them to a kid. People just ain't no good.

Being offended on behalf of someone is bullshit. It's virtue signalling and it's condescending (condescending means patronising, like when you talk down to someone – you understand, right?).

'Oh, you can't joke about those people, *they* can't take it.'

And yes, my sense of humour is not for everyone. But to punch down, you have to be looking down. If you think I'm up high, then you also think the people I've made jokes about are down low. That's on you.

I know they're well meaning, but they might wanna check their privilege. By calling it 'punching down', they're showing their sexism, racism, disablism (delete as appropriate). I think they're the ones who don't see 'them' as equals. Stop including me.

Guess who likes disabled jokes? Disabled people. At least the ones that come to my shows. Who doesn't like to be included? They like that I can see them and I'm not tiptoeing around. When you joke about someone, they're in the gang. It's inclusive.

Of course, free speech doesn't only defend the jokes you like. As Voltaire said, 'I disapprove of what you say, but will defend to the death your right to tell dick jokes about gay disabled Muslims.' Something like that anyway, I'm paraphrasing.

TERRIBLY FUNNY

We don't apologise for a joke. We are comics. We are here to make you laugh. If you don't get that, then don't watch us.

— Joan Rivers

On the day Joan Rivers died, my friend Anthony Jeselnik tweeted, 'Joan Rivers once told me she would die before she'd ever apologise for a joke. I'm glad she made it.'

Immediately, if I hear anyone saying, 'This is no time for jokes,' what I think is, that's a person that can't think of anything funny to say. The only thing you can get wrong is that it might be a bad moment, but we can all admire a swing and a miss. Obviously, I don't subscribe to 'too soon'.

I find comfort in the fact that the joke that will end my career, I've already told it. It's out there somewhere on YouTube and it's perfectly acceptable . . . until one day it isn't.

Terrible things happen and they aren't funny. But a joke is not the thing. Such as rape – rape is never funny. But some jokes about rape are very funny. The joke is not the rape.

Why do jokes about taboo topics? Because we need to laugh to let some of the pressure out. I'm attracted to the transgressive. The mechanism at work in jokes is tension and then release, and with transgressive subjects, the tension is already there.

Would I ever avoid a topic? I look at it like this: there are certain taboos that I know are going to cause controversy and if I'm going to tackle one, I'd better come up with jokes that are funny enough to justify doing it. The reward has to match the risk. If I don't think I've come up with a funny enough joke, I won't do it.

That's too terrible to joke about, is like saying that disease is too terrible to cure. – Louis CK

CUNTS GETTING OFFENDED

A distrust of wit is the beginning of tyranny.
– Edward Abbey

A guy once said to me after a gig, 'That was disgusting, pure filth, no better than last year.' What can you do?

After a show, a lady once asked me, 'Why do you go out of your way to offend people?' Well, curious lady, offending people was on the way to where I was going. It was no trouble at all. Thank you for asking.

Incidentally, it's easier to be inoffensive when you're not trying to entertain people for two hours. Much easier. For two hours a night, five times a week, I'm up on stage making jokes and I've been pushing the envelope for twenty years, so I'm bound to have a few papercuts.

'I just didn't think it was funny' is sometimes a way for people to pretend they're not offended. Why? Be offended. Offence just means you don't like it. It's okay to not like something. And remember, just because you're offended doesn't make you right.

Look, my rule is, I wouldn't say anything that would offend my mother. You've just never met my mother.

A BRIEF HISTORY OF MINE

The noblest art is making others happy.

— P. T. Barnum

The world of showbiz throws different people together. Every once in a while you meet someone and unexpectedly you hit it off. I had a close friendship with Stephen Hawking. Weird, right?

It was at an awards ceremony when I first spotted Professor Hawking and his lovely nurse. We weren't at the same table but later, as I was walking around, I took the opportunity to introduce myself. I sat down next to him and said, 'Hey, we used to be at the same college. I was at Caius, how are you doing?' He most probably wouldn't have remembered me from way back in the nineties. But I certainly remembered him zipping around in his wheelchair.

And then I started telling him some stories. Hearsay about the people on stage. He loved gossip. Rolf Harris was presenting an award for a kid and this was just around the time of Operation Yewtree, and I made what turned out to be a pretty appropriate paedophile joke.

Then I said, 'I've got a couple of jokes about you in my set.' I told him a couple of my Stephen Hawking jokes, and then it was time to come clean about the insane letter I'd once sent him.

When I started doing comedy. I sent Stephen Hawking a letter. It's a well-worn comedic device, a prank – send a joke letter, see if you get a funny response. The letter I sent out was pretty fucking brutal. It basically said, my son's got a similar condition to you. He's properly 'mongified'. He loves to play. I continued, could we set up a playdate with you and him? That was the letter. I know.

Stephen sent me back this beautiful letter, which said, 'I think you're never too old to play, but I'm afraid I'm very busy. Here's a balloon ride, maybe he'd like to go on one. I went on one recently and they can put a wheelchair in the basket.'

He bought a balloon ride for me and my imaginary disabled son. I know. I'm the worst and he's the best. That's the thing with pranks – sometimes the other person wins. And he won. The joke had been about the inappropriate language but he took the meaning beyond the language. Great.

When I confessed all that to him, I felt like the worst person in the world, a proper cock. I wanted a black hole to open up and swallow me – which I'm guessing he would have enjoyed seeing up close.

He said he vaguely remembered. You know, because mostly he thought about string theory and getting through the day, not hanging out and having fun with disabled children. After all, he was a theoretical physicist, not a dolphin.

The day after the awards ceremony I got an email from him. His team had gone to the effort of tracking me down. He asked if I wanted to come to tea in Cambridge. He said, 'The next time you're up, just come and hang out.'

So I did. I went to Cambridge and hung out with Stephen Hawking. I had tea with him and his nursing staff and we chatted for a couple of hours.

And again, I got an email afterwards to say how much he had enjoyed himself.

I figured it would take him so long to type anything that you basically had to be on 'send' and I was willing to talk 'at' him. He had this amazing care team around him who would fill in his anecdotes. You might say, 'Hey, how's it going?' and they would tell you what he'd been up to and you'd chat about it and then he would respond the next day by email.

The next time, he came to a show. By that stage of his life he wasn't eating out a lot. But I made a real fuss of going, 'Come on, come out,' so he did. We had a really good laugh and a wonderful dinner. If you think you're famous, just go to dinner with Stephen Hawking – you become entirely unremarkable by association.

The thing about Stephen is that everyone wanted to meet him. You talk about famous, everyone knew who he was. He used to come to my parties and I remember Elton John being really excited to talk to him. I was like, but you're Elton John. And you realise everyone is secretly really into physics.

As a side note, Stephen Hawking drunk, no difference. I guess the voice modulator doesn't have a 'slur' setting.

He loved musicals, maybe because time literally slows down when you're in the second half of *Les Mis*. He liked going to the shows and I think it was partly because he knew it was a treat for his care team, the people who worked so incredibly hard for him.

The one that stands out is the time I took him to *The Book of Mormon*.*

---

* *The Book of Mormon* is one of the funniest shows I've ever seen. It's by Trey Parker and Matt Stone of *South Park* and Robert Lopez of *Avenue Q*.

Afterwards, the cast and crew said they'd love to meet him, so I did the introductions. I said, 'This is Stephen, he's, er, he's actually converting to Mormonism, he really believes in the Mormon faith.'

And just fucking left it there hanging.

After *The Book of Mormon*, he came back to my place for a curry. It was always super fucking messy when he ate. There's something about being a messy eater: it suddenly makes the interaction informal. You get to forget that this guy is a brilliant and lauded physicist; you get to be friends sharing a curry and hanging out.

I still think of Stephen often. Whenever I'm tempted to complain about any little physical malady I think of how grateful my friend Stephen would've been to have the opportunity to pull a hamstring.

JOKES ON HITLER

I'm struck by how laughter connects you with people. It's almost impossible to maintain any kind of distance or any sense of social hierarchy when you're just howling with laughter.

— John Cleese

Unfortunately, Hitler knew exactly what John Cleese was talking about, and that's why he shut down all the cabaret clubs. It's hard to hate anyone you're laughing with.

Ever wonder why it's called a 'sense' of humour? Because

it's as necessary as all your other senses for survival and when you don't have it, you're at a disadvantage.

To laugh can be an act of defiance. People will laugh in the most stressful and hopeless situations. During the Holocaust, prisoners held in concentration camps found ways to secretly tell jokes and share stories.* And they laughed. Laughing gave them some control and reminded them of their humanity. It helped them cope. The movie *Life is Beautiful* is exceptional. How could they make a Holocaust movie that was funny? Well, because that shit happened. And I think it's okay to joke about the Holocaust.

They say there's safety in numbers. Tell that to six million Jews.
– Jimmy Carr

When you're able to laugh at authority figures, what you are doing is changing the power dynamic. It makes 'them' less frightening, like when you see humour used as a tool for protest. I love a good banner. During the anti-Iraq war march, someone made one aimed at Prime Minister Tony Blair: 'Leave it, Tony, it's not worth it.' At a women's march in London, a banner read, 'What's my favourite position? CEO.' At an anti-Brexit march, one placard read, 'The only single market I want to leave is Tinder.'

---

* In 1939, *The Joke's on Hitler: Underground Whispers from the Land of the Concentration Camp* was published in Britain.

ISLAMIC STATE – MY PART IN THEIR DOWNFALL

You can't laugh and be afraid at the same time – of any-thing. If you're laughing, I defy you to be afraid.
                                    – Stephen Colbert

I remember Jack Dee had filmed his DVD special in London on the day after the 7/7 bombings. I thought, 'I hope that never happens to me' (the Jack Dee thing, not the blown-up-by-terrorists thing – but that too). Fast forward to 13 November 2015 (yes, a Friday): we've got the cameras all rigged up in the theatre and I am doing a run-through of *Funny Business*, my tour that year, which we were going to film the next evening for a Netflix special. The first half is great, we take a little break and people check their phones.

It's hard to remember what things were like before Covid-19, but the UK was on high alert. Terrorist attacks were the most threatening thing at the time. Anyway, that Friday was the night of the Paris attacks. It started at a football match at the Stade de France, trailing through cafés and restaurants, then ended with gunmen taking hostages at the Bataclan Theatre.

The second half was fucking weird. When something like that is unfolding in real time, the attention of an audience gets, well, a little dispersed. It was tense, the heckles didn't make sense, it was hard to get laughs to catch.

The next night we were shooting (which sounds in poor taste). At that stage of the tour, when you're recording a Netflix special, you expect to have to work a little: it's like a five out of ten for difficulty. You're not on autopilot, but you can relax into it.

Only 80 per cent of the audience showed up and they drank fast and way too much. They were bawdy, interfering hecklers. I would say the difficulty rating that night was ten out of ten. I had to be on my game the whole time. It took me nearly three hours to perform two hours of material. Of course, you'd never know watching it back – that's the beauty of an edit.

Here's the thing: once people started to laugh, they stopped being afraid.

And if we stop laughing, the terrorists win – so I guess I did have a small hand in their defeat. #JeSuisCharlie

PART 5
SAD CLOWN

CHAPTER TEN

TOUCHY-FEELY

YOUR MAMA, SHE'S SO DEPRESSED

There's a cliché that all comedians are depressed. I don't think that's accurate. But it's a popular misconception that comedians are the sad clowns of life. It's just too delicious an irony.

Man goes to a doctor and tells him he's depressed. Life seems harsh and cruel. He says he feels all alone in a threatening world where what lies ahead is vague and uncertain. The doctor says, 'The treatment is simple. The great comedian Grimaldi is in town tonight. Go and see him. That should pick you up.' The man bursts into tears and says, 'But, doctor . . . I am Grimaldi.'

In my opinion, it's amazing not how many comics have killed themselves, but how many haven't. Because, here's my amateur Freud theory: I think comedians have often had to look after a sick parent (either physically or psychologically). It's a good question to ask a comic: 'Who was sick in your life, your mum or dad?'

Having to please a sick parent – that's my story. My mum

struggled with depression throughout my childhood. I grew up in an environment where I needed to make things okay at home. I wanted to please my mother, I wanted her to be happy.

I remember one Christmas being in the kitchen doing nothing, not helping at all whilst my mother was cooking. I said, 'Well, you know what, I should get out of the way. I might watch a movie.' And she said, 'No, stay there, you're here for vibes.'

There was a guy in the band the Happy Mondays named Bez, he couldn't play a musical instrument, he couldn't sing and to my knowledge had no musical abilities whatsoever (pretty sure he was the lead singer's drug dealer). He was there for 'vibes'. I feel like I was the Bez in my family.

That's what comedians do for an audience: we talk about life and make it okay. We're here for vibes.

MISERY LOVES COMEDY

The Sad Clown Paradox is where mental disorder meets comedy. It's the 'cyclothymic temperament' (me neither, thank God for Google), a ceaseless instability of mood, thinking and behaviour. It's a never-ending cycle where a child takes on additional responsibilities, which evokes a need for acceptance and creates mental health issues, which in turn leads to a need to self-medicate with humour.

Rinse and repeat enough times and what you get is a comedian. Trauma is the motivation to use humour as a way to form relationships and get acceptance. My question: why is this not called the Jimmy Carr Syndrome?

I'd argue that a lot of depressed people are drawn to comedy as a coping mechanism to deal with depression.

I'd also argue that the tools of stand-up comedy can help you cope.

You could argue that Jimmy likes to argue. But I'd argue I don't.

DEPRESSIVES AIN'T UNHAPPY

I feel I need to make an important distinction here: feeling down isn't the same as being depressed. You may want to check in with yourself when you feel low. Which one are you? Are you clinically depressed or are you unhappy? There's a stigma in our society around unhappiness, but if you're unhappy, you're lucky. It means you can do something about it.

It's appropriate to be down sometimes. It's appropriate to be unhappy if something goes wrong. It'd be weird if you weren't unhappy. If your partner leaves, you're suffering chronic pain, or you aren't where you want to be in life, it's appropriate to be unhappy.

Grief is a good example. I always liked the phrase, 'Grief is the price we pay for love.' It suggests that the level of our unhappiness at someone's passing is in direct proportion to how much we loved them. Grief isn't depression, it's unhappiness – it's entirely appropriate unhappiness.

Unhappiness is one thing; depression is another. If you're depressed, well, depression is caused by chemistry in the brain. It's a physical illness, a biochemical imbalance.

Neurotransmitters are fucking with your brain function. You feel down, you can't sleep, you have fatigue, you're irritable. You have anhedonia: the inability to feel joy.

I think anhedonia is the reason that people who suffer with depression are drawn to the light.

Depression can be just as deadly as cancer, just look at the suicide rate. Suicide is a symptom of depression. It's strange that we don't always think of it that way because the connection is undeniable. In the same way cancer can be thought of as the body's immune system attacking itself, suicide is a result of our minds turning on us.

Depression is a disease, a real actual disease. Now, I know you know that. But do you? Have you ever told a depressed friend to 'snap out of it'? Maybe, you might have. Well, have you ever told a friend with cancer to 'come on, snap out of it?' Same same.

Depression is an illness. And no one is immune.

TAKE YOUR LIFE . . . AND NOT AS AN EXAMPLE

My favourite suicide note, yeah, I have a favourite suicide note: *Betty, I hate you. Love, George.*

As a solution to depression you could try suicide. It's certainly effective. But suicide is a permanent solution to a temporary problem. When I said earlier that all human activity is purposeful, I meant it. Even the people killing themselves are doing it for good reason. It might not seem like a good reason to you. But it does to them. And there but for the grace of God, and an encyclopaedic memory for jokes, go I.

What's the difference between unhappiness and depression? About 200 paracetamol.

It's hard to hear about a suicide and not consider how fragile we all are. We have one life to live and sometimes that's too much. The ripple effect of a suicide is devastating (especially if someone's drowned themselves). The pain you avoid with suicide doesn't vanish, it merely gets redistributed around those that loved you.

A lack of perspective is inbuilt in depression. A happy person isn't someone who's happy all the time. It's someone who interprets events in such a way that they don't lose their innate peace. Here's where comedy can help. Comedy requires you to step back and disassociate. Comedy can help you deal with tragedy by letting you see what happened through a different lens and from different angles.

Comics are good at playing with perspective. There's always another way to look at things. No matter how down you feel, it won't last.

My dad has a weird hobby. He collects empty bottles. Which sounds so much better than alcoholic. – Stewart Francis

If you are actually depressed, what choices do you have? The common consensus is that you should try medication, exercise, or both. Exercise is meant to be more effective than Prozac but seriously, it's hard enough to get someone who's happy to go to the gym.

Dogs are great. If you have a friend who's depressed, get them a dog. Every dog is an emotional support animal. Having a dog means you have to get up in the mornings, you have to get dressed, you have to walk the dog and feed them. And dogs are hella affectionate. If a dog can't cheer a person up, they're truly depressed. What you need then is two dogs.

I'M SAD/YOU'RE DEPRESSED

When I was twenty-five years old, I'd lost my faith, hated my job and my mother had just died. I didn't realise it at the time, but I had it easy. All I was, was very unhappy. Unhappy is all right. Unhappy I can work with. I thought I was depressed, sure. Fair enough, really – a lot of the symptoms of depression are very similar to being unhappy.

Here's the distinction I keep coming back to: it's nature vs nurture. Depression is nature. Sadness is nurture. You can do something about sadness. Just don't conflate the two, or you could end up feeling down.

And at that point in my life I realised that all I needed to do was one thing: change everything.

I instinctively knew I needed a little injection of merriment, levity, joy, humour – a fucking laugh. I was desperate for it. I'd lost my purpose within my family, which was cheering up Mum. And I just pivoted slightly and instead of trying to cheer one person up, I tried to cheer everyone up. I was drawn to comedy like a moth, out of the darkness into a dazzling bright limelight.

WAIT – I'M NOT SAD, I'M DEPRESSED

I had to go back and forth to Australia twice in a month. I was in my hotel in Melbourne when I was hit with crippling depression. God, it was bad, I was lying on the bed seriously considering if there was any real point to anything.

It starts with something like vertigo. It's the sensation of falling within a black void. I became acutely aware of my mortality. I sometimes get it when I'm watching documentaries about the universe. You're looking at the earth and thinking, we're fucking tiny, on the edge of a galaxy. The universe is vast and it's like, 'Ah, shit. I'm going to die.' You really understand your place in it. We're nothing. I'm nothing.

It's also this inability to feel pleasure. It's not about the stimulus not being there; you can see it – the weather is so great, you can almost taste the skin cancer, I'm here in beautiful Australia – but you can't receive it, the receptor for pleasure is all fucked up.

Have you ever experienced a loved one dying and they're painfully thin and you make them their favourite food, but they can't eat it because they've got no appetite? I have. That's what it's like with depression: in that moment you have no appetite for life.

If this is unfamiliar to you, that is fucking great. And if it does happen one day, know this: it's not for ever. Hold on.

Luckily, I knew enough to understand that what I was experiencing was extreme jet lag coupled with the serotonin-stripping effect of the Valium I'd taken to sleep.

And I also knew that it was going to be a bad couple of days, but I'd be okay.

Really nothing is the answer for me. I just white-knuckle it. Easy for me. Because it passes relatively quickly and I can work through it. I mean, literally, I can perform a show on stage mid-depression and mid-panic attack and no one seems to notice. It's an odd experience; you feel very alone. But ultimately getting into a flow state, doing something I enjoy, really helps. It's saved me more than once.

The next night I had a gig in Perth and had a full-on panic attack on stage, during the show. I should have given myself a bit of a break between the two gigs. Later, I heard that Pink took a mental health day once in Australia and I thought, 'What a fucking boss.' I only did the gig because I couldn't work out what else to do. It felt like it'd be more hassle to reschedule. I didn't have the energy to take a day off. And there I was looking at 4,000 people laughing and feeling nothing but isolated. Talk about being the only person in the room facing the wrong way.

Give yourself a little time, be kind to yourself. Who doesn't enjoy a pity party? I'll bring chips and dips.

Here are three tips for when you are feeling depressed, courtesy of the great documentary filmmaker Ken Burns:

1. Remember this won't last.
2. Get help from others.
3. Be kind to yourself.

That's it. Thanks, Ken.*

---

* Also, if you find yourself with sixteen and a half hours to spare, do yourself a favour and watch Ken's documentary on the Vietnam War. It's a laugh riot.

I WORRY IT'S ANXIETY

The brilliant Clive James made this gorgeous observation:

> *Common sense and a sense of humour, are the same thing, moving at different speeds. A sense of humour, is just common sense, dancing.*

I love that quote. Well done, Clive James.

Sometimes I get depression, but anxiety is a constant hum in my life.

I look at it this way: yes, I have the lows of anxiety, but I also have the highs of creativity.

Anxiety is the flip side of creativity – it's a gift. A gut-wrenching, pain-in-the-arse, nightmare gift. But it's the thought that counts. If you're suffering with anxiety, great news: you're a creative person.

The downside to a creative mind is that it's always on. Anxiety: it's your creativity with nothing to do. Give your creative mind something to do or it'll drive you crazy.

When I'm feeling anxious, I try and refocus my anxiety on something positive, I try to give my mind something to do other than worry. Start simple. Do anagrams, solve a puzzle, anything that gets your mind going.

Sometimes I get a full-on panic attack. It feels like I don't belong in my own skin. I can't do anything, can't settle, can't sit still, can't get comfortable, can't eat, can't lie down, can't focus. Sometimes you just have to sit with it. Feeling your feelings looks a lot like doing nothing; feeling your feelings looks like procrastination. And that's a problem when we (the big We, like our whole culture) are addicted to activity.

Anxiety can be useful. Say you're not feeling confident, then worry is good. Anxiety will motivate you to prepare if you let it. People who worry seldom have anything to worry about precisely because they felt worried and that worry made them prepare. And because their worry makes them prepared, they have nothing to worry about. If you don't follow, don't worry.

ATTENTION TENSION

Every journey begins with a single step.
— Confucius (incidentally, they're called 'fortune cookies' 'cause that's how Confucius made his money)

Anxiety can be about everything happening at once. Anxiety can be about being overwhelmed. The task you're faced with is too huge to contemplate, you don't know what to do next so you do nothing.

The way to overcome this is pretty straightforward, really. You take the impossibly huge task of living, and you break it down into little bits. You say, what shall I do today? Right now, right this minute, where can I focus my attention?

You need to work out what's the most important thing that needs doing right now. The extraordinary thing about the human mind is not how much information we take in but how much we filter out. And anxiety is when you're suddenly aware of all the things you need to filter out.

It's like the emergency room in a hospital. Nurses have to work out in triage who needs priority attention. Similarly, your mind is an ER on a Saturday night: you've got ninety-nine problems in your waiting room and you need to work out which one is the most immediate. So go on, what's your gunshot wound?

Do the duty nearest to thee, and thy second duty will already become clearer. – Thomas Carlyle

FEELING FEELINGS FINALLY

Let everything happen to you: beauty and terror.
> – Jojo Rabbit, quoting Rilke

No feeling is final.
> – Still Rilke

There's an old Cherokee story about the two wolves within us, one white and one black. (And yes, the Cherokees are saying that the white one is good and the black one is bad. Little bit racist, the ancient Cherokees, but on balance they were more sinned against than sinning.)

The boy asks his grandfather, 'Which wolf will win?' The grandfather replies, 'The one you feed.' So you feed the white one, right? Yeah, obviously, that's the Western version, that's the one you want to be big and strong, that's the white way.

But in the original Cherokee, the grandfather says, 'They both win.' The story continues, 'You see, if I only choose to feed the white wolf, the black one will be hiding around every corner waiting for me to become distracted or weak . . . He will always be angry and always be fighting the white wolf.'

If only Americans had waited to hear the end of the story. What I'm saying is, you can run from your feelings, but they'll catch up with you.

It's important to acknowledge how you're experiencing the world. Feelings matter. Feelings are what will give us the edge over the AI machines. The emotions you don't like are just as important as the feel-good ones. Seriously, fuck Instagram and your #bestlife; uncomfortable emotions will help you far more in life. They're also the emotions that help you connect to other people.

Putting on a brave face is nothing, who gives a fuck about your brave face? Have you seen comics rant? They're not bottling it up, they're not hiding their feelings. They're showing you how they're feeling their emotions and making the process funny. Emotions are not the problem.

Of course, just because you have an emotion, doesn't mean you have to act on it. That's crazy. That turns anger into something like vengeance, which never ends well – just ask John Wick.

We all use the words 'emotion' and 'feelings' pretty interchangeably. It's close, but they are different: emotions are physical and instinctive. They create a reaction in your body. Feelings are your brain consciously experiencing your emotional reaction: it's where you add meaning.

A feeling is an emotion with A levels. You'll get further if you pay attention during them.

Feel everything. Just keep going.

PART 6

SO, I GOT PUBLICLY SHAMED

CHAPTER ELEVEN

JIMMY CARR'S GUIDE TO LIFE AND ACCOUNTANCY

The short version of the story is that I had not paid enough tax, and after it was brought to my attention, I apologised and paid what I owed. But the long story . . . Fuck. Me.

There's a saying about problems: 'If you have a problem that can be solved with money and you've got the money, you don't have a problem.' Turns out, not entirely true.

When your ass is hanging out and getting kicked in public, it's hard to maintain your disposition, let alone your dignity.

'MORALLY REPREHENSIBLE'

I get 'the phone call' from a paper on a Sunday afternoon in 2012. A guy says, 'Hi, I'm from *The Times*, we're running a story on you . . .' I'm like, 'Shit', and I run through every sin I've ever committed. And it's amazing how quickly your mind runs through every terrible thing you've ever done and said, and every person you might have pissed off. For me, my immediate go-to is jokes. Come on, I've definitely said something terrible – that must be it. And what's the worst that can happen? The headline will be 'comedian tells a joke', it'll be fine, I'll be okay.

But then the journalist says, 'I'd like to talk to you about your tax planning . . .' And I think, 'Oh, fuck.'

What's the difference between tax avoidance and tax evasion? Two years in jail.

Tax avoidance is where your accountant asks you, 'Hey, do you want to pay less tax?' And you say, 'Sure, but is this legal?' And the accountant says, 'We'll see.' Tax evasion is getting paid in cash and hiding the money under a mattress (for clarity I avoided, never evaded). I'd seen tax as a game. You're supposed to do your best to avoid paying and then they're supposed to close the loopholes. And so on.

After that phone call, I knew it was gonna be in the paper, but there's in the paper and then 'in the paper'. There's 'a few paragraphs on page 15' and then there's the front page.

The story hit on Monday.

At the time, I was recording a series of *8 Out of 10 Cats*. We taped on a Thursday and our writing days were on Monday, Tuesday and Wednesday. The same Monday morning that I debuted on the front of *The Times*, I went to work, walked into the writers' room at 10 a.m. like usual. And everyone took the piss and that was all right. The writers joking made the whole thing feel normal.

Meanwhile, there were lots of phone calls with accountants trying to work out why the fuck I had done this and what exactly I owed and how far back it went. For the first time, finally, I was taking an interest in my accounts. This was way too late. It was like locking the gate after the horse had bolted, been shot and turned into a glue stick.

Just as things were getting better and I was beginning to understand what I needed to do, which was clearly pay it the fuck back, things took a turn. On that Wednesday the Prime Minister broke off from the G20 Summit in Mexico. He came from a meeting with Obama and eighteen of the other most important leaders of the world and he walked into a press conference where he spoke about nothing other than my personal tax affairs.

Holy Fucking Shit.

On every news channel in the UK, people could see our Prime Minister call me 'morally reprehensible'. If the Prime Minister of the country you live in, the leader of a right-wing party who personally implemented brutal austerity measures, calls you 'morally reprehensible', you know you have a problem.

But I mean, '*morally* reprehensible'? Really? Had he even seen my act? Morality has never been my strong suit. I imagined parents everywhere, panicked, saying, 'Oh no, what will we do? Now that Jimmy is gone, who will our children look to for guidance?'

Also, in my defence, I have never fucked a pig. (Note to the reader: rumours abound that David Cameron fucked a pig whilst at university. That may or may not be true, but he also gave us Brexit and austerity and some sleazy lobbying so, depending on your political affiliations, fucking a pig may not even be the worst thing he's ever done.)

Still, you have to take your medicine, I understood that. But with that one statement from the PM, it went from being a front-page story that was blowing over to 'Oh shit, it is not going to die down' and all fucking hell broke loose.

It is devastating to be the bad guy on the front page of the newspapers. I had an incredibly visceral response to being publicly shamed. I was having panic attacks, I wasn't sleeping, it was overwhelming, I could barely function. All I could do was wander zombie-like through the week.

When I had those full-blown panic attacks, I didn't have the bandwidth to watch a movie, so you know what my partner and I did? We watched *Downton Abbey*. *Downton Abbey*, I swear it's TV Valium. It was the comfortable, warm blanket I needed. Some people swear by heroin, but have they tried *Downton*?

Now, I'm not a doctor but here's what I'd do with your panic attack: write a list. Boring, right? But boring can be good. Boring will calm you right down. Write down what you have to do and keep writing. Refine the list, make it ever more specific, until the huge looming disaster becomes a series of manageable bite-sized tasks. Take a breath and then go take care of business.

Item number one on that list should be: down time with *Downton*. *Downton* and chill.

'LIFE, DEATH AND TAXES'

> *Get your facts first . . . Then you can distort them as you please.*
>
> — Samuel Clemens

You learn a lot when you're having a bad day. I'm now quite the expert in tax. So here's my advice: if you get a letter demanding payment, do the responsible thing – pop it in the recycling.

Don't worry about the letter, they'll send another letter, those fuckers love a letter.

Just to be clear again, I was avoiding tax, using legal loopholes. Whereas legendary comic Ken Dodd was a tax evader. Dodd got paid in cash for everything. He had a room full of money, literally. When the police eventually searched his home, they found a room full of banknotes. In court Dodd said, 'I told the Inland Revenue I didn't owe them a penny because I live near the seaside.' Legend. Incidentally, he was acquitted by a jury of his peers in Liverpool. Double legend.

Loopholes are a game of cat and mouse played exclusively by the rich – that's how it worked for years. That's still how it works, but not for me. Halfway through 2012 they changed the rules. How come this offshore tax haven is okay, but that one isn't? How come corporations and billionaires get to do it but other people can't? Good questions, but I wouldn't ask them if I were you.

That maybe sounds like a justification – like I'm saying what I did was okay. Trust me, I know it wasn't okay. Trust me, I don't fuck with any of those loopholes any more.

THE SECOND LAW OF JOURNALISM

The legendary PR guru Matthew Freud is a friend and he's good in a crisis – he gives good crises. Matthew told me, 'You are a victim of the "second law" of the press. It's not your fault, it's just your turn.' My natural inclination was to lean in and ask, 'What's the "first law" of the press?' Matthew: 'There is no "first law".'

I admit, I may have indulged in some self-pity, because who else was going to pity me? Self-pity was the only pity I was getting. What were people going to say, other than 'Rich guy; pays what he owes.'

There's a story about a prank Arthur Conan Doyle played. He sent out a letter to five of his friends saying, 'We are discovered. Flee.' One of those friends disappeared and was never seen again. We've all done stuff.

I knew I had to host a topical comedy show where the premise is: what's the most talked-about thing of the week? That's not great when you're the most talked-about thing that week.

The thing about TV is you always think it's the performer who did well, but more often than not it's the producer who has said something great to the performer beforehand. That person was Ruth Phillips, the producer. She said, 'You just have to take it. Don't come back with anything. You can't win.'

That was good advice. The experience was like being the centre of a roast. You get roasted, except you don't get to do a rebuttal. In the end you just go, 'Yup, sorry about that.' Sometimes all you can do is a mea culpa. When it comes to money and super-sketchy tax schemes, there's very little compassion from anyone other than from people with more money than you. Insisting that what I did was not illegal was a weak-ass position and I knew it.

Here's what I said in my statement:

I appreciate as a comedian, people will expect me to 'make light' of this situation, but I'm not going to in this statement as this is obviously a serious matter. I met with a financial adviser and he said to me: 'Do you want to pay less tax? It's totally legal.' I said: 'Yes.' I now realise I've made a terrible error of judgement. Although I've been advised the K2 tax scheme is entirely legal, and has been fully disclosed to HMRC, I'm no longer involved in it and will in future conduct my financial affairs much more responsibly. Apologies to everyone.

But also, to be clear, Matthew was only half right. It wasn't just my turn. It was also my fault. I get it.

A MILLION REASONS I AVOIDED TAX

You want to know how much money I saved in tax? I'll tell you: fuck all. Despite a lot of effort on my part.

I was saving money for a rainy day. Hell, I was more prepared than Noah. They went back through everything. Everything. I paid back money that I saved in an ISA, I paid back money I paid into an Enterprise Initiative Scheme, a scheme set up by the government that had a tax benefit, because they said I only did it to avoid tax. Well yeah, obviously. They went back through everything and I paid back everything.

I paid millions to HMRC for twelve years of back taxes. When you owe that much, if you walk past a homeless guy you think, 'At least you've got nothing. I'm five years of solid touring away from being back at zero.' (Incidentally, I'm not allowed to volunteer at the soup kitchen any more.)

And then HMRC told me, 'You owe us interest on that money.'

And I went, 'But you only just told me . . . I only just got the fucking bill.' Jesus wept!

I tell you what I didn't do when I got that bill from HMRC. I didn't stay at home and wallow. I couldn't afford to. I called my manager and said, 'Book 500 shows. I'm going to work. And this time, don't give me the money. Don't even let me hold it.'

ONLY MONEY

We cannot forgive what we cannot punish . . .
— Hannah Arendt

No one is complaining here. I took the phone call from my accountant about my impending financial ruin on my own tennis court.

However. There are moments in a scandal where you go, 'Oh, I'm gonna lose everything.' When you realise you could lose all of it, you understand how lucky you are and how much you like your life. So, for that insight, thank you, HMRC. And I don't even mind you charging for that life lesson, but may I humbly suggest your rates are a tiny bit, too fucking unbelievably soul-crushingly high?

For me, the worry was less about the money and more about no longer being a comedian. Being someone that people come and see perform live is a privileged position. And that privilege is not for ever. It is for as long as people want you and that can change. I genuinely wondered if I'd ever be allowed to do stand-up again.

I still wake up in a panic, maybe around 5 a.m., I wake up to a panic attack every morning. The disruption to my sleep pattern has stayed with me. I don't like to call it post-traumatic stress because people who are involved in violent crimes or have been to war, they've got PTSD and I certainly wouldn't compare my experience to theirs. And also when shame is a part of an experience, it's hard to feel like you have a right to anything.

I feel like I had a fall from grace but there was a bungee rope. So, I had the sensation of falling from grace, all of the sensation of losing everything, but then the bungee kicked in and I bounced back.

My experience has increased my powers of empathy, and that's no bad thing. Now that I know what that feels like, I'm very empathetic when people lose everything. Jay Z said in an interview, 'I'm not the worst thing I ever did.' And I hear you, Jay.

People fuck up. And people get crazy judgy when people fuck up. And here's the thing: I will joke about anyone, I will joke all day long about shit going down. But if someone's your friend, if you know someone, you should be kind.

That experience gave me a new rule for life: be a good foul-weather friend. The world is full of fair-weather friends. When you're throwing a party, people are going to turn up. But who's gonna reach out when you're on the cover of the paper and being publicly denounced by your Prime Minister? Who is secretly happy you've been brought down? I had a friend, super bright, funny and I thought he was a nice guy . . . Well, I thought I had a friend.

On the other hand, James Corden called me around midnight

that same day the story hit the papers. He was doing a Broadway run of his play *One Man, Two Guvnors*. He rang, just to check in, no judgement, just called to cheer me up. I wasn't in great shape. And then the next night, he called again. And the next night. He was and is a fucking great guy. And frankly, I needed it. James Corden is a mensch.

So, a lesson I learned is, if you have a friend going through hard times, call, text, reach out. People don't forget the friends who do that. And if you don't know what to say, just say, 'I don't know what to say.' It's all good.

In some ways my mistake was relatively easy to remedy because I knew what to do to fix it. The path to redemption was clear for me. But some people have it much worse. They get publicly shamed for things that are harder to punish.

I have a lot in common with Al Capone. They got him on tax too and I'm also going to die of syphilis.

PART 7

LIVING ON THE EDGE

CHAPTER TWELVE

A GENERAL THEORY OF SPECIALISATION

YOU DO YOU

The crowd is there to be entertained, not followed.
— Jimmy Carr (yeah, I'm quoting myself. Wait,
this whole book is a quote by me. Never mind . . .)

You're a unique individual, a snowflake unlike any other. Think of all the special people out there. That's a lot of snowflakes. That's a goddamn avalanche. How will you distinguish yourself?

You've got to find your edge. To a certain degree, we all have an edge. But then we're taught to smooth out those edges and fit in. We're offered a cookie-cutter life by society and if that's your bliss, you are in luck, my friend. There's a book I'd recommend called *How to Be Like Everyone Else*, and it's written by Committee.

We all start out trying to fit in because we're a social animal. But sooner or later you're going to want to find your 'edge', because if you can find your edge then life is so much easier – not as easy as your mum, but easier.

Firstly, take a look at everything you've got. You'll need to be honest with yourself. Be straight. Spinning your qualities is what you do for other people, but for you, you'll want to see yourself clearly: what are your resources, your friends, education, location? What do you have going for you or against you? What are your limits? What are you apt to do? What internal qualities do you have? I'm no Scientologist, but this is an audit. The good news is, instead of it costing you £50,000 and your family, I'm only charging you the price of a book. Beat that, David Miscavige.

Personally, I think it's a beautiful thing not to have a telephone voice. Nobody can compete with you at being you. (If you have an identical twin, ignore this bit. If you have an evil identical twin, probably best to kill the evil twin – although if you think that's a good idea, odds are you're the evil twin. I digress.)

You'll have natural aptitudes that you might not know you have, at first. But there are clues, breadcrumbs that lead you in a particular direction.

Here are three questions to get you started:

What do people say is hard for them, but you find easy?

What is something other people value that you can do?

What would you do anyway, even if no one paid you?

And as long as the answer to that last one isn't 'torture people', you've probably got something you can build on. If it is 'torture people'? You may have a career as a dentist.

GENETIC CELEBRITY

*The thing that makes you exceptional, if you are at all, is
inevitably the thing that makes you lonely.*

— Lorraine Hansberry

There's an idea of 'genetic celebrity'. It's the concept that some
people are so attractive they experience the world as a celebrity would, even though they're not actually famous. They are
treated differently by people. Of course, they're never aware of
their privilege because the world has always appeared that way
to them. But they will be aware. There's an old joke:

*My grandmother said, 'Young men used to be so much more polite
when I was a girl.'*

*'Yes, Grandmother, because the young men of today are not
trying to fuck you.'*

We often take our gifts, our edge, for granted, because having
them just seems part of the natural order of things. If you've got
rich parents, don't hide it. Don't deliberately make it harder on
yourself. There are no extra points for difficulty. You can still
build a work ethic. And if you're from a poor background, use
that chip. Make it work for you. Don't hide.

It's easiest to appreciate edge when you can actually see it and
it's good-looking. Take models. Staring at the face of a beautiful
gazelle-like creature, you know they'd be crazy not to use their
beauty to their advantage. Especially as models are on a clock

(there is a limited time on being super hot – I don't make the rules). That isn't to say they should solely rely on their super-hot edge, but for God's sake, they should use it while they can.

If you're in your twenties, do you know what edge you have? I can tell you, without even meeting you. Energy. You don't even know what an edge that is until you're in your forties. That's why every old fucker looks at you with nostalgia: 'Oh, to have that energy, that vitality again . . .' Well, you have it and it's going to diminish faster than a supermodel's looks – sorry.

When you're young, you not only have energy, you also have ludicrous levels of optimism – that's two huge edges. You know who didn't start Facebook? A forty-year-old. And do you know why? A forty-year-old would have shrugged and said, 'Nah, it'll never work, we already have MySpace.' Which for younger readers was basically a Friends Reunited for the sort of people who weren't on Bebo.

Beauty, energy, optimism. Whenever old people are jealous of youngsters, that's what it's about.

In fact, if there's anything about you that other people get jealous about, pay attention to it: that's your edge.

Lean into it. Use your edge in life. Give them what they didn't know they wanted.

'TONIGHT, MATTHEW, I'M GOING TO BE JIMMY CARR'

When you're in showbiz, there is a moment where you'll suddenly break through. We call it a 'big break' (clearly, we are not scientists, it's not even in Latin). It's the moment where your edge is given an opportunity to shine and, suddenly, you're noticed. Mine might have been Edinburgh in the summer of 2002, when I was nominated for the Perrier. Or it might have been the Royal Variety performance I got off the back of that, which was televised a few months later. After that, suddenly there was a bit of recognition, that first experience of 'Haven't I seen you on the TV?'

But I feel like the real shift happened when I did a show in a West End theatre.

It was right after Edinburgh when I got a phone call telling me that they were doing a tribute to the legendary wit Peter Cook. I guess they figured it'd be fun to have a new face on the bill, because everyone else was a heavyweight: Michael Palin, Harry Enfield, Jonathan Ross, Rik Mayall, Angus Deayton. Plus David Baddiel was also there.

Everyone in the show was being asked to do a classic Peter Cook bit, a sketch or a monologue or a piece of prose. That was weird for me because I was from the circuit and there you just didn't do other people's material. It's like a golden rule of stand-up comedy. We get very judgy about that.

I said, 'I don't think I can do someone else's material. I can't do Peter Cook's material because Peter Cook is Peter Cook and I've been doing comedy for five minutes. I'd love to do the gig but if it's cool with you, I'll just do five minutes of my own jokes.'

And I did. I did five minutes of my own jokes and in a two-hour show, it was the only five minutes that people hadn't heard before, so I stood out. And, whoosh . . . It's not often you think, 'Whoa, that went well.' But I did that night.

My edge was, I was the new kid and inexperienced. I was thirty years old and the fact that no one knew me became the advantage. No one can beat you at being you.

THE WISDOM OF CROWDS

If you're still having trouble with the questions 'What's my edge? Who am I exactly?', you can always ask around. Ask ten people: 'So what kind of person do you think I am?' And be careful, because they'll try and soften what they say. You have to do a little translating. For example:

If they say that people need to 'get to know you', you're a bitch.

If they say that you're 'lively' and that you have a 'big personality', you're an asshole.

If they say that you're 'challenging' or 'opinionated', you're a cunt.

The person who lights up the room doesn't know they're the source of the light; they just think rooms are bright. The particular magic you have, you probably don't know you have, because the impression you give is not about how you feel. I have met a lot of beautiful people and they do not go around feeling beautiful. What they feel is self-conscious because everyone is staring at them and acting weird.

It's a bit like that old joke about feeling sorry for the Queen because she thinks the whole world smells of fresh paint. You might not know you're a funny fucker, you just know everyone around you is always laughing.

There's this story about Don Rickles: Rickles is performing in Vegas to a packed room. He's the biggest comedian in the world at that time. Right in front, there's an empty table and it's reserved.

About twenty minutes into his routine, he's killing it, when who walks in? Marilyn Monroe, who is the most famous human in the world. Suddenly no one is listening to 'the Don' any more, they're looking at Marilyn Monroe. She sashays to the front table and sits down. Now Rickles knows everyone in the room is staring at Marilyn, so he waits a beat and says, 'I thought I told you to wait in the truck.'

I'll bet you anything Marilyn Monroe didn't know what she was doing. She might have known she could make an entrance, but I'll bet you dollars to doughnuts she had no idea of the extraordinary effect she had on people. She probably thought that's what people do when they see someone enter a room: they turn and stare with their jaw on the floor.

When I was on holiday in Greece in my mid-twenties, at one of those Human Potential Movement kind of hippy retreats called Skyros, a complete stranger said to me on the second day as we were dancing the five rhythms under a thunderstorm: 'You should be on TV.' I looked at him blankly. He was right and he was years ahead of me.

THE CHILD-CATCHER

Talent hits a target no one else can hit; genius hits a target no one else can see.

— Arthur Schopenhauer

Careers advisers – what the actual fuck? You talk about your Monday morning quarterback. They don't know you well enough to know what you should do with your edge. Seriously, the only thing a careers adviser should say is: 'I'm sorry, I've got to go, I'll be back when I've sorted my own life out. I may be gone some time.'

The problem with careers advisers is that they're career advisers and chose to be careers advisers; these people thought that was a good career choice. These are not our best and our brightest. It's like getting relationship advice from Johnny Depp.

I think we should take the most successful people in our society, kidnap them, bundle them into the back of a van and make them tour secondary schools around the country. Being a careers adviser should be like jury duty for the successful. You get a letter through the door and your shoulders drop because you know what you have to do. You say to your partner, 'Well, it looks like next week I gotta tell a bunch of sixth form kids what to do with their lives. Maybe I can get out of it if I pretend to be racist.'

I was a victim of the careers adviser. As far as I'm concerned, I was the victim of a child-catcher.

Basically what happens when you walk into the careers adviser's office is there's a bunch of square holes. They look at you and you're this young weirdly shaped thing. And they think, 'Hmm, I think we could jam you into this square hole. Look at that, a perfect fit.'

My careers adviser looked at me and thought, 'Hmm, you seem like a fun creative guy – have you considered working in advertising?'

I said, 'Sure.' I went with it. I'd like to say that I'm not a dumb guy, but that sounds like the kind of thing a dumb guy would do, right? Advertising led to marketing and marketing led to the marketing department of a large oil company – I never intended to rape the planet – sorry, Al and Greta, it just kinda happened.

You may not have been exposed to what you want to do yet. You might be aiming at a target you can't see yet. I had a feeling there was something more, I had a direction but I didn't know exactly where I was going.

It's easier to fool people than to convince them that they have been fooled. – Mark Twain

What is the unpredictable thing you could do? You have no idea what you're capable of because no one does. I had no idea and I like to think I'm insightful as fuck.

CHAPTER THIRTEEN

BE YOURSELF –
EVERYONE ELSE IS ALREADY TAKEN

PEOPLE PLEASING, PEOPLE PLEASE

It's better to be hated for what you are than loved for what you are not.

— André Gide (now I don't know the guy
but I love him)

Lots of people refuse their edge. You've seen it happen. A beautiful actress who wants to be taken seriously, a powerful politician who wants to be likeable, a stand-up comedian who thinks he's a therapist – crazy shit like that.

I remember as a teenager desperately wanting to get off with a girl who just didn't find me attractive. Why did I waste my time trying to change her mind? Go where you're wanted; look for a little bit of encouragement. You're somebody's idea of perfect.

'Don't take it personally' is a great expression. I mean, how could you not? It's a rejection of you. So yeah, take it personally – but don't dwell on it.

How the world sees you and how you see yourself should work in tandem. A little bit of ego, how I see myself and a little care of what other people think. I see myself as a comedian, the world sees me as a comedian, ergo, we're all in agreement. Hooray.

Comedians find their crowd and cater to it, they know to play to their audience. You're not for everyone. The opposite of love isn't hate, it's indifference. I'd rather get a reaction, even negative, than nothing. If you're yourself not everyone will like it, but neither will you get indifference. People either want tea or coffee; what no one wants is a weird mix of the two.

It's heartbreaking for people as needy as stand-up comedians to learn you can't please everyone. I used to be a people-pleaser, but people don't like people-pleasers, so I stopped.

Someone somewhere out there thinks I'm a cunt – right now, they're thinking it – it's like an eternal flame. I could go onto Twitter at any hour, night or day, and someone is saying it.

Focus on the crowd that love you and build on that love. Let the haters hate, they're fine. Please don't spend your life trying to win people over. The result of pleasing everyone is bland: plain pasta and white bread.

Do you remember the kids you went to school with? Not your friends, not the ones you hated, remember the other ones? No, you fucking don't.

Don't try and sell yourself, be yourself and wait for demand.

THE GOOD IS THE ENEMY OF THE BEST

If there was to be a Mount Rushmore of comedy, the four greatest comedians of all time etched in stone, you could debate who the other three are, but Richard Pryor's place is guaranteed. He's on that mountain.

When Pryor was twenty-three and working his way up through comedy clubs in New York City, his life experiences – his mother was a prostitute and he'd been raised in a brothel – did not look all that promising. At the time, Bill Cosby was the best example to young comics in America of how to achieve fame and fortune with his clean-cut, family-friendly material (actually a little too friendly, we discovered later). Pryor did his best to do a 'clean act' and it worked. Within four years, Pryor was regularly appearing on TV shows. He was doing good.

In 1967, a lot was going on in America. Martin Luther King gave a speech in Washington DC as urban race riots broke out. King would be assassinated the following year. For the first time, tear gas was used on American citizens to disperse anti-Vietnam demonstrations. It was a tough election year and Nixon won. You get it, tough times. And it was a tough year for Pryor personally: his mother had died and his father was about to.

In September 1967 in Las Vegas, Pryor was performing to a sold-out, all-white audience and thought, 'What the fuck am I doing here?' And walked off the stage.

Sometimes, the good can be the enemy of the best. What Pryor did was he walked away from good and with a little time became incredible.

It didn't happen overnight. He evolved his act over the next few years in San Francisco and then in predominantly black clubs across the country. He was honest, charming, used his physicality, incorporated words he grew up with, he painted a picture of what it was like to grow up in a brothel in Ohio.

It took seven years. His third album was his breakthrough recording: it hit and hit hard. He won a Grammy for Best Comedy Album in 1974.

In the seventies, Pryor became the highest paid black entertainer in America and he didn't do it using Bill Cosby's voice. It's somewhat ironic that Bill Cosby turned out to be the really controversial one.

Pryor had a good life but he risked everything for a better life. He is considered the most influential comic of all time – but that's only because he is.

CHARM VS CHARISMA

Charm and charisma have come to mean the same thing in our language. We got sloppy. They're actually very different. Put very simply, charm is 'I come to you' and charisma is 'you come to me'.*

With charisma, you want to say 'yes' before you know what the question is. Charisma has got animal magnetism. Charm is seductive, inviting and intimate – the very embodiment of 'I like who I am when I'm with them'.

---

* Johnny McDaid came up with that phrase when we were talking about how charming he is.

This isn't a value judgement. Charismatic and charming, they're both good things to be. The point is, you'll be one of them. Which one are you? Are you charming or are you charismatic? Hard to answer that without sounding full of yourself, right?

You can be charismatic and wish you had charm, or you can be charming and envy people who are charismatic. Ultimately, though, the smartest strategy is to figure out which one you are and lean into it. Because when charismatic people try to be charming, it looks shady. It's like a big person trying to fit into too small a space. People won't be charmed, they'll be suspicious. And when charming people try to do charisma, it looks forced, it's like a small person trying to walk in shoes that are too big. And the reaction will be pity.

You would assume that everyone who gets on stage is charismatic, but actually, nope. Donald Trump was charismatic – even if you fucking hated him, you have to admit it. Trump embodied 'you come to me'. Barack Obama though, have you ever experienced a more charming guy? Obama is all about that 'I come to you' life. And they're both able to hold a crowd.

It's a great game to play. Next up, Angelina Jolie and Jennifer Aniston: which one is charming and which one is charismatic? Angelina Jolie is hella charismatic. That's someone you want to put on a pedestal. But who wouldn't want to be Jennifer Aniston's friend? She's charm personified. And both work – they both got to fuck Brad Pitt. Not at the same time, unfortunately. Though let's take a moment and think about that for a minute.

And another minute.

And . . . we're back.

Have you ever seen the first season of *True Detective*? Matthew McConaughey is from Texas, so you'd assume charming, right? Southern drawl and all that. But no, he's charismatic. When he's doing charm, it's hilariously sleazy (*Dazed and Confused*, anyone?). Whereas Woody Harrelson: one charming son of a bitch. No value judgement: both of them, when they come on screen, not a dry seat in the house.

Now, I'm charismatic. Charming and warm and cuddly – nope. Able to create intimacy in a huge room – nah. I wish I could do that, but that's not my gift. I've got my thing and I work that.

Peter Kay, on the other hand ... He and I had a discussion once, comparing our experiences of being famous. People assume I'm going to be acerbic and sharp when they meet me – something about my sense of humour, I guess – so they're surprised when I'm actually pretty friendly. But for Peter Kay, who's a charming dude, it's a nightmare. People are disappointed if they're not invited over for Christmas. I know I'm a goddamn dreamboat, a total mensch, but I'm aware of how I come across.

It's worth knowing how other people see you. You may be an incredibly sensitive soul, but if they see you as a thug you're going to get frustrated. Never mind what's true, what's important is what you take to be true, and how you can make that work for you.

Charm and charisma are part of your edge. It's less to do with you and more about how you're perceived in the world. You don't get to decide everything about how you're perceived, but you do get to know how to use it.

I'M A CELEBRITY . . . GET ME OUT OF HERE

There are a lot of young people who will tell you they want fame. They think it'll bring happiness.

If you're interested in being famous, having been famous for around twenty odd years, I have a little insight. Right away I'm going to say – it's great. Maybe they're right, I'm famous and I'm pretty happy most of the time. Being famous makes the world a friendly place to be. It's like being the most popular kid at school, it's like being a really hot chick, and who doesn't like that feeling?

I think the people in pursuit of fame are really in pursuit of belonging. It speaks to our caveman mind. Fame has replaced heaven in a secular world: surely everything will be okay if you're famous. It's the land of milk and honey you could have right now.

We're all a little thirsty and fame looks like a cool glass of water.

Our tribe is now so big that we've understandably got a little carried away. We've all had a taste of being rich and famous – it's about belonging and having enough. That's Christmas, right?

But I tell you what, I wouldn't want to be a celebrity. Fame and celebrity are often synonymous, but I think there's a distinction.

Fame tends to be skill based. You're known for what you do. Whereas celebrity is all about the external. The Queen is the ultimate example of being a celebrity in Britain. People are fascinated by who she is, not what she's done. Celebrity is about appearances, it's being a figurehead, it's red carpets and photos of your home on Instagram. Your job is to be you. It's transactional. It is 24/7, 365 days of the year.

When you are a celebrity, 'you', not your abilities, are the product. If you have to chase that high year after year on a national or global scale, it's going to be understandably exhausting.

I'M KIRK DOUGLAS'S SON

There is a legendary story comics tell each other – a parable, if you will: one night at the Comedy Store in London, a visiting comic, an American, rolled up and asked to do a spot. The owner, Don Ward, gave it to him. He got on stage and the audience gave him nothing. Every joke he told bombed and he could not get the audience to laugh. Of course, all the other comics stood at the back of the room watching the fiasco play out with glee.

He couldn't understand what was happening. In frustration and panicked, he bragged of his status, 'But I'm Kirk Douglas's son.' Nothing. At first. Then a member of the audience stood up and said, 'No, I'm Kirk Douglas's son.' And oh, how they laughed. Then another and another. 'No, I'm Kirk Douglas's son,' echoing his father's famous *Spartacus* line. By the end, the whole audience was standing.

He got his laugh and in a way, he sort of got a standing ovation. Just not the way he wanted. The audience killed it. They were the best act in the Comedy Store that night. And those comics standing in the back, they had to try and follow that. Respect the audience. What I'm saying is, if your edge is you dad, you're in trouble. And also, 'I'm Kirk Douglas's son.'

WHAT DO YOU BRING TO THE PARTY?

There are many types of intelligence and I should know, I'm academically gifted. The more you specialise and the more niche the skill set, the higher the reward.

Work out what kind of smart you are and use that. It's not arrogant to acknowledge what you're good at. Look at it this way: we're all shit at so many more things than we're good at. Stephen Hawking couldn't change a tyre. The complexities of quantum mechanics couldn't defeat him, but a high kerb could.

If you keep working on your weaknesses, you just might become average. But if you find your strengths and work on those instead, you will become the best. Maybe not the best in the world, but at least the best version of you. Work on your strengths and when you can, as soon as possible, delegate your weaknesses. Pick what you find easy and focus on that – get great at that. That's what edge is.

What the world doesn't need is more all-rounders.

Look at society and ask yourself, 'What am I bringing to the party?'

YOU SHALL GO TO THE BALL

You might think I had to learn how to say the wrong thing out loud, but no, I've always had the gift.

I got a call from my manager. It was one Tuesday in 2012 and she said, 'It's the Queen's Diamond Jubilee on Saturday.'

'What's that got to do with me?' I asked.

'They need some comedians to do little bits between the performing artists at the concert on the Mall. You just need to do five minutes while they change over the drum kit for Grace Jones.'

How could I say no to that? Worst-case scenario, I'm going to get a story out of it. Well, here's the story.

A gaggle of us comedians were at the concert – Peter Kay, Lee Mack, Rob Brydon, Miranda Hart and me – we were just hanging out for the day with some A-listers. Everyone was there, Elton John, Shirley Bassey, Andrew Lloyd Webber, anyone you could think of who was famous at the time.

Obviously, I wasn't going to do anything edgy; the Queen is going to be there, and I'm a professional. I get on stage. But what I wasn't expecting was to be able to see the Queen. There she was front and centre. She'd got really good seats, I guess she knows a guy. I opened by saying, 'Everyone is really nervous backstage, because we're going to meet the Queen later, and what's the etiquette?' And I said, looking directly at the Queen, 'Just call me Mr Carr.'

Then I introduced Grace Jones, who was wearing a hula hoop, job done.

Later, backstage, I'm in a line-up next to Peter Kay who is dressed as a Beefeater – always great – waiting for the Queen to arrive, and who joins us? Sir Paul McCartney.

Now, no offence to the Queen but in my mind Paul McCartney is a much bigger name. I started a conversation with Paul (he's Paul now, what am I like?) about the lyrics of 'Blackbird'. And Peter, who had been listening in, was like, 'Can't we talk about something normal?' Like it was normal to be there with a bunch of people you'd usually see in a wax museum. But point taken.

So I said to Paul, 'I live in St John's Wood, you live around the corner from me, right?' And he went, 'Yeah, yeah'. And we talked about where the best place to get breakfast near us was. I look at Peter Kay. Normal enough for you? (Actually, Paul recommended a great little breakfast place. Paul really knows his tofu scramble.)

When the Queen finally came along, I did the obligatory 'that reminds me, I've got to buy stamps' joke. It raised a smile (fair enough, she'd heard it before from Jimmy Tarbuck at the Royal Variety in the sixties).

This is how crazy it was: at the end of the performance, we all had to go back on stage for an encore and to sing the national anthem. I'm next to Ed Sheeran. We were looking at Buckingham Palace and Ed said, 'Man, this house is amazing! Must have cost a fortune. How much money do you think she has?' I said, 'Ed, It's Buckingham Palace. You know she has money. Her picture is *on* money. She *is* money. That's how much money she has.'

Stevie Wonder is in front of us, his hand on the shoulder of a guide walking him out, and Stevie Wonder says, 'I don't know the words.'

So I say, 'They're on autocue.' He laughs and he turns around and kind of goes, 'These guys . . .'

Then he gets his harmonica out and just for me and Ed he riffs over the top of the national anthem.

At the party inside the palace I'm teasing Cheryl Cole (I appreciate she has a different surname now but that's what it was at the time, I think), who was also on the bill. I say, 'You're single, right? Haven't you just broken up with someone? I'll set you up with Prince Harry.'

Prince Harry had done an interview the week before with the tabloids (back when he spoke to tabloids) where he said it was really 'tough' being single when you're a prince. Apparently, nobody wants to date a prince because of all the pressure.

I rock up to Prince Harry and say, 'Hey, I read that article where you said it was difficult for you to date because you're a prince. Yeah, because famously, no young girls want to be princesses . . .' I told him about teasing Cheryl Cole all day and how I promised to set her up with him. 'If you come with me and say hi to Cheryl Cole, she'll fucking die.'

He was game, he came with me and I introduced him to Cheryl. Pretty fun night so far.

Sidebar: Prince Harry was right. Turns out being his Mrs is a high-pressure gig – Cheryl, pet, you dodged a bullet.

I'm getting drunk at the party and then there's a tap on my shoulder. I knew I didn't belong there. A tap on the shoulder means I'm getting kicked out, right? I had finally said the wrong thing to the wrong guy. I accepted my fate.

It was Prince William. He reached out his hand and he said, 'Mr Carr.'

YOU'RE SO SPECIAL YOU SHOULD SPECIALISE

There is a reason for the cliché of frustrated, unsatisfied, middle management. Those people didn't specialise.

We live in a specialist economy. In the olden days we all did it all. Just a couple of generations ago we were supposed to take care of everything ourselves. Now, I can't change a lightbulb or put up a shelf. But I can pay a guy who's good at it. It's gone from Do It Yourself to Do It For Me. And as a bonus for him he'll slightly emasculate me when I make him tea. (I know it makes no sense but the guy who does my car stuff or the guy who can fix things around the house does feel a little more grown-up and manly than me. I guess it'll take a few generations to get rid of the gender roles we have embedded deep in our psyches.)

You see, school will teach you aptitude, but it won't encourage you to lean into what you're good at. That's up to you. Getting a C in physics and struggling with it serves no one. Who's saying, 'Wait, what, so you can do physics badly for me? Just what I'm looking for.' To be mediocre is to feel pointless and guess what, that feeling is correct.

If you're a pretty good singer, and you're a pretty good comedian, and a pretty good electrician, then you're pretty much unemployable. No one says, 'This guy is only a reasonably good brain surgeon, but on the plus side, he'll also fit our new kitchen, so let's go with him.'

Your job is to pick something you're good at, get great at it and do that. Nowadays, people are so busy honing their skills and working on their speciality that they don't even have time to notice what's happening around them and laugh about it. Thank God, because that's where stand-up comedians come in.

The more you specialise, the better you do in society, that's our set-up.

It might sound limiting to specialise, but remember I specialised in dick jokes. The possibilities are endless.

BATTLE NASTY

Montreal's Just For Laughs Festival is the greatest festival in the world. Bar none. It's the fucking dream. A great place to hang out and do comedy.

The myth of Montreal is you do a gala and suddenly you'll be a big hit in the States. The first time I went, I was invited to do a gala and ten days later I flew to New York to do *Late Night with Conan O'Brien*. So yeah, it works sometimes, but that's not the point of the festival.

Montreal is crazy, it's a mid-size European city in North America. Their winters are fucking brutal but who cares, the festival is in the summer. It's Canadian, but French. You know how great Montreal is? I'll sum it up in one sentence: French food, American portions.

Everybody is having a good festival because it's by invitation only. The organisers, Robbie, Jodi, Zoe and Bruce, scout the world to find comedians. Montreal always makes the thing I love feel new and fresh and exciting.

I knew how my edge worked in the UK, but you never know if it's unique enough internationally until you try.

I was chatting to my friend Robbie, one of the organisers, and I said how I'd really like to do the Nasty Show. The Nasty Show is where edgy comics are let off the leash. Robbie said, 'Well, I don't think you're right . . . because you're British and you're well-spoken, I'm not sure if it's quite you.' But he booked me regardless.

People will always put you into this category or that, but it's up to you to push yourself and make them see your edge.

Here's the great thing about the Nasty Show. If you have to follow Brad Williams, you have to up your game. I mean, the guy's a dwarf. It's 10.30 at night, everyone's drunk. If you're following a funny midget, you better have good jokes. Because Brad has no shortage. I mean, apart from the obvious.

If you have to follow Bridget Everett, good luck my friend. She had to be put on at the end of the show, because who's going to go on after her? She sang a song for eight minutes and the only lyric I can remember, because I was laughing so hard, is, 'What I gotta do to get that dick in my mouth.' She's a force of nature. Funny bones.

You know that if you're on with Anthony Jeselnik or Jim Jefferies or Amy Schumer, or any of these people who absolutely destroy, it's going to get competitive. You're all going to try to one-up each other in terms of subject matter and in terms of funny.

Before Roast Battles was a TV show, it was a club show. It was started in the Comedy Store in LA by Jeff Ross and Brian Moses.

A Roast Battle is really a joke-writing competition, it's comic vs comic battling with insult jokes. It's like a rap battle but without the gun violence. You each get five jokes to obliterate your competition.

So, it's about midnight, and the club is opposite the hotel where everybody's staying and instead of hanging at the bar, everyone goes to the show, where basically, you watch two people just tearing each other to pieces. Nothing is off limits.

Not that big a deal career wise, but oh, the fun of seeing great performers coming up with real zingers. Roast Battles went on for five nights and they had a league table in the lobby of the hotel so you could see who you were roasting. So, if you won a roast, the next morning you'd look at the name of the comedian you were going to be up against that night, go, 'Who the fuck is this guy?' and then run around asking people, 'Right, what do you know about him?' 'I hear his father has Parkinson's.' And you'd be like, 'Great, I can use that.'

It brought everyone together because you'd sit with your people drinking coffee at the Eggspectations café and go, 'Is this funny? Is this a thing?'

I was enthused to go to Montreal and always more enthused coming back. You leave going, 'Oh my God, I've got to write a new show, I've gotta have new shit for next year.'

That's the thing about edge: once you find it, you can work on making your edge even sharper.

PART 8
CREATIVITY/HACK

CHAPTER FOURTEEN

CREATIONISM

STICK IT TO THE MAN

When we talk about creatives, we have a tendency to think about musicians or artists, we think about people who produce something called 'art' as if it should be reserved for museums and galleries, and only practised by a very few, special people. We put creativity over there and everything else is 'serious business'. Seriously? Fuck that. So dumb. So elitist.

I say this because, before Shell, I worked in advertising. I was something called an 'account handler' which is like middle management. What you do is sort of organise stuff and hold meetings – you know, just busy work. I worked alongside 'the creatives' who did creative stuff: copywriters and graphic designers. It's the dumbest thing. In a company of 200 people, thirty of them were labelled 'creative', as if the rest of us shouldn't even think about doing anything imaginative. We had been put in our place: 'Don't you lot go about having ideas. We've got ideas covered.'

Creativity is not a special thing in a special box in a special room. It's crazy thinking because any business does better if it's open to creativity. Any work can be creative. Architects are creative, as are gardeners, chefs, strippers, cab drivers, nurses, accountants (accountants can be incredibly creative, let me tell you). It's not about what you do, it's how you do it, that's what makes your job creative.

Ultimately, every business has the same competitive advantage – its ability to adapt and change. And in that respect businesses are a lot like people.

Sometimes the word 'creative' is a problem. If the term is too hippyish for you there are other words available: try 'productive' or 'inventive'.

If you work in management you can call it 'thinking outside the box'.

If you're in manufacturing you're an 'innovator'.

If you're an economist, you might prefer 'free thinker'.

If you're a plumber, you're a 'problem solver'.

If you're a four-year-old kid, you might be 'a problem'.

I'm sure there's a word out there you can find just for you in place of 'creative', because you *are* creative.

GET CREATIVE ABOUT CREATIVITY

You've got to think creatively about creativity. You don't have to think of yourself as creative to be creative. I hadn't seen myself as a creative person either. I was waiting for someone to tell me I was funny instead of telling myself I'm funny. I had been waiting for permission.

Here's what I realised: no one was ever going to come up to me and say, 'Hey, you're really creative, you should do creative things.' No. I had to take this into my own hands. I had been waiting for someone else to 'bring me flowers rather than planting my own garden' (yeah, I can be all artsy-fartsy sometimes).

Never mind your 'Who's gonna let you?' thinking, ask yourself 'Who's gonna stop you?'

ALL ABOUT THAT LIFE

Just being alert to what's possible is enough to start. Creativity should be a part of your everyday. You can ease your way into being creative. Try it out. Having a conversation with someone is an opportunity to mess around. You know those conversations you've had a million times before? Change them, inject some fun into them.

I have a famous friend who is always asked to sign the guest book in hotels, and he takes the guest book and he signs it. And then he turns ten pages forward into the guest book and he draws a huge pair of tits. Very juvenile. He then writes underneath the tits, 'lots of love, Tina Turner'. Perfect. It makes him laugh to do it and I'm pretty sure when it's discovered it raises a smile. Being creative should be a part of the everyday, just like fun should be a part of the everyday.

My go-to, if I'm ever asked if I've seen the latest serious documentary (*An Inconvenient Truth* or *They Shall Not Grow Old* or *Mea Maxima Culpa* type thing), I'll always say, 'It wasn't as funny as I thought it was going to be.'

If you do something regularly, you get better at it. So if

you're playing and having fun, you'll get better at it. Are you playing and having fun in everyday life? With your partner, your friends, your colleagues, acquaintances, strangers? Humour can be injected everywhere. It's about adding lightness by increasing your own daily 'dicking around' quotient.

Creativity doesn't have to be nine to five, what about your personal life? In your personal life, how imaginative are you? I'm not asking how much of the Kama Sutra you've worked your way through, but what are you doing that's creative in your personal life? You know, with your friends. Do you still play with your friends? Or are you all growned up?

PRO LIFE

The problem with trying to be creative is that there are a lot of messy first drafts. A lot. If you're a writer, you get down a messy first draft and you create a lot of problems for yourself. But on the upside, what are people good at? Problem solving. If it's not perfect, it's perfect. You see obvious flaws and a solution leaps to mind.

Are there bad ideas? Yes, clearly, there are some terrible ideas (check out the Darwin Awards if you want examples, they keep a list of the dumbest shit humans have done). You'll get more things wrong than you get right, can we all agree on that? The thing about creativity is everyone has ideas, but really good ideas are thin on the ground. If you're a creative person you'll have ideas and almost all of them will be bad. You have to be willing to have bad ideas to get to the good ones.

Shut your inner critic up. Your inner critic will kill those ideas before they get a chance to breathe. I'm a huge fan of abortion but when it comes to ideas, I'm very pro life. Even if you can't afford to raise it, let the idea live a little and if it turns out to be a bad one you can always starve it out or let it play with knives.

Critics are useful. Great critics articulate and assess creative work. When they're great, they actually help shape an era. The problem is when your inner critic thinks it's being creative. Your inner critic is amazing and useful, and you are going to need it . . . later.

What you don't do is let critics into the rehearsal and you certainly don't invite them to give their input during the construction process. Are you crazy? Critics are assholes, they'll tear you apart and skilfully. Imagine if critics had read the first draft of *Catcher in the Rye* or seen the rushes from *Apocalypse Now* or heard Beethoven whistling the *Fifth Symphony*. These brilliant works would never have seen the light of day. (That said, with no *Catcher in the Rye* we might still have John Lennon so, yeah, there is that I suppose.)

Walt Disney literally had different rooms for different tasks. He had a room where he dreamt up ideas called 'the dreamer' (surprisingly uncreative name). A separate room called 'the realist' for working out how to realise his dreams, the practical managerial bit. And a third room, a totally separate physical space called 'the spoiler' where his critic lived. (I'm not sure where he did his antisemitic thinking – maybe he had an underground bunker?)

LIE, CHEAT, STEAL

Don't worry about people stealing your ideas. If your ideas
are any good, you'll have to ram them down people's throats.

— Howard Aiken

Yeah, you heard me. You've probably heard that a lot of creativity is stealing. It is. It's totally stealing.

Stealing is why you study great works inside out, it's so you know which structures to steal. It also helps to know the history of your field if you want to be in an industry that's creative. We're all standing on the shoulders of giants. The modern stand-up comedians owe a huge debt to music hall comics, music hall comics owe a great debt to clowning, clowns owe a lot to jesters, jesters owe a lot to the trickster gods of mythology. And trickster gods owe a lot to human sacrifices. 'Paying your dues' is an expression for a reason.

The key to stealing is this: you can't steal the material, but you can steal the structure. Structure is your friend.

Improv to me is fascinating. If you see an improv show, it's all pattern and no content. Those performers don't know what they're going to say but they do know the structure. The pattern is everything – all they have to do is put meat on the bare bones.

You're going to have to learn how to embellish. You have to make shit up. If real life was interesting, we wouldn't need the *Daily Mail* or so many *Avengers* movies. Lying is a great way to be creative. You know lying, right? It's not you, it's me . . . You look great . . . I love your work . . . It didn't mean anything . . .

Which leads to editing. You might know it better as 'lying by omission', 'not exactly lying' but it's not the truth either, but sometimes it's called 'cheating'. Editing is your Instagram 'best self'. Editing is a lie but it looks like the truth. And the great lesson you learn from faking the truth is that no one really knows the difference, but they really understand truth-y.

Lying well is about balance. If you emphasise the wrong thing, people will think it's not the truth. When you get good at lying, what you're doing is getting good at the structure of the truth.

CHAPTER FIFTEEN

PATTERN RECOGNITION

REMEDIAL CLASS CLOWN

The limits of my language are the limits of my world.
— Ludwig Wittgenstein

I didn't learn how to read until I was around ten. I could recognise words, but putting them together and then making sense of a sentence just seemed like another world. At nine, my friend Vicky was reading *The Hobbit*. Just looking at the size of the book, I remember thinking, 'Good luck with that.' Vicky was nice – at break time she would tell me stories from the books she read.

I was terrible at reading and spelling, but honestly, no one seemed that fussed. Anyway, my parents had their own shit to deal with. Dyslexia hadn't been invented back then. It wasn't a recognised condition where people were looking to help you solve the problem.

No one said to my parents, 'If only Jimmy could master reading, then he could write jokes and get on TV.' You were just dumb or lazy, which is fair enough. There was no question of being kept behind.

It was just shy of traumatising when it came to shit like spelling. I still sometimes get the Sunday Scaries. You know the Sunday Scaries? That's when you're anxious on Sunday night because the weekend is over and you have to go to school the next day and you haven't done your homework. The homework I couldn't do was for the spelling test. I'd sit there on Sunday night thinking, 'Well, it's just not possible, I can't do this, this is crazy.'

There was a lot of reading out loud in class going on for some reason. That was the teaching method. 'The kids can just fucking read stuff out, that'll teach them.' I hated being asked, it was scary. It was so obvious to everyone listening to me. The mouth breathers read in a weird staccato style. That was me, I was one of them (the perversity of choosing a career which requires reading from autocues, the adult equivalent of reading out in class, is insane). Even though no one else seemed to give a fuck, I did. When you're a kid you care about fitting in. And I did fit in, it was just what I fitted into was the special ed class.

I would start the day hanging out with everyone in my class and feeling like I was the same as them and then, in the afternoon, off I'd go to the remedial class. Remedial class is tuition for dummies. No one was mean about it, but there are no secrets in a playground, everyone knows what's what. It was not good and I felt it.

Sidebar: in remedial classes, they used to teach us to read phonetically. A whole series of books were published and everything in them was spelled phonetically. And then we 'graduated' to regular books where words were spelled . . . completely differently. The guy who came up with this was a fuking as hole. Eyem not saain he sistem wis flaad, eyem just saain it diddnt worc for me.

Then there was the dreaded 12+. In the eighties the 12+ was the exam that decided your future, it determined which school you attended for the next six years. By some miracle, I got through it – of course I believed in miracles back then.

The truth is, the incredible power of fear was what got me through. Fear has a lot of energy going for it, especially fear in the shape of humiliation and shame (remember the shark story). Those two are utterly galvanising. Don't fight it. Let them help you. It's like dying on stage in front of your peers, it's terrible and great because it makes you work.

I had a small Collins dictionary. It was a little thing, almost square. And I read it. For hours. I was ashamed that I couldn't read and I spent hours just sitting there, practising reading the words and then spelling them. I became aware I learned differently to other kids.

I have a lot of admiration for people who mispronounce words, because when people mispronounce words I know they're an autodidact, that they don't know how to say the word correctly because they've never heard anyone else use it before. They learned it for themselves from a fucking book. Like an OG. Because a lot of spelling is very subtle. Incidentally, I'm still not confident pronouncing autodidact, I've only ever seen it written down.

While we're on the subject of spelling . . . If you know a dyslexic and they ask you how to spell a word, tell them. Don't do that weird thing where you say it slowly like you've got a brain injury. 'Cil-oohh-et' doesn't get me any closer to silhouette. I'll give you an actual brain injury if you don't give me the letters.

With a thing like dyslexia, your automatic ability to read and write isn't there. You have to think about what words are, which is not an advantage in your academic life. It slows you down. You're breaking a sentence into components and this pattern-seeking affects how you listen and forces you to be creative with language.

Slowing down is actually good because between word-hunting, you find more choices, more possibilities. You have time to ask yourself, 'What else could happen?' A lot of 'what ifs' open up when your mind has to be pliable. I think this is why a lot of foreign comics, where English is their second language, often have strong jokes. It's because they can't take knowing the language for granted. And they're forced to listen for patterns. Blanche Gardin, Felipe Esparza, Gad Elmaleh, David Kau are all great examples.

I have no idea if this is true, but I'll bet a lot of dyslexics are good at wordplay.

I worked my ass off just to get by. When things are difficult, you almost don't remember the process, what you remember is suddenly one summer, ta-dah. By the time I was sixteen and taking my GCSEs, I was doing fine, I was middle of the class, which for me was awesome.

My friend Toby commuted to a better school, a boys' school, a grammar school. My mother suggested I should try to go to this other school. She was friends with Toby's mum.

I remember going for an interview at the new school with a guy named Mr File (and no, his first name was not Paedo). He looked at my GCSE results and went, 'This all looks in order, I'll just have to call your last school, check you didn't rape the matron or anything dreadful, but I'm sure it'll be fine.' He literally said that in the interview. Happily I had not, I had been too busy learning to read.

WAIT, I'VE SEEN THIS SOMEWHERE BEFORE

You're going to need connections to be a success. I don't mean you're going to need to know the right people. This section, thankfully, has fuck all to do with networking. You're just going to use your power of pattern recognition to make connections between things that have never been connected before. Your ability to do this is the backbone of your creativity.

Pattern recognition is the basis of IQ tests and Darwinian evolution. Seeing patterns is great for survival. It makes us better at catching fish, avoiding poisonous mushrooms and getting into college. This is also why stereotyping is such a human reaction. It's how we learn. And it's at the root of why older people say, 'You can't say anything these days,' because getting them to learn new terms, let alone overhaul their attitudes, is an effort. They're tired and old and have to save their energy for remembering the good old days and complaining about millennials and trying to get out of the bath.

Of course, there's a downside to pattern recognition. Stereotyping is nothing but pattern recognition and can lead to some amusing observations or to racism. Be careful and play nice. Don't be like one of those filthy French fuckers.

We're so good at pattern recognition that we can see patterns where there are no patterns. Conspiracy theories are people looking for patterns in a random, complex world. Conspiracy theories are simple solutions to complex problems. Which is a fancy way of saying 'bullshit'.

Don't believe in conspiracy theories. They're nonsense. At least that's what my illuminati overlords told me to tell you.

If you can reliably predict what's going to happen, life will be easier. If you're constantly surprised by what you run into, then you're always starting from scratch. At some point, your brain will explode. So that's why there's a lot of 'wait a second, I've seen that before . . .' and 'this again, huh, I wonder why?'.

What are the patterns in your life? You have patterns too. Not every person you date is crazy, some of that is on you.

CONNECT THE DOTS

Do you remember being a teenager? When you first get an inkling that everyone is masturbating, you're just relieved. 'Oh great,' you think, 'I thought it was just me that really likes touching myself in a very specific way.' But do you remember the first friend who says it? 'Hey, are you guys, uh . . .' That's the stand-up. They take the thing humans do that's embarrassing and put it out there.

In order to be a comedian, initially, the desire is everything. Right at the start, you *want* to be a comedian. But how do you actually go about it? Baby steps. You don't just say, 'I want to be a comedian so I'm going to leave my job.'

Before I even considered getting up on stage, I went to comedy clubs and sat there to watch comedians, and I would think about the wordplay and listen to the pattern of their jokes then maybe add tags in my head. That's how I started to work out jokes.

There are all kinds of comics out there: observational, shock, confessional, absurdist, insult, prop, clowns and then there are the joke comics and that's me: I write jokes, I do wordplay. My favourite thing about wordplay is, well, you've got the whole English language. That'll keep you busy for a while. Which is great, it means you don't have to wait for funny shit to happen to you, you can just go, go, go.

Early on there was a slog, where I didn't think I was getting anywhere, I couldn't think of anything and I actually said to myself, 'I don't think there's any more puns left. I think all the puns have been done, I'm out of puns.'

A lot of creativity is lateral thinking or problem solving. In its simplest form a crossword puzzle is a gentle way to get yourself started on being creative. 2 + 2 can equal 5 – it's why we like riddles and puzzles and games.

I went and bought the *Oxford Dictionary of English Idioms* and went, 'Right, A' and then, going through the entire thing, wrote 400 jokes. There was a page with the term 'fattist', a term for people who are against fat people. I saw that word and went, well that could mean two different things – dyslexia pays off again (and dictionaries).

A large lady came up to me after a show, she pretty much surrounded me. She was livid. She said, 'I think you're fattist.' And I said, 'No, I think you're fattest.'

Sure, some of it is inspiration, but the inspiration came when I was wading through the *Oxford Dictionary of English Idioms* for eight hours. Eventually, it comes more naturally and you go faster. And instead of having to go through the dictionary, you pick it up in conversation. 'Oh, that's an interesting word that can mean something else.'

PROBLEMS PROBLEMS PROBLEMS – I SEE A PATTERN

Emo Philips, Wanda Sykes, Mitch Hedberg, Rita Rudner and Steven Wright taught me how to write jokes. I just picked apart their work and looked for the patterns. Creativity is as simple as thinking of another solution. And how do you do that? Break it down. You look for the pattern.

So, how do you write jokes? For me, it was the same way I learned to read: pattern recognition.

I learned this from my school friend, Pete Maxmin, after I told him I didn't know how to get an A in history. He told me to read his A grade essay. He said, 'You don't copy the essay, you copy the pattern.' Like a dummy, I had thought the important thing about A level history was learning about history. Nope. My friend Pete taught me how to break codes.

Jokes rely on it – that's why it becomes a superpower for every comedian. The initial set-up (the context) is the bit that gets your brain to jump ahead (to make assumptions), which will then be subverted. Surprise is why we like jokes. With jokes there's always something unexpected involved. You think it's going to go in one direction but in fact it goes in BTS.

Intuitively, I broke jokes down. But then I started to do it on purpose. It would start with a joke that really made me laugh. I'd think, 'That's a funny idea. How did they construct it? Where did they start, what were they thinking?' You might get the sense that maybe they started with that phrase . . . and then you reverse engineer it.

Here's an example. After wordplay, the 'rule of three' is the easiest joke to recognise. The first line sets up the expectation, the second line confirms your assumption and then the third line surprises you by subverting your expectation. You can see the pattern is established and then subverted.

Does America really need to be the best at everything? You already dominate the world in economics, military power and obesity.
– Trevor Noah

The Japanese toilet: it washes you, dries you, does your taxes.
– Jim Gaffigan

Neurotics build castles in the air. Psychotics live in them. My mother cleans them. – Rita Rudner

I love jokes, they're magical, it feels right that you 'spell' words. If you put certain words together in a certain order you get an incredible joyful response. I found I had a knack for writing jokes and the more I did it, the better I got. Joke writing is very freeing for me. Jokes that are very clearly jokes from the off meant I could go to all kinds of crazy places in the joke and no one minded. No one takes jokes seriously, it's only when a joke is mistaken for an opinion that the trouble starts. Goddamn Twitter.

CHAPTER SIXTEEN

EDINBURGH 101

THERE'S A FESTIVAL IN EDINBURGH?

The first time I went to Edinburgh I drove up, which is a sign of how little I knew about where Edinburgh actually was. Take the train if you're coming up from London. It's a long-assed drive. Just don't sit next to the Scottish guy who gets on at King's Cross with the sixteen cans of lager. Every single one will be empty by Crewe.

I hadn't travelled in the UK at all until I started doing comedy. I hadn't been to Manchester or Newcastle or Coventry. It turns out I didn't have to get on a plane to experience the world differently.

On the comedy circuit, people would ask, 'Are you doing Edinburgh?' To cover my ignorance I would go, 'Oh, no I don't think so . . .' because I hadn't really heard about the Fringe part of the festival.

Back at university, a dramatic society there, Footlights, had annual fundraisers to take their plays to Edinburgh, and I remember thinking, 'Why would I pay for you to take a play to Scotland? Have we run out of starving children?'

But what I definitely didn't know about was the sheer

scope of the festival: film, dance, art, literature, plays, operas, street performers, fucking everything along with every kind of comedy. It's incredible, it's heaven and it's insane.

The Fringe is not about 'who's going to let us', it's 'who's going to stop us'; it's the best example of that mentality. Because in Edinburgh you can go up and put on your show for the whole of August. It's very *Field of Dreams* – you put on the show in the belief that people will come and see it. The Fringe is for everyone.

There's also the international festival where they'll invite the best of the world's performers. I'm still waiting by the phone for that call.

In 1999, the Fringe wasn't as big as it is now and it was a different scene. Producers and scouts from all over the world would be there. They had an award called the Perrier, and if you won it, it could change your life.*

If you're a comic, you can put on an Edinburgh show and have fun. But it's pretty high stakes. It's expensive and emotionally draining, which means there are winners and losers. Some people put on shows that are now on telly or Netflix, and some people lost a lot of money, their relationships broke down and now they have PTSD and/or an STI.

My friend Iain told me to go to Edinburgh and see shows. 'Don't just try and perform, go and see shit.' Iain knew me pretty well. The Gilded Balloon, which was run by Karen Koren at the time, had a new act competition where you only needed

---

* The Perrier Comedy Award has since been renamed Dave's Edinburgh Comedy Award, which makes it sound like a made-up participation prize from some bloke called Dave.

to be on stage for five minutes. That year, *So You Think You're Funny* was hosted by Peter Kay. This was still very early on in his career, although he already had a pilot for a TV show on Channel 4. Doing the competition meant I had a reason to go and since I was already up there for that and didn't care about being paid, I played loads of shows that were little 'turn up' gigs. Even though it's the biggest arts festival in the world, full of comedians, they still needed more comedians.

Up to that point, twenty minutes of material was the pinnacle because I'd only seen my role models doing twenty minutes in clubs. My heroes were doing hour-long HBO specials, VHS videos or DVDs, like Billy Connolly, Eddie Izzard or Chris Rock. But that seemed impossible and I was focused on what I could do.

The Fringe was my first taste of seeing what people like me could do with hour-long shows. The first few shows blew me away by how good they were. And then I went to see some shit ones and thought, 'Well, I could do *that.*' Thank God (the one I don't believe in) for mediocrity. Mediocrity is inspiring stuff.

The following year, I did a show for two weeks with three other people: Ricky Gervais, Steve Merchant and Robin Ince. We were writing on *The Ricky Gervais Show* so we'd already been hanging around together. *Rubbernecker* was pretty good. We rented a nice apartment and we laughed a lot.

The extraordinary thing about Edinburgh is that everyone gets on with everyone else. Clowns, street performers, character comics, circus acts, ladyboys, burlesque strippers, people from all around the world come and there's an incredible sense of camaraderie.

I like to think of it as a picnic for all the broken toys.

Everybody is doing their thing, sharing venues and trying to get through the month in one piece. There's a collegiate atmosphere, it's kind of like secondary school. Maybe all of life never really moves beyond secondary school. You arrive as the new kid, you have your friends for a while and then eventually everyone splinters off and goes their own way out into the world of showbiz. But you always remember the group you came up with.

THE ONLY SOBER MAN AT THE EDINBURGH FESTIVAL

Lots of people have ambition, of course they do. Everyone who goes into comedy has ambition. I was clear, I wanted to be in the game. I wanted to be accepted in that world. I wanted to do this for a living and for it to be my life. I wanted to do well.

My show was called *Bare-Faced Ambition*. It was called that for a reason. The joke wasn't that I didn't have bare-faced ambition, it was that you weren't supposed to say it. It's frowned upon in British culture.

By 2002, I was nominated for the Perrier. Thank you, 'congratuwelldone' me.

You get one day off when you do an Edinburgh run. For me, it was a Tuesday and I hadn't seen my girlfriend for two weeks. She couldn't get the time off. So I took the train to London in the morning and travelled back the next day. On the way back, I got a text message from my agent, Hannah, saying, 'You've been nominated for the Perrier.'

This was crazy and I was absolutely delighted. A lot of people work very hard on their shows and never get the acknowledgement, the buzz around them or the ticket sales. These were people who had really fun shows. But for me, it felt like the hard work, the not having more fun, the constant pushing, had really paid off. It doesn't always happen and if I hadn't been nominated I would still have gone back. But goddamn, this was nice.

The other shows that were nominated were Adam Hills, Phil Nichol, Noel Fielding, Omid Djalili and Daniel Kitson, who won that year. Everyone was pleased. Daniel is a comic's comic, everybody liked him. Plot a graph and put funny on one axis and ambition on the other. Daniel is in the sweet spot, super funny and with zero ambition (commercially, that is – creatively, he's a very ambitious boy). Daniel doesn't want to be on television or in films, doesn't want a Netflix special. He's happy being super funny and not taking bread from anyone's table. Great.

It really felt like a graduating class. Once you're on TV you really can't get nominated for a Perrier again and I had a TV show coming in September, so I knew that was it.

By the way, my ambition still is the same: for stand-up to be my job.

MY LEVEL OF ENVY – YOU WISH

Comparison is the thief of joy.
  – Eleanor Roosevelt (smart but not as hot as JFK's wife)

There's a difference between jealousy and envy. They get mixed up but jealousy and envy are not the same – only one of them is a force for good.

Jealousy is when you resent what someone else has, but you don't necessarily want it. Jealousy is the motive of the guy that keys your brand-new car. Jealousy is a dick move.

You get this with siblings sometimes, there's a bit too much competition and, well, family is family, what can you do? Maybe a little bit of distance would help? If you're in Norfolk, try sleeping in different beds for a while?

Jealousy ruins lives. 'How did they get that?', 'they don't deserve that'. Jealousy turns into resentment and resentment ruminates and sets in and it becomes bitterness. If you can, try not to get bitter. It's not a good look.

I've got a 'holistic theory of jealousy' 'cause I'm fancy: if you feel jealous of someone, remind yourself that you can't take just one element of their life. You can't just get the career or the status or the awards or the jet ski or the super-hot partner or the mansion or the Lamborghini or the extra spare jet ski they keep on hand in case Dave Chappelle drops round. Nope. You also have to take the drug addiction, the angry ex-partner, the kids who hate you, the parasites who want your money and the press who lie about you, and the ongoing costs of a spare jet ski that no one ever uses. You've got to take the whole thing. Who would you rather be? You or them?

I have to say, there are not many people who I'd want to swap lives with. We all have struggles and we all have to take the good times with the bad.

Look around you, not up.

At twenty we worry about what others think of us. At forty, we don't care what they think of us. At sixty, we discover they haven't been thinking about us at all. – Winston Churchill (well, misattributed to Winston Churchill; of course Churchill didn't say that, he was talked about all the time. He's still talked about. The person who said it is somewhat ironically lost in the mists of time, which seems appropriate.)

And then there's envy. Envy is more interesting, envy is great. Envy is when you really want what someone else has. Envy is pure motivation.

Envy is your subconscious telling you what you actually want out of life. Envy is the answer to *the* question.

Essentially, whatever makes you bitter is bad, and whatever tells you what you want is good. That's jealousy and envy in a nutshell.

WHAT'S THAT BUZZ?

The worst part of success is trying to find someone who is happy for you.

— Bette Midler

When you're a comedian and you perform at the Edinburgh Fringe, the hierarchy is very clear. And forget the reviews, you know who's having a good Edinburgh, just from the buzz.

Every year, there will always be a show with a bit of buzz around it. People will go, 'oh, have you heard', 'he's sold out for the whole run', 'she's doing brilliantly', 'have you seen such and such' or 'funny, just funny'. And there's a little bit of envy being passed around. If you get nominated for an award, it can feel like the whole town's talking about it. If you're an actual resident of Edinburgh, you'll know it's basically a bunch of fucking art students getting overexcited.

In Edinburgh you learn that a five-star review might throw you a little traffic, but the only thing that makes a real difference is word of mouth. And not word of mouth in the general community, word of mouth from comedians. If a comic says, 'This funny person here, they're the shit,' people are going to see it.

I remember in 2001 Ross Noble telling me about these New Zealand guys. 'They're wonderful, we're gonna go, you wanna go?' Of course I wanted to go.

We went to The Caves at 11.30 p.m. to watch Flight of the Conchords with fifteen other people on the first night. The next night we went back, there were sixty people. Afterwards, we could hardly get in. They had to put on extra shows.

I learned that envy is a good thing. You go and see a show that's better than your show and it makes you want to do better. If you see something that's worse than your show you feel like, 'Huh, maybe I'm pretty good.'

If you see a show with amazing material, it makes you want to go and write, to pull it apart and work out what they've done. I remember seeing Harry Hill and Al Murray do a show called *Pub Internationale* and they had great callbacks. They'd set things up in the first fifteen minutes and it paid off at the end of the show. It was joyful and fun and silly and I adored it. I did my best to pick it apart and then I thought, 'Right, I've gotta see that again.'

You see shows with great performances and you just want to get on stage immediately. Envy tells you what you want, envy's good.

EDINBURGH LAUGH LESSONS

I learned in Edinburgh:

1. *The human body is pretty resilient.*
The Edinburgh diet was extraordinary, literally the worst food available in terms of nutrition and hygiene this side of Glasgow, the heart disease capital of Europe. I found quite a good kebab shop, so I was living on a kebab a day and was pretty pleased with myself. It was a balanced diet; it covered all the bases. There was bread, lamb, some salad and some other stuff best labelled under 'miscellaneous'. Sure, a kebab can be one of your five a day. Just so long as you're not eating five of them a day. It's extraordinary how unhealthy you can be and still live. I'm frankly amazed I didn't get scurvy.

2. *The main thing, is that the main thing, is the main thing.*
You're up there to do a show but someone will always want to go do something exciting. There's drinking to be done, late-night hanging out available ... Doing your show involves an incredible level of discipline. Your show, that hour, is what you're living for. Everything else feels like a pull on your time.

Not drinking in those years was the secret sauce. Sure, if I'd drunk I'd have better stories for this section of the book, but what I got instead was a career. I should really have five blank pages here for all the crazy Edinburgh stories I don't have.

My thing was the hang. My show was at eight o'clock in the evening in the dining room at the Gilded Balloon. (If you get hold of a time machine, I recommend you go. Don't worry about booking ahead. There will be plenty of room in the first week.)

My show was an hour long each day, which meant I had twenty-three hours to kill. I killed the time by going to see other shows, everything I could, and became a real cheerleader for other comics. In doing so you become part of a community, you get to know people and they become your little crew. And you hang round before going to the next show. All you've got to do is go to shows and then hang out with comedians for coffee or pizza or whatever and perform. My best times were sitting around coffee shops with Demetri Martin and Flight of the Conchords and David O'Doherty and Russell Howard and Tim Minchin. Looking back now, of course those were the best times. Hanging out with the funniest people on the planet 24/7 – what's not to love?

3. *There are no rooms you can't play.*
There's a show called *Late'n'Live*. It's almost like someone sat down and intentionally created a 'worst-case scenario' comedy show.

What time would the worst show start?

1 a.m.

A terrible idea. Everyone's going to be exhausted. The audience and the performers. Great.

Will they be inebriated?

Affirmative.

So sleepy and drunk.

Awesome.

Will the gig start late?

Of course.

Will the host overrun?

Always.

When you get up on stage, will it start with heckles?

You betcha.

The original room was a Victorian bear-pit, before it burnt down (for the insurance money, I'd wager). There was the audience in front of you and the balcony was almost eye level with the comics so it felt like the crowd was on top of you. You felt like you might die. And you often did.

Here's the thing: it was perfect. Something about it just worked.

Every year someone was the king of *Late'n'Live*. I seem to remember Daniel Kitson having a year where he basically hosted it every night. The next year Russell Howard took on the mantle. And it was so fucking fun. For a while we were the cool kids.

4. We get better in tiny increments.

That's a great lesson.

The reason actors go on about stage acting is because in movies actors only get a couple of takes. But with stage acting, actors get to do the same lines every night then recalibrate, experiment a little. They get to do it better every time and chart their progress. You, as the audience, only get a snapshot of the journey they're on.

If you do thirty shows in a row and are constantly adapting your material and your performance, it won't be the same every night because you'll be trying to make it better. Sometimes, it can feel like it's two steps forward and one step back, but you can try things. You might ad-lib around a bit and if the ad-lib goes well, it'll become an ad-fib (an ad-lib where you know it's gonna happen ahead of time).

5. Perfect it, then throw it away.

Before my time, the thing was to have the same material and hone it for the rest of your career (if you're interested, there's a recording of Morecambe and Wise playing Croydon with the act they'd been perfecting their whole lives – well worth a watch). But with Edinburgh, you have to have new shit every year, you can't do the old stuff. So you get into the practice of burning material. It keeps you sharp because seriously, who would write a new show if they didn't have to?

It really pushes you. I've got friends that are good comics on the circuit. They tried Edinburgh but lost money, didn't get the attention they were hoping for and they got gun shy. They'd wait two, maybe three, years or maybe never go back. And what happened is that they tended to drift. Short-term goals are good and you need them because they ground you. For a while, it was really important to me to get a five-star review in *The Scotsman*. Is it really important? I don't know, but it helped me keep my purpose on point.

I don't know what the equivalent is in the real world, but I know there is one. There will be something you want to do this year that seems really important. And it is. It should matter.

For comics, Edinburgh is an ambition that's attainable within twelve months. Once you're there, you're forced to practise every day for a month. By the end of your run, there's no way you can walk away and not be a better comic for it. No way.

For comics, it's the woodshed, it's basic training, boot camp, weightlifting, a high intensity workout, anything that feels hard doing it but great afterwards.

If you're not a performer, go to the Edinburgh Festival anyway, it's great fun. If you've been to Spain ten years in a row but haven't been to Edinburgh, frankly, I think you're a fool. Do you like fun? Edinburgh is where they make fun and there's nothing else going on in Edinburgh to get in the way of that fun.

PART 9

TALKING POINTS

CHAPTER SEVENTEEN

YOU CAN'T NOT COMMUNICATE

THEY'LL NEVER FORGET HOW YOU MADE THEM FEEL

*They may forget what you said, but they will never forget
how you made them feel.*

— Maya Angelou

Communication is important because you need to get along
with people. And if you don't think getting along with people
is important, then fuck you.

Wait, come back, I swear I'm good at this.

You've heard people say 93 per cent of communication is
non-verbal, right? I used to be sceptical, but I get it now. The
actual words are only 10 per cent of what you hear. The rest is
emphasis, tone of voice, body language, facial expressions – it
all tells you more than the words. I get so much more out of
a conversation with someone face to face than I do over the
phone. It's not hard to figure out why Zoom calls got old real
fast. During the pandemic, it felt like suddenly we were all
cam girls. When you're able to look another person properly

in the eyes, there's a connection. We're an empathetic bunch.

You cannot help but communicate. Communication is the principal way you interact with the world. If words are the meat, communication is how you're going to serve it (apologies to vegetarians and vegans).

Words help you present your view of the world, but you have probably worked out by now that nobody listens to what you actually say. It's like this book. You won't remember every single word I've written, but you will get a sense of what it was about and how I made you feel, you feel me?

It's hard for us to comprehend what it must be like to meet us. The effect we have, the space we take, the energy we bring when we walk into a room. These are all intangibles because we only know what it is like to be ourselves. I think it's because we only ever get to see ourselves in two dimensions. We only get to see ourselves in reflections. Not only in mirrors, but from the reactions we get from other people.

Have you ever been to the Parthenon in Athens? If you've seen a photo, it's nice, right? The photo is nice, but the real thing is fucking amazing. That's like you. The best photo of you is nothing like being in the room with you.

OBSERVATIONS ON OBSERVATIONS

Have you ever noticed how many comics do 'observational' comedy? Or is it just me?

I would argue all comics start off pretty good at observing and we perfect those skills as we develop our act.

Observation is the most common way to gauge context. Where are we? What is going on in the world around us? Who are they? What do they want? Why are they doing that? What are we doing here?

What you mostly learn from comics is how subjective we are when we look at the world. A comic is like an alien, bemused by the world and himself. Everyone is trying to figure out this life; comics are just open about it.

We take the everyday, break it down and see what other people tend to miss, or voice what others don't want to acknowledge. We try to work out what people think they are doing versus what is actually happening. Someone like Jerry Seinfeld can take an everyday interaction and break it down, make links, connect phrasing, and in doing so he's able to make us look at ourselves anew and make it fresh.

Sometimes, noticing what's already there will seem obvious to you, but it's nevertheless an act of creativity. And just because it's obvious to you doesn't mean anyone else has noticed it before. Or maybe people have noticed it before but didn't know how to articulate it.

Comics get good at reading a room. It doesn't sound like anything, but that phrase includes not only the shape of a room and the acoustics, but also the demographic of an audience and the culture of the city you're performing in along with the news of the day. Comics also take the emotional temperature of a room. Reading a room is a soft skill, it's a skill you only really notice when someone fucks it up. Like say, someone crashes into a room being all loud and brash and doesn't pick up on the black suits, the tears and the coffin.

Observation and listening are part of the same thing: attentiveness. Comics talk a lot, but they listen more. When they're on stage it looks like they're in 'send mode' most of the time. But tune in a little closer, you'll hear the audience is playing their part and the comic is constantly listening to the feedback loop coming from the crowd and adjusting their act accordingly.

YOU, MISUNDERSTOOD

God gave you two ears and just one mouth for a reason.
— Every Dad Ever

How you communicate is either conscious or subconscious. My advice: make it all as conscious as you can, as often as you can. Communicating is not about facts. The words you say are important, of course, but they won't matter nearly as much as your attitude and what you do.

There's an old Jewish expression: 'an enemy is someone whose story you do not know'. Sure, if people took the time to know you, they'd love you – but who has the time? If you got to know everyone's backstories, when would you find the time to do anything else?

Humans are acutely aware of intent: why are you doing what you're doing? This is a good thing to know: people will forgive a lot if they believe you mean well. That said, the road to hell is paved with good intentions, just like the road to heaven, and if we could see what everyone else's intentions were, we'd be a whole lot more forgiving about their fuck-ups.

Hanlon's razor: never attribute to malice that which is adequately explained by stupidity.

If you keep being misunderstood, well tough luck, it's on you to be understandable. You're the one talking. There are 273,000 words in the English language and we regularly use 171,000 of them, so if you still find you are being misunderstood, then your problem might be tone, *you fucking idiot.*

Tone affects meaning. Up to 38 per cent of communication is the tone you use. Think of tone as the delivery method, the packaging. The packaging matters. You can say 'the right thing' in a sarcastic way and everyone will assume you mean the opposite.

While we're talking sarcasm, I challenge you to use the phrase 'thanks a lot' without sounding sarcastic. It's like we've baked sarcasm into 'thanks a lot'.

Tone is hard to read in a text. It's tough to tell when people are being sarcastic or just mean. I tend to think people are being sarcastic, but that's difficult to explain in court. 'No, your honour, it did not occur to me to ring the police, I know the defendant texted me to say he was going to put his fist so far down the victim's throat it would look like he was shitting fingers, but I didn't think he'd actually kill him, I thought he was joking.'

Music gives us a clue as to how important tone is. You hear 'Purple Rain' and you know instinctively Prince is singing 'We Shall Overcome'. The lyric doesn't mean a damn thing but the tone of that song – everybody gets it.

Controlling tone is part of what you can do when you listen to yourself, but you can also modulate the timbre of your voice. You know when you hear yourself back on a recording? That is how you sound. It's hard to hear. It was hard for me, too. But if you can learn how to take better selfies, I'm sure you can learn to adapt the sound of your own voice.

JUST WAITING FOR YOUR TURN TO TALK

You know that feeling you get when you're saying something and you suspect the person you're talking to isn't actually paying attention, they're just waiting for their turn to talk? We all know that feeling because we're all guilty of it from time to time. We're not really listening, we're maybe partly listening to them and mostly to our internal monologue, we're thinking about what we want to say and how clever it'll make us sound.

If you really listen, it's very powerful. Pay attention to your partner. They might not have said what they need in so many words but they'll have fucking told you.

Test this out: talk to a friend, ask a question, pretty much any question, and after they've answered, shut the fuck up. Lean into the silence and see what happens. Invariably, your friend will fill the space, they'll expand on their point, they'll clarify their position, they may even find something new about their perspective.

If you want to be a great listener, all you need is this one sentence: 'So what you're saying is ...' and then you repeat what you think they said. That act of acknowledging you heard correctly, that's enough to make you a superstar listener. The bar is very low, honestly, you could step over it. Did you hear what I said?

SAY SOMETHING FUNNY

The end of laughter is followed by the height of listening.
— Jeffrey Gitomer

Here's a tip: learn a joke. Loosening up and letting people laugh with you increases the perception of your status and intelligence. Just telling a joke shows confidence. And although it pains me to know this, it shows confidence regardless of whether your joke is funny or not. Your joke doesn't even need to land, just the act of telling a joke lets the world know you're confident and open. But if your joke is funny as well, you've just displayed competence.

Confidence and competence! No wonder clowns get so much pussy. Of course, it could also be the big shoes. Clown dicks are no joke.

'Getting along with people' is what humour gives you, which is why it's easy to laugh someone into bed. The tricky part is laughing them into the taxi home afterwards.

People trust people with a sense of humour because it charms and disarms. If people are laughing, it signals that they're paying attention (and we're all a little thirsty for that, right?). People are more likely to remember what you meant when it's done with a sense of humour.

We comedians gauge *how* to deliver our jokes by listening to the audience. The audience lets us know what we need to do to press them for bigger laughs. We want to work with them. It's why the shape of the room matters and why we test out the sound system. You need to hear us and we need to hear you.

There's a reason stand-up isn't a written medium: jokes need to be brought to life. (I know I've written down a lot of jokes in this book – what can you do?) Your voice gives the joke context, who you are gives the joke context, what you're doing gives the joke context. How many arguments contain the words 'but that's not what I said'?

One of my favourite noises at a comedy show is a laugh followed by a sharp intake of breath. The laugh means the joke worked and the sharp intake of breath reveals how taboo the audience views the subject matter. But I like that they couldn't resist laughing anyway. It means their moral compass kicked in, but too late. The audience didn't want to laugh, but I made them. If you want to sound smart it's cognitive dissonance: they've got two conflicting thoughts in their heads at the same time. It's so much fun when an audience lets you play with them. That's good, clean, grown-up fun.

FUN STUFF TO SAY

Comics work hard at finding the right words to express themselves. Have you ever heard a comic say something that stuck in your head? A little observational remark that just nails it? It expresses the frustration we were feeling but couldn't articulate, until a comic did. It's so fun to do, it makes sense of the world, and there's a comfort in knowing your ill-defined feelings of exasperation and annoyance are expressible.

I look out for what I call 'sticky phrases' – and no, that's not code for dirty talk. Sticky phrases are turns of phrase that once you hear them you can't wait to use them.

Why say 'that's really gay' when you could say 'as gay as a bag of wigs' or 'as gay as cum on a moustache'? Why not have some fun? Well, because I'll get cancelled, and no disrespect to anyone who's ever 'put their pyjamas on the wrong way'.

Sure, you could say vagina but why not say 'twinkle cave'?

You could say that the lady in question found you attractive but better to say 'she was wetter than a submarine with a screen door'.

There are women who are attracted to funny men. They like a guy that can make them laugh. We could explain all that or we could just say 'Chuckle Fuckers' and let people figure it out.

'I'd rather not' is a perfectly acceptable thing to say but isn't it more fun to say, 'I'd rather shit in my hand and clap.' The bonus is, you won't be asked to clarify.

You could say 'this needs more gravy', sure. But why not say 'it's as dry as a Nun's Nasty'?

THE ART OF PUBLIC SPEAKING

For a dyslexic boy, reading autocue (which you have to do a lot of when you host TV shows) is challenging, but there's also a big difference between the written and the spoken word.

One day we were recording at the BBC when I bumped into Anne Robinson backstage. I was nervous and she said hello, she thought she'd seen me on something and I said, 'Yeah, I'm just taping this thing and going through the autocue script.'

We were constantly changing stuff, right up until show time, which meant I didn't always have time to rehearse.

Then, bless her, she gave me a tip. 'I have a trick,' she said. 'After every phrase, I put in a comma. It shows me where to breathe in the sentence when I'm reading autocue.'

It was so simple but it made a radical difference. It changed the prose into something you can fucking say. If you punctuate a sentence, what it gives you is markers making it easier to sound natural. And when you're hosting TV, it's important not to have a phone voice. It's why when some people are starting out as hosts on a TV show they do a kind of weird voice. Like a middle-class mum taking a phone call from a bishop. If you want to be naturalistic, those commas really help. If you're doing, any public speaking, yourself, lots, of, commas, is, a, pretty, good, hack.

I really hope I'm not fucking with Anne Robinson's money by revealing she's actually very nice.

CHAPTER EIGHTEEN

CONTROL THE NARRATIVE

'YOU' THE VERB

The privilege of a lifetime is being who you are.
Joseph Campbell (of course he'd say that, he's
Joseph fucking Campbell)

We're all faking it. The clearest example is first dates. 'First-date you' is the best version of yourself. First-date you is terrific; you're clean, you're dressed as well as you're ever going to be dressed, you're listening more than you usually do and you're not checking your phone every thirty seconds. If you don't like someone on a first date, that's a red flag, because that's the best that person can do. Equally, if you get rejected after a first date, that's gotta hurt. How can you not take that personally? That was you at your best and they said, 'No thanks'. Ouch.

Some men accuse women of cheating, like, 'She wore make-up and a push-up bra.' No dummy, that's salesmanship and thank the lord for salesmanship.

You only really meet your wife when you're getting divorced.
– Chris Rock

We're all playing the same game. We're all putting our best foot forward. Even if you're a make-up-free vegan type, you're working an angle (just FYI, if you tell anyone other than a waiter that you're a vegan, you're the problem).

On any given day, in any given hour, I don't say that many funny things. But put me on a stage in front of 3,000 people and I'll say three funny things a minute. Am I being inauthentic? No, I'm giving you the 'edited highlights' of me.

(WHAT'S THE STORY) MORNING GLORY

You are the story you tell yourself.

You should listen to the voice in your head, unless of course it's telling you to kill, kill, kill . . . In which case, seek medical help and for God's sake, put down the nail gun.

But seriously, when you're alone and you're talking to yourself, what do you tend to say? Are you cautious? Insecure and then overcorrect to grandiosity? Do you give yourself a hard time?

What you think about yourself and how you define yourself will determine what you end up telling other people. You can't control your narrative when you're a mess, it's like trying to herd cats.

You'll be lucky to find five people in the world who are genuinely interested in you. The real you, the 'warts and all' story is for close friends, lovers and your biographer. Most people are strangers. What do you tell a stranger you are? What's your story?

It's important, because the story you tell other people often dictates what happens to you. Do you say, 'I'm a single mum who has just gotten out of an abusive relationship. I have no money and I'm on benefits.' Or do you say, 'I'm a writer and mother'? J. K. Rowling chose the latter. She chose her narrative and through it she showed you what she thought of herself. (She also thought of herself as a woman and, as it turned out, that was controversial.)

There's a great sequence in the Alan Parker movie *The Commitments*, when the band members are queuing up to collect their welfare cheques and they're excited. Because it feels so much better to be an unemployed musician than an unemployed plumber.

I was ten gigs in and telling people I was a comedian. Now, you could've said I was delusional and I wasn't a comedian yet, but I wasn't lying about who I was, I was stating my intent. What you say to other people reminds you of who you want to be. The story you tell helps keep your purpose in place and your ambitions on track.

When I started telling people 'I'm a stand-up comedian' as opposed to 'I work for an oil company', the conversations became understandably different. One led to a conversation about comedy and laughter and fun. The other led to a furtive look over my shoulder for someone more interesting to talk to.

GOOD JUDGEMENT

Good judgement is the result of experience and experience
is the result of bad judgement.

— Mark Twain

Look, we make snap judgements about other people all the time. And those 'other people', they're going to make snap judgements about you too. Go ahead and make your peace with that.

We all go to stereotypes when we first meet people. Are they loud, short, clever, blond, punctual, old, young? You tend to quickly pick the most obvious traits when describing other people and make an assessment. Think about when you meet someone; in a few short minutes, you have an idea about how they vote, their sexual orientation and their views on global warming. Nobody captures all the nuance that makes up a person. We're in a hurry and there's too many of us.

People are against profiling in airports, as if it's only happening in airports. Profiling happens everywhere all the time. And if you're a member of a minority group, you already know that.

I know I read as slightly stiff. I don't look like I benefited from a mum who was charismatic and fun and warm and affectionate. I look like I was built by a nice old man called Geppetto and got my wish to be a real boy.

And I would say, don't fight your stereotype if it helps your situation. When I'm introduced as British in America, I'll tell you what I don't do: what I don't do is correct anyone. Americans think I'm very British, sitting somewhere between Hugh Grant and Mr Bean – fine. Let's go with that.

The quote 'You see the world not as it is, but as you are' has two levels to it. Not just in how you see, but also in how the world sees you.

When Melania Trump was asked if she'd be with Donald Trump if he wasn't rich, she said, 'Would he be with me if I wasn't beautiful?' Touché, Melania. Touché.

'YOU' – THE ELEVATOR PITCH

Humans are fucking shallow. You've stepped in puddles that are deeper than humanity.

Now that you know this, you'll find you have more control of how you're perceived than you think. You get to decide what you're going to wear, how clean you are, what you smell like, whether you make eye contact, what kind of gestures and facial expressions you make, even what sort of accent you have. That's a lot of control.

What do you want to say? What do you want people to think when they meet you? Simplify yourself for others. What do you want their 'takeaway' of you to be?

Think of it as a trailer for the movie of you. It's a little snippet full of promise. When you meet people, don't go into a long exposition scene explaining all the boring parts of your life; focus on the exciting bits, the action sequences, the bits where Jason Statham punches a giant shark in the face. Why should people be interested in you? Because you have something to give, a great story to tell. It's got a giant shark in it, for fuck's sake (all interesting people have shark stories, right?).

You can be authentically yourself wearing make-up, with a hair transplant, in a suit and with whitened teeth. I do it all the time.

Look, I had very 'British' teeth, which is the American way of saying bad teeth. And I had a hairline that made me look like a vampire's accountant. So I had both of them fixed. Now when I smile, it looks like someone opened a fridge door. And I didn't so much add hair as do a redistribution.

INSTA-GRATIFICATION

If you look at a photo of an influencer on Instagram and compare it with what you see in the mirror, you'll feel terrible. Of course, your life seems messy and complex in contrast. Stop comparing your inside to other people's outside. #bestlife #blessed #seriouslyfuckingstopit

Also they're much younger, richer and hotter than you. So yeah. There's also that.

That Instagram influencer is casually posting a photo that it took 300 shots to get and they've used filters. They've done the work of editing for you so you can feel bad about yourself. Thanks, Instagram influencer.

Incidentally, Mayans used to believe photos stole your soul. It turns out maybe they were right. Not one photo, one photo is fine, but thousands upon thousands are the problem. Have you seen what taking Instagram 'seriously' does to people? Living your life on Instagram has no downside other than robbing you of your soul. Mayan people were way ahead of the curve on this one.

I FEEL MANIPULATED

You know you can manipulate a situation, you can spin it and tell a story. And you'll be in good company; it's what God did when he knocked up a nice teenage Jewish girl.

Comics are manipulating you the whole time. Comics tell you their story and they edit and highlight areas so you see what they want you to see. For a comic, their 'stage persona' is the audience's perception of them. It's made up of all the assumptions and the snap judgements people make about you while you're up there.

Guess what? We all try to manipulate the people around us. Comics are just really good at it. It's good bullshit with slices of truth. Manipulation is a great skill with negative connotations (maybe I'm just saying that so you'll like me – hard to tell).

Wear a suit, don't wear a suit, suit yourself both literally and metaphorically. Just be aware, you create your artifice. Give people a cheat sheet: what do they see instantly? What do you want them to see?

A person in striped pyjamas: an escaped prisoner.

Man with a neck tattoo: knows where to get drugs, fine with minimum wage.

Woman in a checked shirt with buzz cut and a moustache: enjoys hockey, good at pool, oh let's just say it, lesbian (apologies to any clean-cut lesbians reading).

BE THE SIGNAL, NOT THE NOISE

One lesson from business I understood and applied to stand-up comedy is branding. You're selling your speciality.

I can be deeply serious and academic, bookish even, but it's not what I do best. I can be depressed and anxious, but I don't share it all that widely (well, now I have). I'm a world-class bullshitter, but I don't want people to think of me as a liar. I have a huge penis, but I don't let it define me.

You know when you meet a type of person, say he's an old Etonian, and you think, 'I've met this guy before.' And you haven't, you've just met old Etonians before, you've met his 'type'. Once again, it's pattern recognition and it's a huge time-saver.

But if you can show people something different, if you can make them do a double take – then they feel like they've never met anyone quite like you before. What's going to make you stand out on a planet where everyone is clamouring for attention? What I'm saying is: don't be a basic bitch.

Sometimes we get in the way of ourselves by being a little too much. How much useful 'signal' are you sending out? How much useless 'noise' are you making? The 'noise' will muddy the 'signal'. If you have too many things going on at the same time, you can't count on people being capable of seeing the 'real you'. I mean, have you met people?

One of the great things about performing is you get to edit out your own noise. You get to be pure signal for two hours on stage. It's fantastic. Don't believe me? Buy a ticket. Be amazed.

PART 10

WORK IS MORE FUN THAN FUN

CHAPTER NINETEEN

10,000 HOURS OF WHAT?

WORK SMART

There's a delusion in our society regarding meritocracy. It's the idea that people who work the hardest will be the most successful. I don't agree. Meritocracy is a myth.

Work ethic feels like some Protestant bullshit that people have bought into. 'If you work hard then you must deserve success' – something about it feels, I want to say, German, there's something so self-righteous about it.

True meritocracy lies in working smart, in how you apply your hard work. You know what's really hard? Recycling plastic in a Brazilian favela, that's hard. Mining for cobalt in the Democratic Republic of Congo, real hard. Repaving roads in 40° heat in Qatar, that doesn't look fun. You can work as hard as you like in manual labour, you'll never be rewarded. The people born into those worlds will never have the life choices that those working in tech in Silicon Valley have. Of course, you don't choose where you start, but you do get to decide where you finish. If you don't have a choice in life, work hard. If you do, work hard and smart.

If something is too hard, maybe you're not good at it.* If it feels hard, maybe you're not doing it right. Stop, take the time, rethink what you are doing. If you work in a job and it takes you twice as long as the next person, maybe that is nature's way of telling you to do something else. Maybe it's not for you.

When I did exams at college, I remember my friend Oscar always talking about how much time he put in studying. But no one gives a damn about how many hours you spent revising – it wasn't about how long you studied, the hours you put in, it was about how well you did on the test.

You'll know if it's right because it'll come easy (just like your mum). It will be the line of least resistance. Sometimes people say to me, 'It must be nice, you just get up there and tell a few jokes, it's easy for you . . .' And I say . . . I say, 'Yeah, it is.' Because it will be easy if you're leaning into your edge. This isn't about what's worthwhile or important, it's about how niche your chosen path is.

My mother was a nurse, it's a caring profession, it would be hard to overstate its value, but it's not rewarded in our specialist economy because a lot of people can do it (not me, I'd have to care). Rule of thumb, if they advertise your job on TV, they're not paying you enough.

Think of the jobs that are the easiest to acquire in our society: low barriers to entry, no qualifications required, no specialist skill set needed. Fruit picking is the lowest paid and least valued and least satisfying, no matter how much you like strawberries. If you were to say to me, 'But the thing is, Jimmy, I'm incredible

---

* There's an important caveat here: this doesn't apply if you're just starting out. If you're just starting, enthusiasm will get you through.

at picking fruit,' I'd say, 'Guess again.' If the guy on his first day is getting paid as much as the guy who has been doing it for twenty years, that's not a good sign.

Old Guy: 'Hey, what about all my experience picking apples?'

New Guy: 'Mmmm, I think I've got it.'

Say you get a driver's licence, you can then take jobs that require a car, but if you get an HGV licence, you can do a little better in a lorry.

Now, if you can pass your accountancy exams, you can do even better than the driving jobs – we reward a high boredom threshold. And if you can pass your medical exams, you can do better than an accountant. So far, so obvious.

Notice it's not about hard work. Hard work is not the metric. Do fruit pickers work hard? Yes. Do nurses work hard? Hell, yes. Do they get paid as much as Premiership footballers? Nope. Is life fair? Great, you're getting it, but not as often as Premiership footballers.

THE RESULTS ARE IN

There are different versions of you in the world, but it's all perception. I think I'm a very successful comic, but I'm not a Hollywood star. If Will Ferrell suddenly had my career he'd fucking kill himself (but he'd still do it in a funny way). 'Success' is a perception. But what's the metric? From whose perspective?

You might as well be working in the same currency as the rest of society, and that currency is results.

You might judge your work on satisfaction, and it's hard

to argue because that's your internal metric. But results are where other people measure you against the world. The real reward in society is if you can find satisfaction and happiness in something you can specialise in, which is also in demand.

It's all about the results. If I turn up to a garage and ask the mechanic if he's fixed my car and he says, 'No, but I've been working on it for thirty hours. And I love it. It's my passion. I've always seen myself in overalls and I like the smell of grease, I like the whole thing really . . . I'm just not good at the actual fixing of the cars. But as I say, I worked really hard for thirty hours non-stop. The car still doesn't run. Here is your bill, sorry it's massive.'

What you want to hear is, 'Yeah, we fixed it, it was easy for us.' That's the point of going to a mechanic, a specialist. We judge people on results. People can be sniffy about blue collar jobs, but those guys are judged on what they've achieved and deliver on the regular.

I'm not saying you should do what I do, I'm saying you should do what you do.

I lost a few years trying to live up to an expectation I thought others had of me. Don't make that mistake.

QUIT SMART

If you can't decide, the answer is 'no'.

— Naval Ravikant

Quitting because it's too hard is not acceptable. If it's just hard, what you want to quit is complaining.

Don't quit until you've got a plan. Don't quit school until you have a job, don't quit your job until you have a career, don't quit your career until you have a better option. Don't be an idiot. Don't quit Harvard unless you're starting Facebook.

If you're leaving college, make a plan. If you're fifty and successful, make a plan. People say, 'Don't quit your day job.' I agree, even if you hate your day job, don't quit your day job . . . unless you have a plan.

Of course, there are times when quitting is the right option. When you were a kid, did your parents want you to persevere with the piano because they 'weren't raising a quitter'? Well, your parents were wrong. Quitting frees you up to do other stuff. You were right, the piano wasn't for you (apologies to Elton John if he's reading this).

'IF YOU CAN'T QUIT, YOU MIGHT AS WELL GIVE UP'

In your life, you start more things than you finish, and you try more things than you like and you make more friends than you end up with. If your reach exceeds your grasp, you're going to have to get good at quitting stuff.

Delusion is the opposite of quitting. Check out the scene in LA if you want to see the proof. The problem with Los Angeles is that people that don't succeed don't leave. It's not for me to say, but there's a lot to be said for moving back to Omaha and being the prettiest person in town. Why not move on? You could be a ten in Omaha, instead of an LA six. And that's coming from a guy who is an LA five on his best day.

Sometimes the thing you want to be good at is not what you have an aptitude for (see *Britain's Got Talent* for details). The heart wants what the heart wants. But you'd be crazy to follow your dreams, unless your dreams are what you're best at. If you happen to have a dream that you're the best at (family and friends' votes don't count), go on ahead. Otherwise, dream something smarter, dream something better suited to you.

I'm not saying don't be a quitter. I'm saying, if you're going to quit, quit smart.

OH, THE PLACES YOU WON'T SEE . . .

In your life you're going to do great things. But there are so many more amazing, wonderful things you're not going to do.

If you cure cancer, you're the guy who didn't cure heart disease and AIDS. You monster.

You're going to have to quit a lot of things to do one thing well, and you're going to have to not be in some amazing places to be where you are.

NOT MY FUCKING PROBLEM

Make two lists. List everything that is your problem that you need to take responsibility for and do something about. And then make another list of all the things that are not your problem. That's my favourite list.

You'll find the second list infinitely longer than the first. Be grateful you don't have to deal with that shit.

Think of it as a more detailed version of the 'Serenity Prayer': God, grant me the serenity to accept the things I cannot change:

Global warming – not my problem.

Trans rights – not my problem.

Kim Jong-un's weird haircut – not my problem.

Dick jokes – I'll get right on that (I guess technically any joke about Kim Jong-un is a dick joke).

With all those global problems, ask yourself, what can you realistically do? Pick a small thing and do it: recycle, be respectful of people, tell your friends if they look ridiculous. Do what you can and move on. It's so much better than moaning about it.

WHAT CAN YOU DO?

Getting there isn't half the fun – it's all the fun.
> — Robert Townsend

You know that brilliant Malcolm Gladwell book, *Outliers*? In it, Gladwell claims that to master any skill at world-class level, you need to practise it for 10,000 hours, with the proviso that you practise correctly.

What I think is interesting is why someone would spend 10,000 hours doing anything. What could you bear to spend 10,000 hours doing? What's going to hold your interest?

I see 10,000 hours as a litmus test of 'Do I love this enough to spend 10,000 hours on it?' Because that's what the 10,000 hours is: it's the doing. And frankly, I don't think that number is even close to what it takes to master anything. I don't think it includes the listening, the watching, the reading, the travelling, the waking up in the middle of the night with half an idea, the obsessing about it whilst you're doing something else . . .

When I started stand-up, I did over 300 shows a year for the first five years. I've cut back to 200 live dates plus TV shows and corporates. Only an international pandemic slowed me down. Why? Willpower, hard work, determination? No, I found something I really liked doing and didn't stop.

That's why a job is a fuck buddy and a career is a lover (which I think makes a zero hours contract a serious sexual assault). Without love, you're just getting screwed.

In school, I noticed this pattern: I did well in classes I liked and in dull classes I goofed around. There's a huge difference between a kid being forced to read a book for school and a kid that's reading a book because they want to read the book. And the likelihood of being able to recall the information, what do you think that would be? (FYI, if you're being forced to read this book for school, your school is fucked.)

But why are you reading Gladwell and not some other writer? Maybe it's because he spent years honing his writing skills. You're interested because he's interesting and has an interesting worldview. And Gladwell has a gift for writing. He loves what he does.

So, ask yourself, how much do you enjoy this activity? You can have anything you want, if you want it badly enough. But what are you willing to sacrifice to get it? You can have anything but you can't have everything.

MORE FUN THAN FUN

Fuck hard work. Do 'the work', sure. You have to do 'the work'. 'The work' is the important thing, it's the most interesting thing.

If you have to work and you really don't enjoy the work (and you'll always have to work at things), that's a hard life. If you only like the result, but not the process, that's also a hard life. You can't work like that just because you want a result; you've got to be enjoying it, the grind, the journey, the whole thing. Like Malcolm Gladwell: he doesn't just enjoy the books and articles, the results of his labour, he enjoys the act of writing itself.

I don't know much about Usain Bolt, but he worked for about fifty seconds every four years, the rest was training. If he didn't enjoy the training, that'd be a hard life. If you love the whole process, you'll stick with it even when it's difficult.

There's not much that sport, entertainment, friendships and parenting have in common except one thing, it's application. Constant effort is the unifying element across the board. How do you keep up constant effort, you ask? Well, what you do is a little bit of work, but often. Often is the key word in that sentence. I don't work hard, I work frequently. You can go a long way on frequently.

Writers will moan, 'You don't know how lonely it is, how hard it is . . .' You love it, you liar, you fucking love it, you're on your eighteenth book. Sure, there will be some tough days, some shitty days during the process, but you know it's a thing that once you get going, it won't feel like work. It may feel like effort, but it won't feel like hard work.

If you get to work towards something, that's a privilege. Pressure is a privilege. If you enjoy what you're doing and you're good at it and you can live on it and it's not separate from the rest of your life, well, that's the *ne plus ultra* of living. You won life's jackpot.

THE START OF SOMETHING

The first gig I did was in a place called the Tut and Shive on Upper Street in Islington, North London. The pub ran comedy nights upstairs and on a Sunday newer comics were welcome. I went to an 'open mic' night and it was pretty good, so I went the next week. But this time, I asked the compère, Andy Fox, if I could try five minutes the following Sunday. He was like, 'Sure, why not.' Part of me wanted to say, 'Why not? Why not? Because I've never done this before, I'm not a comic, are you crazy?'

The thing about being a comic that's magical is this: if you believe you're a comic then you are. We're very much like Tinker Bell in that respect, only with comics we only die if we don't believe in ourselves (a lot of us also share an attribute with Peter Pan in that we 'never grow up').

The following Sunday, my school friend Hiroshi and I met in the afternoon. I mentioned the gig to him. I said, 'Hey, I'm gonna go and do a comedy show tonight.' He said, 'Great, yeah,' like it was nothing, like he was saying, 'That sounds about right.' That was all the encouragement I needed: someone not being actively hostile to the idea was enough.

That evening I did five minutes of . . . let's call it comedy. That was where the big transition happened, up on stage in front of, maybe, twenty people in a tiny pub. It felt like, 'Okay, this is something . . .' Now, I don't know how much talent I had, but I definitely put the hours in. I certainly worked harder at stand-up than anything else I'd ever done.

The first joke I wrote was: 'Boxers are always talking about their working-class backgrounds and about how "there was only one way out". I grew up middle class, we lived in a cul-de-sac, there was only one way out.'

Not great, but joke-shaped.

I found my voice early on. There were already strong indicators of what my sense of humour tended towards, in what I found funny. But what you like isn't necessarily what you're like. I like lots of different styles of comedy, but I didn't know what my sense of humour was until it found me on stage.

THE BEST-LOOKING GUY ON THE BURNS WARD

Comics are not famous for having a great work ethic. Because they don't. So, when I was first on the circuit, I was considered a hard worker by stand-up standards. This was called 'cheating', because in a field where doing the bare minimum is the norm, working at all seemed amazing. Being the hardest-working comedian on the open mic circuit is like being the best-looking guy on the burns ward.

But successful stand-ups? They work their arses off. Most of us are never 'off'. We're on the road way more than we're at home.

What comics are smart about is that they do something they love. They love what they do and so what they do is not work. This is their secret. The problem with loving doing stand-up is that work is more fun than fun. Would I like to perform in front of thousands of laughing people or . . . or what? I don't need to hear the other options. I'll take option one.

Work-life balance is important, apparently. You need time off or you'll burn out, something something . . . I don't know what to tell you. If you burn out before you've even gotten anywhere, good luck to you. I've been on the road non-stop for twenty years, and I have to tell you, it's not the years, it's the mileage. But it's hard to say no when you're being asked to do your favourite thing.

CONSCIOUS INCOMPETENCE

You have to learn craft. Even when it makes you forget your initial inspiration. You have to learn craft so that you can recognise the 'good' accidents.

— Francis Bacon

When you're starting out in any new endeavour, first comes unconscious incompetence. You are like a foal learning to walk, it's adorable. You are blissfully unaware of what you don't know how to do yet. You are unconscious of your own incompetence.

Next comes conscious incompetence, if you're lucky. At this stage, you have a better idea of what to do; you just can't do it. It's like learning to drive: you can't find the gears, but at least you know what gears are. You try to indicate and the windscreen wipers come on. You're terrible at this and you know it. You're painfully aware of what you can't do.

Then comes conscious competence. Your learner plates are on. You can drive when you concentrate, but if you lose focus for one minute, you're going to wrap the car around a fucking tree.

Finally comes unconscious competence. You're driving and you're not even thinking about it. It's muscle memory, it's intuition. You'd even have a hard time explaining what you're doing to anyone else, because you're no longer thinking about it. This is the dream.

When you're at the start, you learn skills, the trade, the craft. Your goal may be to be the greatest of all time, but you'll have to start with the ABCs like everybody else. Unconscious competence is about getting to the level of mastery with the craft.

So, if you're not doing anything for the next 10,000 hours, do what you do. What else are you going to do?

DUMB KNOW-IT-ALLS

Every expert I've ever met has always said, 'Well, it's complicated.' And every person I've met with an opinion in a pub has said, 'It's simple, let me explain . . .'

This is the Dunning–Kruger effect, where people overestimate their abilities. Why would they do this? Because they don't know enough to evaluate their competence or even their incompetence. These silly fuckers don't improve because they think that what they know is the limit of what there is to know.

The effect is essentially a form of self-delusion. It combines a lack of knowledge about your own ability with a misperception of the abilities of others. Essentially, you're a dummy who thinks you're super smart, while at the same time assuming smart people are dummies. In other words, the less you know, the less you know what you need to know.

The scary thing is, you can be unconscious of your own incompetence. But if your attitude is 'every day is a school day', then you can learn from every experience and from everyone you meet.

At this point I know so much about psychology that I could probably write a whole book about the Dunning–Kruger effect. And it would be the best book about the Dunning–Kruger effect ever. I bet I know more about it than Dunning and Kruger combined.

WHAT HAPPENS IN VEGAS

When you perform in Edinburgh you get venue passes, so you get to see all the shows you want to for free. In 2002 I saw Johnny Vegas's show five nights in a row.

The first time I saw it, I thought it was so chaotic. He absolutely destroyed for the first ten minutes, the audience was in the palm of his hand, and then he lost them, the gig crashed over the next twenty minutes and he only brought them all back to a crescendo at the very end. It was operatic.

I brought a friend the next night and we watched it from the back of the room and it was not exactly the same, but remarkably similar.

By the third time, I got a handle on it: the trick of performance. He knew exactly what he was doing. To all intents and purposes, it was the same show every time. This incredibly chaotic, shambling wreck of a man was actually hitting all the beats in the show and doing it night after night. And he didn't make it look easy either, he made it look extremely difficult, but it felt fresh every time and he brought us with him and made us feel like it was totally spontaneous, that it could only be happening right now. It's an amazing skill. It's a great sadness Johnny doesn't do more stage shows because he's incredible.

Sidebar: The first time I met Johnny Vegas was backstage before doing *Late'n'Live*. He was laid out on a filthy mattress. He looked and smelt like maybe he was the reason the mattress was filthy and he was drinking a combination of Cointreau and Baileys, which he referred to as 'luxury Gaviscon' (to this day Johnny claims it's a cure for acid reflux – to my knowledge Johnny has no medical credentials). He was drinking pints of the stuff. As he was downing it, he struggled up, put his hand on my shoulder and said, 'Don't be like me. You've gotta be yourself.' It was sweet, he's a sweet man, but I was like, 'Yeah, don't worry about that, we're different types of animal.'

CHAPTER TWENTY

BEST-LAID PLANS

I LOVE IT WHEN A PLAN COMES TOGETHER

Making a plan is smart, it's 'MBA graduate from Harvard Business School' smart. Having a plan is the difference between doing something and nothing happening.

Harvard sent a survey out in 1979 and found that the 3 per cent of graduates from their MBA who had their goals written down ended up earning ten times as much as the other 97 per cent put together within just ten years of graduating.

And that's fucking Harvard Business School – do you know how hard it is to get into that programme? Have you ever met someone who went there? You'll know if you have, they never stop going on about it (have I mentioned I went to Cambridge?).

Having a plan was the factor that predicted success. The good news is that the barriers to having a plan are low. All you need is a pen, some paper and a little thinking time. The amazing thing to me is that 97 per cent of Harvard Business School graduates thought, 'I don't need a plan, I'll wing it.' I guess 'What They Don't Teach at Harvard Business School' is: make a plan, dummy.

A 2017 study done in the UK by the Department of Education found that the most important behavioural factor for success after university was having a plan. I see a pattern here.

You know when you look at someone and think, 'That guy, he seems to have it all worked out.' He hasn't got it all worked out. He's got one thing worked out. He knows where he's going . . . it might be the only thing he knows, but that's enough.

You don't need it to be a good plan or the right plan, just a plan. I didn't leave my cookie-cutter job to become a TV host, tour the globe and become the British poster boy for cosmetic dentistry. I left to be a comic, I left with a direction and it led me on. The plan isn't what you're gonna do, it's who you're gonna be. Wherever you are in life, have a plan. Don't worry, nothing will go according to plan, but take the time to make one.

APPLICATION WELCOME

I'm all for pursuing desires. However, there's a difference between a dream and a delusion. For me, that's about what you can practically do with your dream. If it has no next step, then you're dreaming. If you have a dream that involves some Svengali who happens upon you whilst you sit at home in your pants, you've already lost.

I wish someone had told me after university that you get judged on what you do, not what you say you'll do. Christ, people talk a good game. Having ideas is not the same thing as being creative. Creation is execution, not inspiration. Talking about a film script, podcast or app is not the same as writing a film script, doing a podcast or making an app. There's a lot of talk (and often, especially in show business, that talk is fuelled by cocaine).

Many people have ideas, but very few take the steps to make the thing they imagine. You only have to compete with those few. You put the hours in and you get satisfaction, but you don't get results? There's a name for that: that's a hobby.

The modern-day example: 'I've got an idea for an app, it's the Tinder for . . . whatever.'

The difference is application. The Tinder people made a plan and went and built the complicated thing. What the Tinder people didn't do was just talk about it and high-five each other.

Did Leonardo da Vinci invent the helicopter? Nope. He drew a great picture though. His picture looks a little like a helicopter, but it isn't one.

I have a cure for cancer. It comes in a little green pill and it's a hexagonal shape. You take it with water and the stuff in the pill finds your cancer and kills it for you. That's my idea. I had an idea. That's what people who talk about apps sound like to me. They know as much about creating apps as I do about biomedical science (fuck all).

Of course, you might not be there yet. But you get it, right? The metric is not the amount of effort you put in, the metric is the results you get out. You can polish a brass coin for a hundred years, it'll never be gold.

Peter Cook was at a party and asked someone what they were up to. The guy said, 'I'm writing a book.'

'Oh really,' Cook said. 'Neither am I.'

NO MORE HEROES

Heroes are great. They're so brilliant and flawless, why wouldn't you love a hero? Chances are your heroes are famous. And that's the main problem with heroes. Heroes are inaccessible.

What you really want are role models when you're starting out. Role models are people you admire, but they're closer to home than your heroes. Role models are more useful than heroes, because you can actually have conversations with them.

You're looking for people who are a little bit further down the road than you. If you're lucky you'll have many role models on your journey. They're people you click with, they take time with you, they'll be able to answer your questions, they'll be able to show you what you need to know. But the best thing about them is that they love what you love. If you're lucky, you can convince one of them to mentor you.

In Philadelphia, back in the late nineties, a veteran comic, Keith Robinson, took a young Kevin Hart under his wing. Happily, Hart also had the ability to take the help. With Robinson's tutelage, Hart was pushed into stratospheric success.

The great Garry Shandling took a young Judd Apatow under his wing. Shandling did a phone interview for Apatow's high-school radio show. Years later Shandling hired Apatow to write for *The Larry Sanders Show*, Shandling's Emmy-Award-winning HBO series. Eventually, Garry pushed Apatow to direct and then be a showrunner. Apatow went on to write and produce critically acclaimed television series and movies you love.

Role models are people you admire not just for their ability, but also for the way they present themselves, for their attitude and character.

Look for them. They're everywhere. Find people who fit what you need at the time. They can be nurturing, encouraging and empathetic, or like a drill sergeant – exacting, challenging or combative. They come in all kinds of packages. And crucially they're people who also want the one thing you really want: they want you to succeed.

In every field, you'll meet people who will be your Brokeback Mountain of inspiration for a time. People you can talk shop with and who galvanise you, who remind you why you love doing what you do. 'I wish I knew how to quit you ... Neal Brennan.'*

GOALS ARE THE GOAL

Your current habits are perfectly designed to deliver your current results. Are you happy with that?

If you're not happy with the current state of play, here's what I'd do: take your life's purpose and break that down into manageable, smaller goals. Goals, rather than 'a goal'. Goals are your plan broken down. They should be hard enough to be a challenge but still realistic. Have a timeline to give yourself a sense of forward momentum.

Prioritise important things. Frankly, if that's news to you, you

---

* Neal is a good friend and makes me want to be a better comic. Check out *3 Mics* on Netflix.

shouldn't be reading this. There is a book about a very hungry caterpillar that I think you'd like. Sometimes, though, stuff can sound important when it isn't. You have to keep asking yourself, 'What do you want?' And if the answer is to play more Xbox, then you are incorrect. There are such things as wrong answers in life.

You might want to lose a stone in weight. That's a goal. A system would be to exercise first thing in the morning. A checklist would put exercise in your diary.

Heroin addicts in recovery programmes find that doing all the little rituals, robbing their mums, getting the works out, heating up the spoon, looking for the last viable vein in their big toe, all the practical things they need to do to take heroin, gives them mini highs. There is pleasure in deferred pleasure. I'm saying get high all the time.*

Break down your purpose into daily goals and then find the high in the everyday of the goal. Get lots of little highs.

LITTLE HIGHS

The way you judge yourself is up to you. In my world, it could be the validation of other comics, critics, television execs, the audience . . . Your internal metric is more important than external measures of success.

The answer to someone who tells you that you've failed as a comic is, 'Well, I'm not done yet.' Unless you've finished your set, in which case, get off the stage.

---

* Apologies to Snoop Dogg for any copyright infringement.

When I first started doing comedy you could do the Comedy Store in central London, drive to Balham in South London to do the Banana Cabaret, where you would do two shows, and then drive back to the Comedy Store. I was getting paid, the clubs were packed, I was in the zone the whole time. People were laughing, I got to hang out with other comics. It was great. For me, that was success.

IT'S ALL IMPORTANT

Even when you love your work, there are things around your work that you'll have to do. Usually tedious and boring admin. Sometimes the periphery feels like a distraction from the work you'd rather be doing. It isn't. It's all part of what you want to do and where you want to go. I say, love that too. Life is not just a highlights reel, it's the whole shebang (*The Hole She Bang* would be a great title for a porn star's autobiography).

As a comic you better fucking love planes, trains and automobiles, because that is your life. And I love comedy. I love everything about it. I love sitting in airports. I love driving down the M1 at 1.30 a.m. with my stereo blasting to keep me awake. I love getting up at 5 a.m. and catching a bus across a fjord to make a flight. I love it all. Look, when you're a jobbing comic, you're driving up and down the motorway all the time. You basically live in comedy clubs and service stations. Put another way, you're essentially a salesman, a door-to-door salesman of dick jokes.

The vision, the life's journey, the purpose, that's all valid. But what are you doing at 9 a.m. on Monday morning? Take care of that and the big stuff takes care of itself. A life's journey is a lot of days strung together.

Two boys go to ride ponies. But the owner of the ranch insists they shovel manure out of a stall before they get to ride. One of the boys hates it. He complains all morning. The other is whistling and smiling as he works. 'What are you so happy about?' asks the first boy. 'Well,' says the second boy, 'with all this shit, there must be a pony.'

Life is full of shit – but there's a reward for getting through it. Sometimes it's just the lesson.

CHAPTER TWENTY-ONE

TIMING ... FINALLY

NOW, WAIT A MINUTE

The last time doesn't exist. It's only this time ... there's only now.

— Bill Murray

In comedy, timing is everything; it's one of our superpowers. Timing is what landing punchlines is all about. There's a delayed gratification to any well-timed joke. You have to wait patiently for the better outcome, you have to have all the 'time' in the world.

The secret of telling jokes is 'playing in the pocket' of the rhythm. Stand-up is an exercise in manipulating time. A skilled comic can make an hour seem like the blink of an eye or stretch out a moment. This is the magic of live performance.

But comics also know all about timing when it comes to grafting. Comics have to put their 'time' in. You can get frustrated with the speed of your progress, but what's the point? You might as well enjoy it, because you can't rush it.

The practice of being a stand-up comedian puts the performer in a state. Before the show you might be sweaty and nervous. Early on in my career I'd be almost throwing up. But then suddenly you're on stage in front of people, you have a clear role to play: all you have to do is make them laugh. You haven't the time to think about the future or the past, you have to be in that moment.

I think that's why so many performers have a hard time off stage, because it's such a perfect zen moment when you're performing that the rest of life can feel clunky.

ONE NOW OR TWO LATER?

Here's an old joke:

> *The young bull says to the old bull, 'Why don't we run down the field and fuck one of the cows?' The old bull replies, 'No. I've got a better idea. Why don't we walk down the hill and fuck all of them.'*

There's a famous experiment, you've probably heard of it, it's called the Stanford Marshmallow Test. Basically, you take a little kid, you put them in a room with a marshmallow (the experiment dates from the seventies when everything was pure sugar), you tell the kid that once you leave the room they can either eat the marshmallow or wait ten minutes and get an even bigger one when you come back.

Only 30 per cent of the kids were able to hold out for the whole ten minutes. And those were the ones who ended up doing better in school, with higher self-esteem than their peers. They were also less likely to abuse drugs and become obese (begs the question: what the fuck did they put in that second marshmallow?).

It turns out kids nowadays can wait a minute longer than their parents' generation and two minutes longer than their grandparents'. I'm guessing sweet treats are less of a rarity these days.

They tried the Marshmallow Test on men on Death Row and they all failed. Of course they did. Basically, a lack of impulse control can literally land you on Death Row. Or maybe guys on Death Row don't feel they have the time to wait for that second marshmallow. Maybe they were worried if they waited too long, it would've ended up a toasted marshmallow.

This is called 'deferred gratification'. The Marshmallow Test is where you learn that you pay for everything. Eventually.

BODY POSITIVITY

I am not fat, but what I am is hungry some of the time. The model and philosopher Kate Moss once said, 'Nothing tastes as good as skinny feels.' Turns out our Kate totally gets deferred gratification (just not when it comes to cocaine, if rumours of nineties excess are to be believed).

'The body keeps a record': what you eat, what you drink, your emotional traumas, high SPF sunscreen. Your body wears all that.

Humans like instant feedback. We're not calibrated to perceive processes through time. So, one day of running a mile is nothing, there's no difference, you can't see any change, you can't perceive it. But if you run a mile every day for a year, in 365 days you'll be a different-shaped person. And you'll also be 365 miles away.

Why not be totally hedonistic? Why not be overweight and out of shape and a little hungover? Because people are goddamn animals. People read that shit in a second. If you value you, we know to value you. Bad people prey on the weak and they don't find the weak through ESP, they just look around.

Now, I like junk food, who doesn't? I have also been overweight from time to time. I think there's a link. With junk food you can see how you'll be shaped by your choices – literally.

Another reason to take care of yourself is the long game. Have you ever seen a really obese ninety-year-old? Nope. The trade-off for all that deliciousness now is no future.

Of course, we're all going to die. And there were people who pushed away the dessert trolley on the *Titanic*. Make your own choices – just don't not think about it.

TIMEFUCK

All we have to decide is what to do in the time that is given to us.
> — Gandalf (it's a twelve-hour trilogy, mate – I
> think you got enough time)

Time is a headfuck. You can only live in the present. But your head could be ruminating on the past, hoping for the future or wishing the day away. You can have too much time or not enough. You can waste your time or it can slip away.

The medium is the metaphor. Watches and clocks make us think time is a certain way. Since the invention of clocks, our perception has changed. Time is no longer eternal; time is measurable. We used to think of time as seasons and days, and now we think in minutes and hours.

The smartest thing you can do with money is to buy time. There's enough money to go around, there's plenty of money but time – time is running out. At some point your perspective will change. Time will become more important than money.

Would you give up all your worldly possessions to be half your age? I think so, yes. I'd fucking love to be twenty-five again. If you think, no thanks, I'd rather keep my stuff and stay closer to the grave, then I don't think you're really gettin' this time thing.

Time is the most precious resource we have. If you don't believe me yet, go to a hospice and ask around.

DEATHBED REGRETS

Thank God I'm an atheist.

– Jean-Paul Sartre

I know I'm right about prioritising later, because, uh – every religion ever. All religions are about living a certain way now so you have a better next life.

Even if you don't believe in a next life, living for it is still a good way to go. I may not believe in a 'next life' literally but I do believe in a 'next life' metaphorically. I hope to be living a very different life in twenty years' time and I know what I do now will have a direct effect on how good that life is going to be.

A priest asked Voltaire on his deathbed to renounce Satan and his evil ways. Voltaire responded, 'Now, now, my good man, this is no time to be making enemies.' Oh, Voltaire you funny fucker.

The number-one deathbed regret is not having had the boldness to live the life you wanted, which is sad. If you live your life fully, maybe when you're on your deathbed you can say something funny like Voltaire.

What are you going to do with this finite and precious resource? What matters to you? Come on, quickly. The clock is ticking.

HOW MUCH FUN CAN YOU HAVE TODAY . . . WITHOUT TOTALLY FUCKING UP TOMORROW?

Do the things that make you happy within the confines of the legal system.

— Ellen DeGeneres

There are some amazing comics you've never heard of because they had so much fun. So much fun, you wouldn't even believe it. Maybe it was worth it. They were living for today. Do you know what day it is today for those comics? It's tomorrow.

It wasn't just an Edinburgh Festival thing. I didn't have all the fun I could've had during the first twelve years of comedy. I didn't even drink. And it wasn't an AA thing; there's no great rock bottom story to wow you with here, I just wasn't 'getting out of my head' because for the first time in my life I liked being in my head. I knew at last what I wanted to do, who I wanted to be and how to go about it. And even though, looking back, twenty-five seems awfully young to find one's calling, it felt like I was playing catch-up.

When after a show, if I got asked, 'Do you want to come for a drink and some delicious cocaine?' my answer was always along the lines of, 'Thank you, but I've had such a lovely day, I want to do it all again tomorrow.'

The hard work of learning your craft and getting good at it is about delayed gratification. Being a comedian is a task without end. You can always be getting better. Those never-ending tasks in life, those are the things that bring happiness. Sure, you could not do the work, go for the pleasure and comfort of doing nothing right now. But ultimately that doesn't lead to happiness.

'Live every day as if it's your last' is terrible advice. It'd largely be tearful goodbyes to loved ones and screaming in pain. How about 'Live every day as if you're going to do something great in twenty years'?

People are constantly telling you to live in the moment. What? Don't live in the moment. The moment is the cutting-edge of now, the moment is giving into compulsions and living recklessly.

Never mind The Power of Now, how about The Power of Later? Obviously there's got to be a trade-off and a compromise, and it's good to know a little about your internal economy. There's a law of diminishing returns. An ice-cold beer on a hot summer's afternoon feels pretty great – but five of them? Ten of them? One speedball – golly gosh – but four and you're in a body bag (I barely know what a speedball is but some of my readers might be hardcore, shame to leave them out).

You can fuck yourself up in the future. People have had a terrific time in their twenties and then never saw their thirties. The 27 Club of rock and roll is not a list you want to make: Brian Jones, Jimi Hendrix, Kurt Cobain and Amy Winehouse.

There's such a strong and natural preference for 'now', 'right now'. Because 'now' is where you are all the time, so it feels like for ever. Have you ever had street food in South America? Delicious. While you're eating it. And what does your future hold? Amoebic dysentery.

Again, all self-help boils down to choosing the long term over the short – I did say that right at the start, I'm nothing if not consistent.

Once again, if you're on a tight schedule or a slow reader, here's the whole book right here: prioritise later.

BETTER LATE THAN NEVER

The future is already here – it's just not evenly distributed.
— William Gibson

Where you end up is important; when you end up there, not so much.

Here's a list of folks who made it, but made it late:

- Toni Morrison was 39 when her first book, *The Bluest Eyes*, was published. She went on to win a Nobel Prize in literature when she was 62.
- Stan Lee was 39 and had no real career prospects when he wrote *Fantastic Four* after his wife suggested he experiment with stories he actually liked.
- Vera Wang was 38 when she left her cushy job as a *Vogue* editor to work for Ralph Lauren. At the age of 40 she set out to be an independent clothing designer.
- Martha Stewart was 41 when her first lifestyle-plus-cooking book was published.
- Steve Carell was 42 when he joined *The Office*.
- Samuel L. Jackson was 40 before he got real attention as an actor. He was 43 when he starred in *Pulp Fiction*.
- Rodney Dangerfield got his break on the *Ed Sullivan Show* at the tender age of 46.
- Jane Lynch was 40 when she acted in Christopher Guest's mockumentaries. And she was 49 before she landed her Emmy-Award-winning role in *Glee*.
- Morgan Freeman was acting the whole time but it wasn't until he was 50 that he found overnight success.
- Ray Kroc was a milkshake salesman and was 52 when he bought McDonald's and franchised it.
- Christoph Waltz was 53 when international success was thrust upon him after years of solid performances on stage and television in Germany.
- Miguel de Cervantes was 56 when he published the first

part of *Don Quixote*. He had a whole lot of living to do before he settled down to write full time.

- Harland Sanders, AKA Colonel Sanders, was 62 when he franchised Kentucky Fried Chicken after twenty years of running a restaurant and hotel.

I love that list – that list takes a lot of pressure off. It's never too late.

CHAPTER TWENTY-TWO

BREAK THE BANK

I CAN MAKE ME RICH

The good news is, there are 'get rich quick' schemes that work, but sadly they only work for the guys running the schemes.

How much money is enough to give you the peace of mind and the security you need? There is no answer, other than your own.

There's a reason billionaires exist: it's because some people became multi-millionaires and it wasn't enough. Right now there are billionaires working very hard to make a trillion. Why? 'Cause it's not about money for them – it's about the pursuit of money. Money is the way they keep score; money is running the show. They're working for money – but literally. Money is their boss.

If you need props around you in order to prove to yourself that you're a success I'll let you in on a little secret: if you're not good enough without it, you won't be good enough with it. And face facts, buying a Porsche won't make your dick taste any better.

'Fuck-you money' is the concept of getting enough money that you can say 'fuck you' to anyone. What's the figure, the I-never-have-to-work-again figure in your mind?

You'll never have enough if you think like that. It's much easier to change your mind about money than to become a billionaire.

And whilst we're here, why would you never want to work again?

Oh. You work in a factory that turns chicken carcasses into nuggets? Yeah. Okay. I get that.

At a Long Island party given by a billionaire, two authors were talking. Kurt Vonnegut teased Joseph Heller that their host had made more money in a day than Heller had earned from his bestseller *Catch-22*. Heller responded, 'Yes, but I have something he'll never have – enough.'

FINANCIAL PLANNING WITH JIMMY CARR

Money is the ultimate example of the Marshmallow Test. If you're spending more than you earn, you can do that for a while, but at some point you're going to have to pay. However, earning more does not mean you have to spend more.

Welcome to Financial Planning with Jimmy Carr. Yes, this is happening:

1. Wait. Can you wait? If you can wait, wait. Wait until you can afford it.
2. Earn more.

3. Spend less.
4. Pay your taxes (that's an expensive mistake I'll only make once).

I always thought Doomsday Preppers were crazy. But they do what most of us have forgotten to do. They have a war chest, they're ready for the apocalypse. They're spending resources on their future worst-case scenario. Most people don't even save for a rainy day. I blame rainy days; rainy days are not motivating.

How retailers seduce you is by giving you the thing right now. Back in the eighties, people stopped getting richer, the politicians couldn't live with that, so they allowed more credit. We got into a habit of owing money. Don't buy in.

I understand of course that a lot of people don't have a choice. They borrow money because they have to, to buy food for themselves or shoes for their kids. Fair enough. Do what you have to do and sincerely good luck. What I'm talking about here are the extras, the luxuries. Do you need that PlayStation right now? Has your laptop really become obsolete this week? Is your penis genuinely not big enough today?

If you wait, you get two things: you get the thing and you get the feeling of achievement. If you don't wait, your impatience costs you. There is a percentage charged, there's an APR on right now. It's easy to think you have stuff when you're actually renting stuff.

I look at it like this: everything costs two times the price. So, take a phone that costs £1,000 (I know they'll try and hide the cost in an easy monthly payment plan and three-year contract, but those things are expensive). You will have to earn the £1,000 and pay tax on what you earn in order to buy it. So really what you have is a £2,000 phone. By the time you've saved the money up, there will be another phone and you'll want the new, new one. Most stuff you can get in a mall is obsolete in two years.

Money is human happiness in the abstract ... – Arthur Schopenhauer

Once you spend your money, you've got something. If you keep the money, you *could* have anything. But things are not as valuable as experiences and experiences are not as valuable as people. Spend your money accordingly.

I don't want to go all Buddhist on you, but happiness is clouded by unlimited desires. Every desire you have is an axis where you might suffer. Buddha himself would suggest not desiring anything, but even then you're desiring Nirvana, 'the state of bliss', so it's a catch-22, you fat enlightened fuck.

I'm sort of 'Buddhist Lite': I'd say desire just one thing. You can have anything you want – you just can't have everything you want. As Steven Wright so wisely said, 'You can't have everything, where would you put it?'

LEARNING TO EARNING

I didn't turn a penny for a year after leaving my day job, I mean nothing. I was living off my redundancy money.

The things you own end up owning you. If you've ever bought something you can't afford, you know what I'm talking about. The payments on that BMW Z3 nearly prevented me from quitting my job and starting comedy. That's crazy, a thing could have stopped me from living my life. A thing I thought I wanted.

In fact, I got rid of the BMW and bought a Rover 75. The best way to describe it? It was a mock Tudor Jaguar. It was a 'split-second Jag'. If you were in a hurry and had a squint, you could be fooled into thinking it was a Jaguar. But then after a second glance, you'd think, 'Oh no, wait, it's a piece of shit.' It ran on liquid petroleum gas (LPG), which was a thing at the time. It was a super-cheap car to run – good for the jobbing comic. To sum it up, my car was the opposite of a 'fanny magnet' – even Harry Styles would struggle to get laid in an LPG Rover 75.

Letting go of the little sports car was so easy, because it represented excitement, adventure and freedom and I had all that good stuff in comedy. You don't need something to represent what you already have.

I was lucky I started out bored in a boring job. If I'd done comedy from the jump, I'd never have known how lucky I was. Which was lucky.

If I was going to give any young comedian advice, I'd tell them to do a business course. Anyone in the arts, really. Pick up a book on running a small business, because that's what you're doing whether you're a comedian, a musician, a painter or whatever.

Sometimes people in the arts enjoy being ignorant about business. They'll talk like they think they're the shit because they're not interested in 'the bucks'. They think being interested in money is shallow and somehow your art will suffer.

It will not hurt your art to think a little bit about marketing to your audience. Longevity in the arts is about being able to sustain yourself. You can look at Jay Z, Damien Hirst, Andy Warhol, Dolly Parton – all great artists, and all great business people.

LIVING OFF MY WITS

I'd been doing comedy for about a year when a booker, a guy by the name of Geoff Whiting, calls me. Man, that guy can talk. He's a good guy, but not one for a short telephone conversation. This is cutting a forty-minute conversation down to the bare bones. Essentially he said, 'I'll give you eighty pounds if you go and perform on a bill for twenty minutes in Plymouth.'

I said, 'Fucking yeah!'

Plymouth is only a five-hour drive away. He said he could sort out accommodation but I said, 'Don't worry, I'll drive back.'

So basically it was a ten-hour round trip to perform for twenty minutes. I would say I was in Plymouth, all told, for ninety minutes. Eighty quid just about covered fuel and expenses (a bacon double cheeseburger from Burger King, fries from McDonald's – the dream road combo), but only because I was paid cash in hand. And I was (come on HMRC, you've got to let that one slide).

I'd left a job making thirty-something grand a year but I was so fucking excited by those four twenty-pound notes in my hand.

Earning money is always great but gamblers will tell you nothing's sweeter than money won. I would suggest that money made from having a laugh is a whole different level. Within six months I was literally living off my wits.

PART 11

DON'T LEAVE LUCK TO CHANCE

CHAPTER TWENTY-THREE

TALENT + HARD WORK = YOUR LUCK

LUCKY FUCK

My second oldest friend, Matt Thick, his father, John Thick, a wonderful man, had a lovely turn of phrase. He would say, 'Be lucky.' He was a chauffeur and he was a happy man.

At the time, I remember thinking that it was kind of a ridiculous thing to say. It didn't make any sense to me because how could you 'be lucky' on purpose, when the very nature of luck is arbitrary? But I liked the phrase and I liked how he delivered it.

But I get it now. When you break it down it makes sense. The root of the word 'happy' is German for luck. So to be happy and to be lucky means pretty much the same thing in German. That's the sense in which I take it – if you're happy, you're lucky. It's a reminder to me that being happy makes you lucky. Not the other way round.

Now I say it to people. 'Be lucky.' And what I'm really saying is, 'Be happy. Follow your heart, spend your time on the things you care about and with the people you love.' But if I said all that every time I'd get nothing done.

The phrase implies you really can make your own luck. You are your own luck.

Incidentally, I don't think it's any coincidence that I met my partner as my mother was dying. When your heart is breaking it cracks open. The great gift of grief is that it makes you receptive to someone else. Even in grief you can get lucky.

OUR LITTLE SECRET

I'd rather my generals be lucky than good.

— Napoleon Bonaparte

A good Christian man kneels at the altar and prays: 'Lord, I've always been an obedient servant, I've never asked you for anything. I'm sixty-five now, please let me win the lottery.'

Nothing.

Then next week, the man prays at the altar again: 'Lord, no one has been a better Christian than me, please let me win the lottery.'

Nothing.

The third week, the man kneels at the altar and says: 'Lord, I've been a faithful, observant Christian, please let me win the lottery.'

A booming voice from above: 'Buy a ticket.'

How lucky are you? Like, were you born looking a certain way, do you have a wealthy family or are you a natural athlete? Were you born in a first world country? Most of us are already lucky. But did you know you can enhance the luck you have?

Have you read *The Secret*? Well. I can save you £10 here and now – don't. It should be called *The Bullshit*. It's basically a book about how if you really wish for something it will come true.

But you can be lucky. That's a fact.

Learning your craft is you buying your lottery ticket. The more craft you have, the more tickets you have. Success is never guaranteed but what you're doing is increasing your odds.

And why not buy a ticket for the lottery? Sure, you probably won't win. But nature has already bought you a lottery ticket for ball cancer. So why not hedge a little?

Luck is also about showing up. I'm lucky, I was in the right place at the right time. Where was I when I was 'discovered'? In a comedy club working. How often was I there? All the fucking time.

The harder you work, the luckier you get.

Luck is what happens when preparation meets opportunity.
– Seneca the Younger (very old now, of course)

Fortune favours the brave (not the indigenous people of North America – those Braves got wiped out by Europeans in a genocide). The brave are not afraid of failure, they're afraid of not taking chances.

Have you ever seen a person with an incredibly beautiful partner and you think it's a mismatch? I made a whole show about this very premise, *Your Face or Mine*. I'll tell you what that lucky person did: they asked that beautiful person out.

Lucky people put themselves out there. They got the job because they applied for the job. If you ever see someone you think is talentless but successful, there's a couple of things you should keep in mind: one, they will have a skill you do not rate for whatever reason and if you can work out what it is, you should learn it. And two, it will be because they have put themselves out there.

CHAPTER TWENTY-FOUR

BROADCAST NEWS

BREAKING AND ENTERING

Of course I believe in luck. How else does one explain the success of those we don't like?

— Jean Cocteau

TV is a really fun party to be invited to but at some stage your name drops off that invite list.

You've got to keep up with your main work. The fact that I never took any time off from stand-up is what I believe kept me in the game. My first Edinburgh show was in 2001 and then I kept coming back for the next eight years even after I got my first TV show. Edinburgh shows require an hour of original material. Looking back on it, I could have had a year off. It wouldn't have had a detrimental effect. But I felt like a shark, like if I stopped moving or slowed down, I'd die.

Early on I'd be asked to join a writing room where you'd sit around with a bunch of other writers and maybe a couple of producers, which I really enjoyed. It was then that I met Iain

Morris, who was working as a producer. He's a good guy, a good man with a great sense of humour. A couple of months later he gets a job at Channel 4 and he says, 'Do you want to come in? Maybe we should do something.' And that something was *The 11 O'Clock Show*, which was already an established show and the starting point for a lot of big comics, most notably Sacha Baron Cohen and Ricky Gervais.

Not to get on my high horse, but I think there needs to be more opportunities for young performers to be on TV and get used to it before they get their big break. It's the reason *Saturday Night Live* produces such incredible stars. Each performer is only required to come up with five minutes a week for a couple of years. No one has to carry a whole half-hour show, they just have to develop their thing. Initially you don't know what you're doing but if you are given the space and you work at it, you will get better.

Being in television at that time was a bit like the experience of doing Edinburgh. There were a lot of people doing the same thing but doing it in their own way, like David Walliams, Matt Lucas, Rob Brydon, David Mitchell, Leigh Francis, Miranda Hart and the like. No one could do what the other ones did; we each were doing our own little TV shows and there was a lot of energy. We were given a lot of chances.

GOOD LUCK

It seems like I started in television at the best possible time. Now, would I have known I was entering the TV game at the perfect moment for me? No. But I suspect we're always living in the right time, in some golden era. Maybe everything just looks yellow to you.

The truth of the matter is, early on I tried writing narrative stuff and it didn't come naturally, you only have a finite amount of time and energy. So I decided to focus on what I could do that worked. And that's how I found out I'd been a TV host the whole time.

There are a lot of ideas for TV shows; everyone has ideas. It helps to have a good production company backing you. TalkBack was a good company for light entertainment.

What you do is you start with an idea and you have meetings about these ideas – a lot of meetings. And then about 1 per cent of those might be made into a pilot. The point of a pilot is to see if it works in reality rather than just on paper. Quite a bit of money is spent and mostly, they don't work. I got lucky, I got very lucky. The pilots I did tended to work.

Every once in a while, one of those pilots actually gets commissioned.

Your Face Or Mine (2002) was a silly idea – it was a game show about looks and mismatched couples. A couple had to choose who they thought was the most attractive when presented with random people. If the audience agreed with them, they won money. This escalated until the couple were asked who in the relationship was more attractive. If the audience agreed with them they won more money, which they could then split in their subsequent divorce.

It got commissioned. They said, 'We're gonna make six of these.' And then they phoned back. They went, 'Actually, we've got a slot in the schedule at six o'clock every day. We want to put it on every day, can we have forty-five of them?' I went, 'Great, yeah, we'll make forty-five.'

Because we'd negotiated my fee on the basis that it was going to go out once a week rather than every day, they went, 'Can you do it for less?' And I went, 'Noooo, no I can't.' And they said, 'Thank you, see you in the morning.'

And that is the story of how I bought my first house.

BIG FAT CATS

After *Your Face or Mine*, we came up with a show called *Distraction*. *Distraction* was based on the premise that we asked people questions and whilst they answered, we would distract them. Maybe when they pressed the buzzer, we'd electrocute them – fun. Or we had them in a little toilet cubicle where you could just see their head and their little feet and their pants around their ankles, and rather than pressing a buzzer to answer a question they had to do a little pee. More fun. It was like they were at a pub quiz in Guantanamo Bay.

We couldn't believe they let us make a pilot. It was a crazy idea, almost like one of those insane Japanese shows. But they did and we made it, which was the weirdest, most bizarre, ridiculous experience. And then – it got commissioned for a series. We made loads of them. We sold it internationally and I got to host the American one made for Comedy Central. It even got nominated for awards.

The Big Fat Quiz was Jonathan Ross and me, sitting in his

kitchen, talking and reading some 'end of year' quiz in a news-paper, going, 'This is really boring, we should do one of these but make it more fun.'

We went to Channel 4 and said pretty much that: 'We should do an end of year quiz, it'll be really fun.' And they went, 'Yeah, here's two hours, great.' Jonathan produced it, I hosted it, and every year we keep doing it.

8 Out of 10 Cats was the show that really hit. *8 Out of 10 Cats* is a topical panel show about everything. We did a pilot and we were asked to do way more of them and then basically made twelve a year for, I want to say, the last hundred years.

CHAPTER TWENTY-FIVE

START AND KEEP GOING

GOTTA START SOMEWHERE

Writing is like driving at night in the fog. You can only see as far as your headlights, but you can make the whole trip that way.

— E. L. Doctorow

You better work, bitch.

— B. J. Spears

I don't know what you want to achieve, but I know how you'll do it. You'll start and keep going. Do you know how Michelangelo painted the Sistine Chapel? He started and he kept going. How did James Joyce write *Finnegans Wake*? He started and he kept going. How did the people at Bletchley Park decode German ciphers? You got it, they started and they kept going. Even God took a week to create the earth. He didn't just have an idea for everything and then go do God stuff, he put the days in.

IN PRAISE OF FAILURE

The man who puts on his armour to go to battle should not boast like one who takes it off.
    – The Bible, 1 Kings 20:11 (I was raised Catholic,
                       it's hard to shake)

Everybody talks a good game. Try something and fail and then we'll talk.

Failing a GCSE in French is devastating at the time – you think your life is over. How will you ever know where the *bibliothèque* is? You're shitting yourself. A girl breaking up with you is an existential crisis: is life even worth living? Failing is devastating when you're young because you're not used to it. When you're young, you're just inexperienced. If you fail enough, you'll find that failure is nothing to fear. Fearless doesn't mean you have no fear, fearless means you fear less (wow, that's corny, but I stand by it).

Avoiding situations where you might make mistakes is the biggest mistake of all.

The reason it's hard to think clearly in stressful situations has to do with cortisol, which floods our system and interferes with our capacity to think straight. The enemy of cortisol is laughter, which as you now know releases serotonin, dopamine, endorphins and oxytocin. Or as it's collectively known by clinical psychologists, the 'good shit'.

GET IT WRONGER

You can always edit a bad page. You can't edit a blank page.

— Jodi Picoult

There's even a saying about writing: don't get it right, get it down. You can edit later – you have a delete button on your computer, this is why computers are better than typewriters (also they're much lighter, and you can't look up 'lesbians taking milk showers' on a typewriter). If you're worried about being right, getting it right, doing it right, being perfect, that's all ego. That's all fear, that's all anxiety, it's everything but actually doing the fucking thing.

Be bad. Be gloriously and ridiculously bad. Stink up the place. Have the courage and the conviction of your suckiness. Failure is incredibly freeing, unless you're an escapologist.

Being wrong reminds you that nobody, and I mean nobody, is wholly right. I mean, even David Bowie was in *Tin Machine*. Getting stuff wrong, and acknowledging that, frees you from being defensive. And being defensive is the quickest way to shut down creativity.

Being wrong is hard – I mean being totally wrong, 100 per cent wrong. It's hard to get stuff perfect and it's hard to fuck up perfectly. But it's pretty easy to get stuff half right. And when you have something half right, then you have a draft, you've filled the blank page. You've got something to work on. Getting it wrong is how you'll defeat procrastination.

Remember: the worst art is the art that never got made. Well, that and the movie *Cats*.

GET DOWN

I write jokes down all the time. Comedians are constantly taking notes, jotting down ideas, details, random thoughts. At the heart of every comedian there is a writer. They take these nubs and try to turn them into material they can perform. The focus is usually on the stage, because that's the glamorous, fun bit that everyone gets to see. But the writing and rewriting are just as important. The jokes are the bullets, the comic is the gun.

Getting an idea down as you think of it is a great habit to get into. No one remembers the exact phrasing the next day when they try and retell the story from the weekend.

'The faintest ink is more powerful than the strongest memory.' That was said by some Chinese dude hundreds of years ago and we remember it perfectly, because he wrote it down. We don't know who said it, because he didn't sign it. Point made.

THE JIMMY CARR EXPERIENCE

Patience picks its own winners.

— Old Man Phrase

There will always be a time when things aren't going to go according to plan. Now that can happen in different ways.

In military speak, it's known as 'known knowns', 'known unknowns' and 'unknown unknowns'. So shit you have to prepare for, shit you have a contingency for and shit that just happens. That is the essence of experience – the more you know, the better able you are to react.

We don't start with 500-seaters, we start in the upstairs function rooms of pubs. Even Eddie Murphy started in a local talent show. We start with small risks and then take bigger ones.

Sure, the first time you get aggressively heckled on stage it's stressful. But the second time, not so much, and the thousandth time – you start having fun. The 'known known' is your routine – you've prepared your act. The 'known unknown' is someone shouting shit out – it's going to happen at some point, you don't know what it's going to be but you've got a generic comeback prepared. The 'unknown unknown' is when something crazy happens and you fucking embrace it.

I was performing at *Late'n'Live* one Edinburgh and a guy shouted out, 'My mum died of cancer.' And I said, 'I wasn't talking about mums and I wasn't talking about cancer.' 'No,' he said, 'but it was funnier than this.' Well played, my friend, well played.

How you get good in a situation is to be in that situation over and over again. Eventually, you'll get used to it. Have you seen *Groundhog Day*? Life is a lot like that. (Incidentally I have an idea for a sequel to *Groundhog Day* – we re-release *Groundhog Day*, call it *Groundhog Day 2* and just show the original movie in cinemas.)

I UPSET THE BOSS

In 2018 I did a benefit show in New York City called 'Stand Up for Heroes' in aid of wounded servicemen at Madison Square Garden – not the main room, you understand, the little theatre on the side which has a capacity of just 5,600.

That year Seth Meyers, Jim Gaffigan, John Stewart and I were in the line-up. Oh, and Bruce Springsteen. Fabulous.

My picture was on the wall, so they recognised me when I arrived. They said, 'Hello, Mr Carr' and they pointed at the stairs, 'Your dressing room is up there and so is the green room.'

At the top of the stairs, I saw an open door and as I entered, right in front of me, I saw a vision in double denim (aka – the Canadian tuxedo) and I thought, 'I might as well be friendly, we're on the same bill. I guess I'll hang out with the the Boss.'

I walked up to him and, 'Hi, I'm Jimmy, I'm one of the comics, I'm on tonight. I listened to your *Desert Island Discs* on Radio 4. I just recorded *Desert Island Discs* a couple of weeks ago and I listened to yours a week out from when I did mine and changed all my selections. Because you picked the greatest songs but you earned the right to do that because you're a musician. So, instead of showing people how great my musical taste is, I played the songs that meant the most to me.'

And then we chatted about how great the format is for *Desert Island Discs* and his stage show and his book. I grabbed a bottle of sparkling water and ate some carrots and hummus from the craft table. I'd pulled up a chair and was very relaxed. Then after about fifteen minutes I glanced up and I saw a sign on the door, which was still open, and where it should have said 'Green Room', it said 'Bruce Springsteen'.

I said, 'Is this the green room or your dressing room?'

And he goes, 'It's my dressing room.'

And I said, 'Oh. I should probably go, shouldn't I.'

And he went, 'Yeah.'

I picked up my bag and disappeared off to my little dressing room down the corridor, feeling ever so slightly totally fucking mortified.

What do you do? Are you going to be embarrassed for the rest of the day or are you going to lean into it? I leant into it.

After my sound check, I was wandering past his room and I could hear him and his wife, Patti, they were singing. I popped my head around the door and said, 'Yeah, practice makes perfect, keep at it.'

He laughed.

I asked, 'Are you, uh, how many songs are you thinking of doing tonight?'

He said, 'I'm going to do five songs.'

'Are you going to do covers or your own stuff?'

'My own stuff.'

I drew in a sharp breath and exhaled. I shook my head and went, 'Well, if you're sure.'

It was fun. He was a genuinely funny, great guy. He offered me tickets to see his show – there's a reason he's the fucking Boss.

What could we take from this? You might find yourself in a cool situation. You might think you're the shit. But I know and Bruce knows I fucking embarrassed myself.

I'm fine with that – embarrassment now is worth it for the story later.

FUCK GENIUS

As I've said, heroes are okay but role models are better.

Now geniuses are another thing entirely. They're godlike and they are already mythic because you don't have access to them, you don't get to see up close their struggles and the blood, sweat and tears, or their hard work. They don't actually help you work out how to develop. When you're introduced to an arena with a genius, the only way a rational person can respond is to go, 'Well, that's ridiculous, I could never do that.' You think they have magical, God-given talent, you think they're special. That their success was inevitable. It wasn't, it was 'evitable. Most of them started out with 'promise' or 'aptitude' just like you.

Let's take a moment to all feel inadequate together. It'll be a bonding exercise.

Don't aspire to genius, aspire to being pretty good. You don't want genius. Genius is hard and not just because of the loneliness of trying to communicate an idea no one else can conceive, or because you'll only be acknowledged after you die. There are three ways to be a genius and you don't want any of them.

1. You have a serious mental or physical illness, usually schizophrenia. Van Gogh, Thelonious Monk, they both had schizophrenia. You create originally because your

brain and chemistry are all fucked up. You create despite your illness rather than because of it. And as a genius you usually die really young. If you're reading this and Kanye is still alive, well done Kanye.

2. You have to go into the wilderness for no less than ten years. Usually because you're rejecting the status quo, but more likely because the status quo rejected you. Scientists get this a lot. This is a lonely way to live, isolating with crippling self-doubt. A few examples would be Barbara McClintock, Raymond Carver, James Joyce and Chet Baker. Usually you get bitter. The most extreme example is the Unabomber, Ted Kaczynski. He was a maths prodigy, but that's not what people remember him for.

3. You're pretty good and then you have a major, debilitating disease that leaves you profoundly handicapped. Beethoven, Matisse and my mate Stephen Hawking are excellent examples.

Okay, there's two more.

4. You have a successful parent, already in the field you're in, like Mozart or Picasso or Michael Jackson. These parents are either pushy or absent and you'll end up either selfish or needy. Great. Michael Jackson of course famously didn't blame his father. He blamed it on the boogie.

5. You are a child prodigy. I fucking hate child prodigies. And with good reason. What they do is 'master' something that an adult has already come up with: chess, a musical instrument, perspective drawing, perspective drawings of

musical instruments on a chess board. What they're best at is making other kids hate themselves. And statistically, only a tiny percentage become actual adult geniuses. Most quit and come to the conclusion that it was a curse.

None of it is fun as far as I can tell. Comedy genius? I fucking hope not.

FUCK A GOAT

> *Critics of mass culture have a trick of weighing the worst of the present with the best of the past.*
>
> — John Gross

GOAT: Greatest Of All Time. Fuck those guys, and I say that with love, as a few of my friends may well be contenders for that title.

You have to swing the bat a few times before you hit the ball. Even the greatest, even Chris Rock has to swing the bat. When you see Chris Rock on stage and he tells a brilliant and funny joke, you don't get to hear the fifteen other jokes he thought were good and didn't make the cut. You haven't heard all the different wordings and variations on the joke that did make it.

Again, the problem is judging your beginnings and middles on other people's results. It never ends well comparing other people's outside against your inside. You only see Picasso's *Guernica*, but you haven't seen the sketches that he did before-hand. There are twenty different versions he painted that he wasn't happy with. You only see the end product and so as humans we look at that and we go, 'Wow, it's so easy for him, one and done, no net.'

This is relatively new. Unlike most of human history, you're inundated with the greats and it's intimidating because in terms of cultural history we've kept everything. We are surrounded by the greatest of all time, all the time. So, we judge the painting on the fridge against a fucking van Gogh.

People in porn are fucking, frankly, like porn stars and if that's all you've ever seen, that might be a little bit intimidating. You're looking at some guy with a weapons-grade penis, and then you look at yourself and you're thinking, 'Well, what am I going to do with this?' Creativity is a lot like pornography: there's a very high standard of fucking going on.

It's inspiring to witness genius. It's motivating and challenging and mind blowing, but the obsession with being a GOAT is counterproductive to doing anything other than disappointing yourself.

Go ahead and look at Billy Connolly or George Carlin, someone who's had a forty-year career, someone who's a 'pioneer' in an art. By all means tell yourself, 'I'm not at that level, I'm not that funny.' But don't get hung up on that comparison. Of course you're not at that level. Relax. Idolising GOATs is just another type of procrastination. Do something that's not as good, do something different – just do something. Just do you.

It's great to remind yourself: you are not competing with a GOAT. You know who you're in competition with? You, last year.

Here's the thing:

There is nothing noble in being superior to your fellow men. True nobility lies in being superior to your former self. — Ernest Hemingway (somewhat ironically, I don't love his later work)

TALENT IS CHEAPER THAN TABLE SALT

There's another delusion in our society: talent.

People talk about talent like it's a superpower. Talent is just your 'edge' plus the hard work you put into it.

Raw talent means nothing. Without the application or hard work, raw talent is a guy in a bar telling you he 'coulda been a contender'. Coulda, woulda, shoulda . . . Raw talent is just 'edge' without smart, applied work over time.

Being a heavyweight boxer is hard. Like, really hard. They train for a fight like, well, like heavyweight boxers train for a fight. The training takes over every minute of their life. Turns out boxing is a very labour-intensive way of getting irreversible brain damage.

Here's how little respect 'the work' gets in our culture. In movies, when we hit the bit where the central character does all the work, we break for a montage. There are a lot of quick cuts, an inspirational song, and the sense that something is being achieved, because no one really wants to see the slog. The saying goes, 'you win or lose a fight in the gym'. But if you watched *Rocky*, you'd be forgiven for thinking, 'I'll just run up and down some steps in Philadelphia in time to "Eye of the Tiger", and I'll be good to go.'

People see a comedy special – an hour of stand-up – not the 10,000 hours it took to get there. People see one step when it takes a million.

Our culture is full of bullshit, mythical stories about how someone's incredible raw talent leads them to unbelievable success. And legendary tales of how someone's incredible hard work leads them to unbelievable success. Unbelievable is right – it's always a mix of the two.

We see the sports star winning, not the blood, sweat and doping that got him there.

INSPIRATION IS FOR AMATEURS

Inspiration is for amateurs; the rest of us just show up to work.

— Chuck Close

Yeah, Chuck, what you've done there is, you've got into a flow state at work – that's why inspiration came easy to you. Think of every great thing that has ever been done – all of it happened in flow states. And sure, not everything you do in a flow state is genius but every bit of genius was done in a flow state. You have to be open to your subconscious mind and ideas popping into your head.

I remember asking a comic how Eddie Izzard did it and my friend said, 'I think Eddie just vibrates at a different speed to everyone else.' Total bullshit. In fairness, I did ask an alcoholic.

Inspiration is nothing more than getting into a flow state.

Early on, it'll happen once in a while. It won't be dependable, but you'll get a taste. Some people have a little ritual. I guess it's valid if it works, but it'll still work without superstition.

You've felt flow, right? In a flow state you focus on the process, not the result. It's worth finding something in your life that gives you flow. Ideally, it's your work, your job, your moneymaker. But if you can't do that, get yourself a hobby that gives you an outlet and some satisfaction. Go with the flow.

Multitasking is hugely overrated. If you want another secret for getting into the flow: don't give yourself too much to do. If you can, do just one thing. One. Really focus on that one thing and you'll end up doing it incredibly well. Focus is the secret sauce.

If you had a choice between investing in an all-rounder and investing in someone that just did one thing – you'd choose the single-minded person every time, right?

I know people will say 'It just popped into my head,' but what they really mean is 'My subconscious mind did this because I did all the groundwork.' Your conscious mind is a court stenographer, your subconscious is the man who got O. J. Simpson off, motherfucking Johnnie Cochran.

'It came to me in a dream!' That's the myth of creativity. A lot of time is spent romanticising those 'Eureka' moments when the truth is those lightning bolts couldn't have happened without all the work they put in. Inspiration is nothing without implementation.

And you know what will keep you busy while you're waiting for your muse? You could get good at your craft . . .

CHAPTER TWENTY-SIX

QUIT QUITTING

STAND UP AND STAY UP

Failure is not falling down. Failure is falling down and not getting up again to continue life's race.

— Richard Nixon

And you can take that to the bank, 'cause that nugget of wisdom is from Tricky Dicky, a guy who really knew about fucking up.

For me, writing is the job. Writing is the gym and performing is the cookie jar. Performing is the reward.

When I'm on stage, I try to remember what I was thinking when I wrote each joke and try to be surprised by it again. Almost like fooling myself into thinking that I don't know where this is going.

Part of performance is in the space between the words. During that time, you think about what you did last time and how you could elicit a better outcome. You calculate, 'How long does that pause need to be?'

It's amazing to me that if you fumble a word, one word in

a set-up, you lose none of the meaning, but you lose maybe 50 per cent of the laugh because the fuck-up has distracted the audience.

You're constantly editing when you're performing, but you're also reviewing at the same time. The unconscious part of your mind is essential so your conscious mind can deal with the room. And when I say deal with the room, what I mean is this: you're having a conversation with 1,000 people so you're constantly looking around, you're trying to make eye contact with everyone. When you're selling the joke, you're saying, 'Follow me, I know what I'm doing, this is going somewhere.'

I look like I stand pretty still on stage. I do move, if you're looking at my toes. At the beginning, I'm on my toes. And then there's a point in which I can move back onto my heels. But as soon as anything unforeseen happens, I'm back on my toes again.

The first couple of years of doing stand-up, I don't think I used my heels once. I was on my toes the whole time, on high alert. It felt like there was a constant fire drill, an emergency, it was all fight and flight. DEFCON One-liner.

The sensation of enjoying doing comedy at the beginning only happens in the briefest of moments. You enjoy having done a gig more than the actual gig. It all seems to happen so fast, very much like the first few times you have sex.

After spending more and more time on stage, you get better at working out when you need to be in emergency mode. As time goes on you think, 'Okay, they've come to see me, we're five minutes in, they're laughing in all the right places, it sounds good, we can relax, we can enjoy this now.'

BE A HACK

The show doesn't go on because it's ready; it goes on because it's 11.30.

> — Lorne Michaels (legendary producer
> of *Saturday Night Live*)

Perfectionism is just another word for 'procrastination'. What, you're going to be perfect at your new job on the first day? Not possible.

I know people who are trying to stop smoking, they have one cigarette and say, 'Well, that's it, I guess I'm a smoker again.' Man, you had one cigarette. But there's something about having a perfect record: if they can't have that, they're not interested. Why? Nothing about the rest of their lives would suggest that would be the case.

How come 'the arts' get away with being talked about like a super-precious creative commodity when, here's the thing, a lot of the arts aren't really creative? There are a lot of cover bands out there. That's what the Royal Philharmonic Orchestra is, by the way, it's a cover band for Mozart. There are by-the-numbers sitcoms, daytime soaps, generic pop tunes and hack comics.

If you're called 'a hack', it's an insult. Hack comes from hackneyed, it means predictable, unimaginative, trite, clichéd, derivative, corny and unoriginal. You can do that, use hack as an insult if you like. But if you're trying to be creative, I'd say being a hack is a good place to start.

And maybe, go ahead and come up with ten bad ideas for jokes, or whatever the equivalent is in your world. (Unless you're a surgeon, where ten botched surgeries sounds like a class action lawsuit waiting to happen.)

The American Professor Brené Brown has a TED Talk about how she changed her opinion on the whole 'if you can't do it 100 per cent, don't bother' mindset. Specifically: any workout is better than no workout. Cooking a so-so family meal is better than not sitting down with your family to eat at all. It's a pretty good TED Talk, not perfect, but it's all right.

UR FiEND DYSLEXiA

Two wrongs don't make a right, but three lefts make a right.
— Andrew Clements

During the whole of human history, our species progressed through a combination of natural selection, mutation and adaptation, all tiny steps in our evolution.

We're the product of millions and millions of accidents. The human race is a product of fuck-ups. So if anyone ever calls you a 'fuck-up', they're 100 per cent right, we're built from fuck-ups. Don't be afraid of fucking up.

Personally, I am the result of a fuck-up. My mother bought a Dutch cap – which is a contraceptive device placed in the vagina. Well, it's supposed to be placed in the vagina, but apparently it pinged across the room as she tried to get it in place, somehow the mood was not lost and my mother thought, 'Sling it up me.' And here I am. It's worth noting, there's a thing called oversharing with your kids. Did I need to know that? Nope. But funny story, Mum.

Getting things wrong taps into creativity. Creativity is the art of picking the right accidents, rather than quitting when we get it wrong. Be creative. Don't think of it as 'not right', think of it as 'lateral thinking'. A lateral thought can look like an accident. A thought that starts one way and then goes off in 'Strangeways, Here We Come'.

Getting things wrong happens all the time. How many times have you misheard something? A song lyric, directions, instructions, a safe word ... This is me all the time. I often get things wrong because I'm dyslexic (this book is co-authored by spellcheck).

Culturally, dyslexia is linked to creativity because sometimes two wrongs make a Wright Brother. When you're both seeing things wrong and hearing things wrong, you have to be alert. Sometimes when you see things wrong and hear things wrong you get things right because you have to improvise.

Spelling seemed so important to me when I was a kid and the truth is, no one gives a fuck about it.

My finals at Cambridge, it was fifteen hours of exams. I'm sitting there writing essays frantically against the clock, my penmanship has never been great and my spelling has always been, let's just call it, auriginal.

I got a note in my pigeon hole. Wait, how do I explain a pigeon hole to the youngsters? It was like a physical manifestation of an email account. And people would put pieces of paper with your name on them in there for you to pick up later. God, I feel old.

Anyway, I got a note in my pigeon hole saying, 'Come and see your tutor' and she said, 'You need to sit in a room and read your exams out loud to a lady who will type them up because the person who is marking your papers said "Um, I can't read this."'

It's encouraging that I'm in the same academic category as John Maynard Keynes. When he wrote his exam papers people didn't understand them, because he was so far ahead of his time. When I wrote mine, people didn't understand them because they looked like they had been scribbled by a toddler on cocaine. The point is, we're both misunderstood.

I've got to say that dyslexia, once again, came up trumps. Because when you're reading your essay to a nice lady who's typing it out for you, you basically get to do a second edit, you can make changes, you have a shot at making improvements. Wait . . . I think I may have cheated in my finals. Shit, no take-backs.

FAIL WELL, FAIL OFTEN, FAIL UP

If at first you don't succeed, try, try again . . . then quit. No use being a damn fool about it.

— W. C. Fields

I've missed more than 9,000 shots in my career. I've lost almost 300 games. Twenty-six times I've been trusted to take the game winning shot and missed. I've failed over and over and over again in my life. And that is why I succeed.

— Michael Jordan

If you had an exam and you wanted to pass it, you'd do lots of practice exams. In the practice exams, you can fuck up. You can run out of time, go blank, whatever. You do enough failing in practice, it's hard to fuck up the main event.

> *Experience is the hardest kind of teacher. It gives you the test first and the lesson afterward.* – Oscar Wilde (famously sent to Reading jail for being gay – I mean, bad enough going to jail but Reading, Christ)

Being 'experienced' is another way of saying 'I've fucked up many, many times before, so go ahead, you can ask me anything, it won't faze me.' If at first you don't succeed, all it means is you've used up all your beginner's luck.

I've failed at more things in comedy than I've succeeded at. I've written more jokes that aren't funny than ones that are. And I've come up with more TV shows that haven't been made than ones that were. I've failed more in comedy than you.

My failure is the secret of my success.

YOU FUCK UP

> *There is only one thing more painful than learning from experience, and that's not learning from experience.*
> – Laurence J. Peter

We are all crazy. We do dumb shit; we are human. If you know yourself a little, you know the ways you fuck up: there will be a pattern to them. The problem with most plans is that they are designed for your 'best self'. But your 'best self' might not turn up every day.

When you make a plan, remember to build in room for fuckwittery. You don't have to do the fuckwittery, but if you build it in, it's less likely to blindside you.

And while you're at it, if you have a plan to go into an office and sit at your desk and work for eight hours solidly, why not also plan to fly to your office with a jetpack? I mean, if we're living in fantasy land, why not at least have fun.

DON'T FAIL THE SAME WAY TWICE

Failure is the condiment that gives success its flavour.
— Truman Capote

I'm a big fan of failure. But don't forget that the key word in the phrase 'learning from experience' is 'learning'. The trick is not to fail the same way twice.

If you've failed 999 times, what should you do? If you keep doing what you've been doing and you expect different results, you're crazy. I think it was Einstein who said it was 'the definition of insanity' (also someone wearing a suit made from human skin is a red flag).

Like I just said, it's okay to make mistakes because the point of 'learning from experience' sort of suggests that you're learning, right? You're not an idiot. You're going to fail differently each time. You're going to fail creatively. You're going to take chances (you understand I'm not advocating armed robbery or intravenous drug use here). Better to regret the things you've done. Or better yet, don't regret, just remember. When you win, you win, but when you lose, you learn (corny again, sorry).

HABIT FORMING

I write only when inspiration strikes. Fortunately, it strikes every morning at 9.00 sharp.

— Somerset Maugham

If you practise something enough, it'll become habitual. So, ask yourself: what do you want your habits to be?

There are no changes other than lifestyle changes. You can go on a diet. Diets work, but they only work for as long as you're on that diet. (The word 'diet' comes (via Latin) from the Greek word 'diaita', meaning 'a way of life'. Fuck me, I had a great education.)

You can go on holiday to relax and you'll be relaxed for as long as you're away, but when you come back to your life, it'll be as stressful as ever. And now you've got the added stress of being pregnant with a Turkish waiter's baby. The main stress coming from not knowing exactly which Turkish waiter.

These are temporary fixes but it's the day-to-day where the game is played.

Don't waste your time doing short-term stuff. Create a system; create a habit. Willpower alone will not beat your environment, so make a good environment for yourself.

Good habits are everything. It's like brushing your teeth: you do it four times every day (these teeth were expensive, I'm gonna take care of them), not every other day.

Mikhail Baryshnikov has said that you can see in prima ballerinas 'the accumulation of the choices they have made in their muscles'. That is all of us, even us middle-aged white men who can't dance.

If you don't like dance, try Aristotle: 'We are what we repeatedly do; excellence, then, is not an act, but a habit.'

A lot of getting better is repetition. When you're learning a skill, what you're doing is laying down a layer of 'muscle', embedding it into your body so you can get on and think about the next thing, the more fun thing, the creative thing.

THE COMFORT ZONE ISN'T FOR ME

I noticed that my hands are shaking and my palms are sweaty – but I say to myself, Okay, be nervous now and then get to the work.

— Garry Shandling

A man sees a magician put his palm over an open flame. He asks the magician, 'How did you do that trick with the candle without hurting yourself?' The magician replies, 'The trick is not caring about the pain.'

A famous comic, who shall remain nameless, was determined to make his failing marriage work and his strategy was to stick it out. He said, 'My wife doesn't realise how much discomfort

I can take. I have a high tolerance for discomfort.' I'm frankly surprised he didn't include that in his vows.

The first time you're on stage, there's so much adrenaline that afterwards you can hardly remember what happened. You just know it was great. And like a junkie, you chase that high for the rest of your career. But at some point, it starts to feel normal. And as soon as that happens you need to change it up. If I get too comfortable on stage then I know I have to try some new stuff – 'cause uncomfortable is where the action is. I say, get comfortable with being uncomfortable. It's better to be uncomfortable than bored.

There's a ton of discomfort on the way to success in stand-up. That's fine, because it's important to get out of your comfort zone. A comfort zone sounds like a soft play area. It's not appropriate for adults. Your comfort zone is no more than a set of self-imposed rules. They're guidelines, it's what you're used to. Comfort zones are conservative – they're literally conserving the status quo. Like I said earlier, when it comes to you, it's best to be a progressive.

When you look back on your life you won't remember sitting on the sofa watching TV, you'll remember the uncomfortable times. You'll remember the times you struggled, the sweat, the tears, you'll remember when you overcame adversity. Those are the great moments of your life.

Sometimes comics will say, 'Oh my God, I could never go back to the trenches, to the clubs, to working that hard for that little money!' That's just ego talking. The job never changes. The venues get better, but it's the same gig fundamentally. For most comics, our attitude is 'Fine by me, it's a great life!'

If you are going through a hard time, just give it five years. Those are going to be your war stories. I remember the Frog & Bucket in Manchester putting us up in a 'hotel' above a pub a few doors down from the club. Of course, it turned out to be a filthy brothel (I'm not being prudish here, it was objectively unhygienic). Would I go back and stay there if I had the chance? Nope. But am I grateful for the experience? Yes.

IT'S A MARATHON, NOT A SPRINT

Thankfully, perseverance is a great substitute for talent.
— Steve Martin

Resilience looks like repeated failure right up until you succeed and then it looks like it was preordained. People think that you were always going to succeed. You're busy getting better, enjoying the journey and then suddenly . . . you get lucky. Well, I'll be damned.

DOCTOR FEELGOOD

I hated every minute of training, but I said, 'Don't quit. Suffer now and live the rest of your life as a champion.'
— Muhammad Ali

You could have food poisoning or flu or crippling jet lag but luckily when you get on stage Doctor Theatre lifts you up.

Doctor Theatre is another word for adrenaline. And the doctor will always help you out. And, sure, there is a price to pay afterwards, but you can get through a show.

There was a corporate gig, I think it was for Microsoft, at the Hippodrome in London in the round. I was only doing half an hour, less time than a software update. I drove to the show and I got there at six o'clock and I felt like I was dying. Constant vomiting. I couldn't eat and couldn't even keep water down. Cold sweat. Awful.

My manager, Hannah, had come to the show with me, which is unusual as I usually travel solo. I like to think of myself as a 'professional killer' and 'killers' work better alone.

I walked on stage, dry-heaving, but once I started and for the next half hour, I was fine. But as soon as I walked off stage, I was clutching my stomach. It was like my brain told my body, 'Leave him, he's got work. Hold, hold, we'll get him in thirty minutes. Okay, go.'

Hannah had to drive me home in my car as I was busy lying down in the back seat throwing up into a waste paper basket.

She'd never driven an automatic car before so she'd hit the brake like it was the clutch every fifty yards, saying, 'Oh shit, shit.' And every time she hit the brake I'd fall off the back seat into the footwell. As I say, I'm not a medical professional, but I'd say that's not a treatment for norovirus.

PLAY NICE

No one becomes successful alone. There are so many great people who have worked well with a partner or in a group and then they separate and never make anything exceptional afterward. They shone because of the chemistry they had together. If you have something like that, respect it because it's another kind of luck that's come your way. Look at the Beatles. It's harsh but true to say after he left he never hit those musical heights again – oh, Ringo.

That is why you have managers and agents and producers and writers and make-up artists and lighting, a whole industry. It takes a village to raise a child and an industry to sustain an adult.

Here's a great rule for life: don't be a dick. You have to learn to play well with others.

Being a TV host is like being made head boy on the first day of a new school. Everyone around you is on your side and then there are these incredible people called 'producers' and it is their job to make you look good.

You also have comedy writers who are sort of like comedians' less evil twins. Comedy writers are like comedians in that they love to be funny. What they don't have are the personality disorders that require the adulation of complete strangers. They're happy spending the day trying to make each other laugh.

The person on autocue (a little shout-out to Sophia): you definitely want to make friends with them. It's you and the person on autocue against the world, especially if you're doing live TV. Live TV is fantastic. Once you finish you can go home and there's nothing anyone can do about it.

You should be nice to everyone, really, it doesn't matter how big you get. Be. Nice.

Be nice because it's the right thing to do, it's the best way to act in the world and it is what good human beings do. Being difficult and diva-ish or petulant just makes you hard to deal with, it doesn't make you more authentic or creative or real.

But ... if you need a reason to be nice, here you go: the person that brings you your coffee, one day that person will end up running a channel. And I know this because the person who used to bring me my coffee ended up running a channel. Those people, their careers will be as long as yours.

Also, if you ever meet me, don't make eye contact.

YOU OR YOUR TRIBE?

There are people who like to belong to a tribe. Their very identity is tied up in family or a gang or a group. Purpose and ambition for the individual is less important in these circumstances, just as the individual and the self are less important in a tribal culture.

In the West, we're obsessed with individual identity and I can't help but feel that's because we collectively feel like we don't belong. At least we have that in common.

The army is a perfect example of tribal culture. In the army, individuality and purpose are not priorities. You rarely meet a soldier who's 'gone his own way' and decided green really isn't his colour.

SWINGING WITH FRIENDS

Friends are a great example of how you can make your own luck.

Everyone is a swinger when it comes to friends. Your best friend doesn't mind you having other friends; they don't get jealous. You can have a good time with another friend and tell your best friend that and they don't get bent out of shape.

You have to ask yourself, what do you want from your relationships? Who is important in your life, where do you spend your time? When do you like yourself most?

You can drop friends, fire them if they're not good for you. 'Friends are the family we choose.' Be around fun people, be around people that get you. In a list of qualities, likeability is a huge bonus. People like likeable people. Nice things happen to likeable people. And likeable is a broad church. If I were to give my child a gift, it would be likeability.

Love is unconditional, non-judgemental regard. You can love someone and not be friends – see all families for details. Friendship is conditional: it's a contract, a bond.

Love can be unconditional. Relationships cannot. – Vienna Pharaon

My whole theory of relationships is that we are with people not because we like them but because we like who we are when we're with them (obviously we like them as well but you get my point). What I learned to ask myself is, 'Do I like who I am when I'm with this person?'

330

Remember: a friend is just a stranger you haven't alienated yet.

HEEEERREEEE'S JIMMY!!!! 2

Nice guys finish first. If you don't know that, then you don't know where the finish line is.

— Garry Shandling

When you're a comedian and you travel around the world, you're on your own a lot of the time, so camaraderie is especially important.

After doing my first spot on *The Tonight Show*, I thought, 'Oh, I guess I'm done.' As I said goodbye to Jay Leno, he asked me, 'You're in town on your own?'

'Yep,' I said, nodding. I sure was. I didn't know anyone at the time in LA.

Jay asked, 'What are you doing?'

I said, 'Nothing.'

He said, 'You want to go see a movie? We're all gonna see the new *Terminator*. Schwarzenegger's on the show tomorrow so we're all going to drive over and watch it.'

I went, 'Great', thinking he's going to hook me up with tickets.

But then Jay went, 'I'll be two minutes, I'm gonna grab my keys.'

After Jay got his keys, we walked outside together where there was a beautiful '57 Corvette. 'I'm a car guy,' he said. No shit. Well, I just happen to be a car guy too. I said, 'I really like cars.'

And then he said, 'Well look, we've got two hours to kill before the movie starts. I'll drive you to my garage.'

On the way over to his garage, Jay and I chatted about what was the ultimate car, we got on to talking about McLarens, then we moved on to vintage Bugattis and the Bentleys of the 1920s.

We arrived.

I want to explain something. I've been to garages before. I've even been to rich guys' garages where they have a collection of cars. He had said 'garage' so that's what I was expecting. What I wasn't expecting was two hangars, like aircraft hangars, full of the most amazing car collection I've ever seen in my life. He's got fucking everything. This was back before people had really heard of Jay's car collection, you can see it on YouTube now. I had not thought I would be in the Smithsonian Museum of Motors.

I got to start up a rocket bike – I mean it was unbelievable, so fun. He had the McLaren, the original McLaren, so I got to sit in the McLaren (if you're not into cars you'll be super bored, just skip this paragraph). He showed me the first electric car (all the doors still attached), which was from 1909 or something. In LA they had these little electric cars that you could scoot around in and the oil companies put a stop to it.

It was actually a little annoying to have to leave to see the new *Terminator* film. I felt like saying, 'Oh, you still want to go and see this movie?' I just wanted to keep wandering round, looking at these wondrous machines.

He grabbed another car, I think it was a Stingray, can't

remember the year, luckily you don't care, to drive us to the cinema. We joined the rest of the crew from the show, who were all there for the movie too. Afterwards, we grabbed something to eat. Jay then asked me, 'Where are you staying?'

I was in some shitty out-of-the-way hotel, but he offered to drive me back. Who does that? He was the host of a show that records every day and he took time out to show me some sights along the way.

In the car, we chatted away about stand-up and the greats, and who we liked and what we were into. As he dropped me off, he said, 'I play Hermosa Beach on Sunday. I play a club there, the Comedy and Magic Club.' Which is only one of the friendliest and best clubs in America, as I was to find out. 'Come down, do a set,' he suggested. I thought, 'This is one of the best dates I've ever been on.' Honestly, I would have, if he'd asked, I would have made out with Jay. Not even the double denim would have put me off. What a fucking gentleman.

I went that Sunday night, and I got looked after like a king. Got to do a set and watch magicians and comedians. Fucking great.

Basically, what I learned is that Jay Leno is a good guy and if someone's in town and they don't know anyone, you're in charge of them, you take them under your wing. You're their guide, even if it's just for a couple of evenings. I'll never get to pay Jay back but I'll pay it forward.

PART 12

LOVE IS REVOLUTION FOR TWO

EPILOGUE

SENSITIVITY TRAINING

SWEET KAROLINE BA BA BAAA

One doesn't realise the price of freedom is loneliness. To be happy is to be tied.

— C. S. Lewis

I do not look like a love-at-first-sight/kismet kinda guy, but I guess I am.

My manager, Hannah, rang to tell me, 'They want to see you for an audition.' It was at Thames TV, just off Tottenham Court Road. They were devising a new panel show and wanted comics to come and audition, to do a little run-through to see who was right for the pilot.

I was just starting out, a jobbing stand-up doing the circuit. I showed up and there, in front of me, I saw Karoline. Back then she was a producer at Thames, which meant on that day she had to herd us comics. The woman I was going to be with for the next twenty years, minimum (let's see if she likes what

I write), sat in the room where I auditioned. Straight away I knew I really liked her. When you know, you know, you know?

Right out the gate I was as funny and charming as I could be. I did my run-through and right afterwards, and I mean immediately afterwards, I phoned Hannah and said, 'I can't even work with that girl, she's fantastic, but I can't concentrate around her. Also, I think I'm gonna ask her out.' Hannah asked, 'Who is this? Put Jimmy on the phone.' (This was back in the days when you could ask people out in the workplace. I guess my love story is a case of sexual harassment working out.)

I found out later that one of Karoline's tasks that day was writing notes on us, the comics and presenters that had been asked to audition. Uniquely, I've got an actual written record of the first impression I made on my long-term partner. She wrote, *A one-note comedian with the eyes of a rapist.*

It was like she'd known me her whole life.

I also found out later that when I called her at her office to ask her for 'maybe, dinner sometime', she had put me on speakerphone. Apparently, she wasn't so sure she wanted to accept, but her boss encouraged her, saying, 'It's a free meal, go.'

She agreed. Gotta love a girl with an appetite. She told me she'd heard of this fancy place called the Ivy, and wanted to go there. I can't remember why we didn't, but we went to another fancy place called the Hemple. Remember, I was a poor comic, but I also really wanted to impress her.

We agreed upon a time for me to pick her up at her flat in Bassett Road, the wrong end of Notting Hill. I was ten minutes early. I knocked on the door, she opened it and said, 'You're too early, I'm not ready, come back in ten minutes.' Back to the car I went.

While waiting, I listened to the soundtrack to *Magnolia*. All the pieces are by Aimee Mann. I really love it. It's a fantastic soundtrack, beautiful music. I'm quite finickity about music, I take it very seriously.

When Karoline got in the car (ten minutes later), she went, 'Oh, what's this noise? I hate it.' I said, 'Fine', turned it off and put on Magic FM. Compromise, I love it.

The Hemple was a beautiful minimalist hotel and restaurant in West London. We were given a glass of champagne each. I was fully teetotal, straight-edge at the time, so she drank mine. She had two glasses of champagne on the bounce before we had a single thing to eat.

My food came in a banana leaf. I'd never seen anything like it. It was so fancy. A guy with a scalpel cut open the banana leaf and my Pad Thai burst out, like 'pooooooof!' It is to this day the best Pad Thai I've ever had.

Karoline's meal arrived at the same time. If someone was making a movie of Charles Dickens' *Oliver*, and their job was to get the gruel looking just right, cinematic, like the gruel to end all gruels, it was like that. It was the perfect gruel, grey and sludgy. I believe it was called a mushroom risotto. It was awful. She ate very little and drank another two glasses of champagne.

She also kissed a guy she wasn't quite sold on yet.

And that was it. That was the night. I took her back to her place, she invited me in to chat and kiss a little. It was a nice evening.

You know how people like to play it cool, you don't want

to call too soon, you like to keep people guessing. You want to keep things a little mysterious, tease them a little. I left her house a little after midnight. When I'd got to Shepherd's Bush roundabout, which is about seven minutes away, she called me. She had waited all of seven minutes.

I asked her, 'Did you leave something in the car?'

She went, 'No, I was just checking in, wanted to see if you're okay.'

And as I drove home, we chatted for like an hour. I thought, 'This is great. This is it.'

She was a little bit slower to catch on. I would say I'm an 'acquired' taste. There are guys out there with moves and manoeuvres, that's like some Second World War shit, and that's great. I'm more of a World War One kind of guy, it's more a 'war of attrition'.

There is a level of understanding a person has to have to be in a relationship with someone who's trying to be a stand-up comedian. You have to be pretty self-sufficient, because comics are on the road a lot. It helped that Karoline was in television and had a job with long crazy hours. For me, it sort of felt like I was cheating on stand-up comedy when I was with her. But somehow, I managed to maintain both of the great loves of my life.

I'm a night person, she's a morning person. I'm a big-picture person, she's all about detail. When you fall in love with someone, you're not thinking about how your skill sets will work together. You just think, fucking hell, she's nice. There's too much lust early on to really think at all. You're not making a game plan about how this is gonna work, but we're a really good little team.

BE A HYPOCRITE OR BE THE SAME PERSON FOR EVER

Last question: what's the last heartfelt thing you changed your mind about? If you can't think of an answer, if you haven't changed your mind about anything for a while, then you haven't been thinking. All you've been doing is rearranging your prejudices.

There's a real taboo in our society about changing your mind. Look how interviewers rip into politicians, pointing out how their opinions have differed over the years. But the world changes, circumstances change; it's not flip-flopping, it's not a lack of consistency, it's growth.

Politicians aren't supposed to change their mind on anything, ever. But if they didn't we'd still have slavery, prohibition, women being treated as second-class citizens and we wouldn't have gay marriage – hell, Obama ran on a 'no to gay marriage' ticket, but he was smart enough to change his mind.

I'd rather be a hypocrite than the same person for ever. – Ad-Roc, who is now Adam Horovitz but who will forever be a Beastie Boy

I'M KIDDING . . .

The last heartfelt belief I changed my mind about was having kids.

I'm a straight white man. That's already a life with easy

settings. But not having kids is like entering a cheat code. That's a really *really* easy life.

I was dead set against it, adamant. I did not want kids. I thought we had gamed the system. Karoline and I were living as a gay couple. I say 'as a gay couple'* but what I mean is that we were living a lovely, hedonistic, fun life.

We went on holidays, saw our friends, jetted around the world, we were spontaneous, did what we wanted because we felt like it and it was great. Absolutely great. People wonder why the pink pound is so valuable. It's because the 'pink pounds' haven't got a snot-nosed kid that needs to go to a singing class in the park. Of course they're doing brunch.

One thing that made me not want to have kids for twenty years was how close I had come to being tied down. The payments on that dumb car nearly stopped me from doing comedy. After that, I didn't want to own anything or owe anyone. When I bought a house, I saved up and bought it with cash. I bought it two years after I should have bought a house. I waited until I had the money and then I bought it. The same with my next house. I saved up and bought it when I had the money. That's how much I didn't like the responsibility of owing anyone anything. The first time in my life I got into any kind of debt really was when HMRC came calling. Yeah, it turns out I didn't have the money after all.

I have a huge amount of respect for people who have made

---

* I know gay people have kids now, sorry gays. We've ruined being gay. Now you can get married and have kids. Liberalism has ruined your fabulous lifestyle. Being accepted – it's not all fun and games.

the decision to not have kids. I clearly remember the conversation that started the whole ball rolling.

It was over dinner with our friends, Victoria Coren Mitchell and David Mitchell (and yeah, I'm naming names, they've got to take some responsibility). They'd had a baby.

Vicky started out by saying, 'Yeah, I get that you don't want kids, but imagine this. Say there's a shop, it's about a mile away and the two of you could go. And in that shop there's a tiny little, foot-long creature that doesn't do anything, it just sort of sits there and looks like a mix of the two of you in miniature. You're not curious? You wouldn't want to have a look?' Well, yeah, you'd wanna go, you'd want to have a look, you'd be curious. And then Vicky adds, 'Oh, and it's really expensive, super expensive.' As if that's a sweetener.

When you have kids, what happens is that you increase the capacity for things to go wrong. Real wrong.

Vicky said, 'When you have a kid, all you do is you raise the stakes. What you've got is skin in the game.'

Incidentally, Vicky's a gambler.

I thought I already had skin in the game. After all, I risked my life for a more interesting time. I thought I was all in but then it turns out no, no you could be *more* in.

It's like this: it's fun to play dollar roulette in Vegas, right? It's a dollar a spin and you really can't lose that much money because there's not that much on the table. And then you up the stakes and on every spin, you're playing for the fucking house. That's the difference between having a kid and just playing for a dollar.

Having a child is not a safe bet. If you have a kid, the stakes are so high. It could be the best thing you've ever done. It could be like the lottery when the Euromillions pot is £160,000,000. It's a life-changer. The high when you win is like, 'Wow, we had a kid.'

But then, one of the pregnancies doesn't work out and it's a low fucking low.

I have a couple of friends who have lost a child and they never got over it. I've experienced grief. Losing my mother was very difficult, but it was at least in the natural order of things. The stakes, when you lose a kid, mean you'd be broken.

PARENTAL GUIDANCE

You don't so much 'change' your mind about having kids because, I don't know if you're familiar with the nitty-gritty on how babies are made, you will need to involve at least one other person in the process, if not more. I don't know what people are getting up to these days.

We went through the fur baby stage. We had dogs that I'm sure a rational person might say we loved too much. I admit, I didn't think I wanted dogs. But Karoline informed me that I did. How did she do that, you ask? She bought a dog. And she was right, I did want a dog. Dogs are excellent training for having a baby. A dog can't tell you what the matter is, it needs constant attention, and you can fuck up a little bit with a dog. It's great practice. So if a dog runs into the road, it'll probably be fine or if the dog runs away in the park, someone's going to find it and bring it back because it's got a little tag on its collar. You don't really want to learn that lesson with a kid.

There were a lot of discussions in the early stages – we would just mention it, you know how you do. It was tentative, like we were testing the waters or saying it out loud to hear what it sounded like. We would have conversations like:

'What are you doing the next eighteen years?'

'Nothing I can't move around.'

'Have you had enough sleep?'

'I think I've slept enough.'

'Yeah, but do you think you've had enough lie-ins for a lifetime?'

Karoline noticed if someone had a baby, I would always pick up the baby and make a fuss over them. If there's a baby around, they're sort of the celebrity. Babies pull focus in the room. It doesn't matter who walks in. 'Oh, there's a baby.' They demand attention. It's really nice. I like holding them. I like the smell of them. Karoline used to say, 'If we didn't have a baby, I'm pretty sure you were gonna steal one.'

What became obvious was that something was missing. We'd built a big house but there were just two people living in it. People would visit, they'd look around and say, 'This is a family home . . .' They could see there was a kid missing. And not because it'd been abducted (Christ, another thing to worry about).

And then, eventually, one night she said, 'I'm not taking contraception any more.' And I said, 'But what if you get pregnant?' And she went, 'I wouldn't mind a little version of you.' Great line, flattered the ego, unthreatening, almost casual.

I went, 'Why not?'

DAD BIBLE

If you want to have a family in your forties, the chances are nature is not just going to take its course without some assistance. We had to have a threesome. Of course, our threesome involved a doctor. Spoiler alert, it all worked out, we're still good friends.

It's a long-assed journey. It feels like you're having a baby for about three years and nine months. Because there's the pregnancy, then there's before, when you're trying everything you can to get pregnant.

There are disadvantages to being an older father. But the advantage is that it's not an accident. This is not a 'I guess the Dutch cap pinged across the room and here you are . . . Sometimes shit just happens.' It's more, 'We really wanted you. We had our heart set on having you. We went out of our way to create you. You are here on purpose. No pressure, kid.'

Sometimes when I'm walking the pram, I'll see another dad in the park and he'll give me that weary eyebrow raise, like, 'Oh, they got you too.' And I'll think, 'Nope. This is the best. I wanna be here. I want this.'

Here's a sidebar, let's call it *A Brief Story of Spunk*.

We're in the doctor's office, and he says, 'I'm gonna need a sperm sample. Would you like help from an attractive Russian nurse?' He genuinely put it that way. I looked to Karoline before saying, 'Yeah'. The doctor presses the tannoy button on his desk and says, 'Send in the attractive Russian nurse.' And this gorgeous, could-have-been-a-model, six-foot-tall Russian nurse walks in called Vlad. Big bloke.

Vlad said, 'Would you like to masturbate in the cup?' I said, 'I'm good, but I'm not ready for competition yet.'

Then Vlad led me into 'the mastubatorim', where you have what I'd call a 'heritage wank'.

I masturbate as much as the next man, maybe more, I am on tour an awful lot. But I haven't knocked one out to a magazine since the eighties. And magazines were all they had. This is a fertility doctor on Harley Street. Where do they even get magazines these days? It was literally like masturbating as a seventeen-year-old.

Then you come out of the room and hand over what looks like the tiniest bit of spunk and go, 'Um. I've er, got the, eh, here's the stuff.'

If you watch pornography (and who doesn't) and you had to guess how much a human male ejaculates, you'd go, 'I dunno, a pint?' There's been times I thought I've done a pretty decent Jackson Pollock painting on a tummy. But no, they give you like a thimble and you can't fill it.

The answer for how much a male ejaculates is, by the way, about 10cc.

Quick quiz: name three bands with names referencing male ejaculation.*

---

* 10cc, The Lovin' Spoonful, Pearl Jam.

SON OF A GUN

Children are the living message to a time we will not see.
— Neil Postman

You know the thing about liking who we are when we're with certain people? I like who I am when there's a baby around. I like the paternal side of myself, the dynamic. I like who I am when I'm with my child.

I'll say this though: one thing that changes is your capacity for anxiety and worry goes through the roof. If you think you've maxed out on anxiety, wait until you have kids. I was not prepared for the low-level background noise, the constant worry about this little creature. I guess anxiety isn't just the flip side of creativity but also the downside to love. But just try getting that sentiment into a greetings card.

Being a parent is like having a procedure where your heart now lives outside your body. – Elizabeth Stone

I feel like a man now. I was a forty-five-year-old boy before. It's not about age, it's about your life stage. I'm no longer afraid of what I might become if I have a kid. I think a part of me thought I was going off on an adventure and having a kid meant I would have to settle down and be boring. Wrong.

I thought my mother didn't really get a chance to get out there and live because she had kids. She had three boys that loved her but she never got to do anything. And I felt like I was so similar to her that that could be my story, so I'd better not have kids.

I thought she lived vicariously through us – poor Mum. But now I realise, like a dummy twenty years later, 'Oh, the kids were the thing.'

AFTERWORD

THE LAUGHTER MATH

I've almost finished this book. I hope you enjoyed it.

The idea was to write something that would give you an impression of who I am.

So if you read it you'd have a pretty good idea of what I'm about.

For better or worse, I think it worked. This is what I'm about.

Here's what I've learned rereading the proof copy:

I should do more of this stuff. I do some of the things that got me here some of the time. If I did more of them I could do more. Now, I know that sounds obvious (bordering on crazy) but you get what I mean.

Like a teenage boy in his bedroom with a laptop, I'm amazed at how far I've come – but who knows how much further there is to go?

I'm certainly not one of the greats, but I've got a shot. It is possible. One day I could be on the Mount Rushmore of comedy. That's the goal, the ambition, the true north. And I like the goal because there's something I can do about it right now.

I'm a work in progress – let's see where I end up.

JUST THE TIP –
TAKE IT FROM JIMMY CARR

I figure the smart way to end the book is with some advice, the 'Now That's What I Call the Greatest Hits Gold, Best of, Compilation of Jimmy Carr Life Advice'.

TO DO'S AND TO DONT'S

Make a to-do-list. Make item one on the list 'Make a To Do List'. Then cross off item one – done. Doesn't that feel good?

You've already achieved something. Now write down everything else you're going to do in your life and start ticking those things off. Start and keep going.

MAKE HARD CHOICES

Hard choices, easy life. Easy choices, hard life.

– Jerzy Gregorek

It's pretty simple.

If you can be hard on yourself now, you can be fit and rich and happy and all that good stuff in the future. But you do have to start now.

NO CAN DO

The ultimate productivity hack is saying 'no'.

Say no to anything you don't want to do. It's a hard choice in the moment but then you don't have to do the thing you don't want to do – score.

'Do you want to go to IKEA this Saturday?' No.

'Can you pick me up from the airport?' No.

'Do you want a shot of Jager?' No.

'Do you want to marry Steve from the chip shop and have his ugly kids?' No.

FAKE IT

Pretending to be a better person and being a better person are indistinguishable to the casual observer. Pretend to be happy and after a little while you might just be happy. The mask becomes the face.

BE ON THE RIGHT SIDE OF HISTORY

Increased individual freedom is coming. There will be gay marriage in Saudi Arabia – I may not live to see it but mark my words it's gonna happen. So if there's an argument at a family dinner table, don't take Grandad's side, take the kids' side.

ASK YOURSELF 'WHAT DO I WANT?'

Ask yourself that question all day every day.

What do I want to eat?

What do I want to get out of this conversation?

What do I want right now?

What do I want in forty years' time?

That's the only question in life.

COMPARE AND DESPAIR

Green is not a good colour on you – or anyone else, for that matter.

Comparison is only useful if you keep it about you. Compare where you were to where you are, and where you are to where you want to be.

DO HAPPY

Here's the secret to happiness: expectations exceeded. That's happiness. Do more; expect less.

The difference between crushing disappointment and being pleasantly surprised is expectation.

GUILT-FREE SELFISH

Your job is to find out what makes you happy – then do that. It's why, when the oxygen masks fall from the overheads, you're meant to put your mask on first before you help anyone else.

DON'T LEAVE LUCK TO CHANCE

Luck is your talent and hard work plus time. You can't win the lottery if you don't buy a ticket – each day of hard work is a ticket. It could be you. Good luck.

TIREDNESS IS THE SOFTEST PILLOW

Work hard both physically and mentally. Because working works: a tired dog is a happy dog.

YOU'LL BE JUDGED ON YOUR RESULTS

Having ideas is not the same as doing things.
    Being creative is all about the execution.
    Life is a doing thing, so go do things.

TAKE CARE OF YOURSELF

A 10 per cent change in diet is equivalent to a 100 per cent change in exercise.
    Exercise is the icing on the cake – the cake you shouldn't be eating.
    All diet books and exercise regimes say the same thing: eat less and move more.

STAY OUT OF THE SUN

Save money on anti-ageing creams and surgical treatments in the future – just stay out of the sun. All tans are fake tans, you're the colour you're supposed to be. All they're selling at the tanning salon is skin cancer. Trying to be a different colour will cause problems – see Rachel Dolezal for details.

THE TRIPOD

Health and work and home are the three legs of the tripod holding up your life. If any one is off, you're out of balance. If it's all three, congratulations, you're having a crisis.

Pro tip: deal with health first.

DISPOSITION IS AS IMPORTANT AS POSITION

You see the world as you are, not as it is. So, if you don't like it, you just have to change you.

People with bad attitudes can fuck right off. I'll be frank: if you meet three cunts before noon, odds are you're the cunt.

FUCK THE BEGRUDGERS

It's a very Irish way of saying 'haters gonna hate'. Some people will hate you just because you don't hate yourself, and I hate that.

EDGE

Lean into what you're good at and lean into what you've got.

The world is full of people with curly hair and straighteners. They're fighting a losing battle.

NO EXCEPTIONS

If there's a universally acknowledged truth, then it applies to you.

When someone says they're the 'exception to the rule', you can easily see that's bullshit.

But it's so much easier to fool ourselves.

You can be exceptional, but you're never the exception. No exceptions is the rule.